ARCHITECTURE IN CONTEXT

ARCHITECTURE IN CONTEXT

CONTEMPORARY DESIGN SOLUTIONS BASED ON ENVIRONMENTAL, SOCIAL AND CULTURAL IDENTITIES

promopress

CONTENTS

FOREWORD

Quality architecture is not just a matter of formal and aesthetic excellence, an exercise imposed from "on high" to be mechanically reiterated. Architecture entails the complex process of transforming a given landscape, which in turn requires analysis of that landscape's historical, social, economic, administrative, environmental and cultural features. A fundamental, though by no means exclusive, requirement of any sound architectural design is the understanding of the context into which a building is to be placed. That means not just considering the climate and environmental aspects but also how people perceive a particular environment and the existing social networks making up the local way of life. The perception of space - be this a natural or urban context - is a complex process encompassing customs and ingrained behavioural patterns, features that often become apparent only after that space has been altered. The architect's job is therefore to be a sort of "guide", at the forefront of understanding the effects that spatial changes will have on people and their way of life.

Examples abound of exquisitely aesthetic yet "empty" architectures; gorgeous buildings but mere containers. Conversely, there is a long list of positive experiences where a single building or architectural intervention has triggered a series of changes in the surrounding environment, transforming the way the whole area is perceived and lived in. Here, architecture is a means of regenerating and re-qualifying a rural or urban setting, a positive inductive process in which a single work of architecture has knock-on effects in terms of improved urban quality. It is an example of a single element having a wide ripple effect.

Architecture and sociology go hand-in-hand. Richard Rogers has said that "you cannot think of architecture unless you think of people". In other words, the success of a project must be measured by the extent to which people appropriate a place, start living and being in it, accepting it and feeling it theirs. That sort of result can only be achieved if the architect understands the underlying cultural and social character of the place.

Architecture must aim to re-establish contact between places and between people and places, to be part of an environment that is enhanced by its presence.

Placing a new architecture in context can be described from

two angles: in social and ethical terms on the one hand, and in environmental terms on the other. The first is all about cultural continuity. It is a metaphorical, abstract process, a subjective and individual endeavor to create architecture that responds to the "mental images" an individual or a collective has of what can be included in a given environment without wreaking havoc with people's lives.

The second aspect concerns more readily identifiable criteria: objective features designed to create efficient modern buildings that sit well in their setting. Sustainability, energy efficiency, modern innovative technologies, features that align with the local climate and natural environment, aesthetic excellence and quality materials are all measurable and quantifiable. The aim is to maintain, or reinstate, a morphological continuity of form, color and construction technique. This is architectural design in the classic sense of the word, an objective exercise aimed to place a given project into a specific place according to functional, spatial and formal criteria in keeping with the geographic features of the site and the existing building typologies to ensure the new building is a good physical fit.

Whatever the scale of the brief, architectural design must consider and blend both these approaches. The result may be a building that enters an area on tiptoe, discreetly fitting into context as if not wanting to be noticed. On other occasions, the same approach will lead to the creation of iconic buildings that stand out for their imposing, unabashed contrast with their surroundings.

This volume presents a selection of projects illustrating all of the above aspects. Some constitute real "architectural events" while others are discreet and retiring. All have a measurable impact on their environment; all show a marked sensitivity to the context of which they are part.

The Plan

FROM PLACE TO PROJECT

How do you design a building that stands out while fitting in? A creation that enriches the site while respecting its surroundings? In the Middle Ages, the great cathedrals were radically different in scale and style from the urban fabric, yet they have always been treasured for their beauty. Bruno Taut made an argument for the Stadtkrone, a secular building that would replace the cathedral as the domininant feature of a city, strengthening its identity.

The Eiffel Tower performs that role in Paris, and Jørn Utzon's Opera House is still the unchallenged emblem of Sydney. Fiercely contested when first proposed, they are now cherished for their relevance: Eiffel expressed the daring of 19th-century French engineering, Utzon the exuberance of sailboats in the harbor. Both are one-of-a-kind but responsive to context. There's a place for one or two such icons in a city, but when everyone competes for attention or pursues form for form's sake it leads to the visual chaos of Pudong in Shanghai, and the capitals of the oil-rich Gulf States.

The twenty projects gathered here are linked by their sensitivity to nature and neighbors, materiality and scale, climate and culture, as well as the intangible spirit of place. The architects' strategies are as varied as the forms of expression. Most of these buildings have a high level of sustainability - for context includes the planet itself.

Several examples occupy former industrial sites and strive to create a new sense of place. Hamburg has transformed its former docklands into the new community of Hafencity, and the Elbphilharmonie anchors that development. Herzog & de Meuron placed their crystalline complex of concert halls, hotel, and apartments atop a brick warehouse, and the wave-like roof perfectly captures the maritime spirit of this proud port city.

The Île Seguin, just beyond the boundary of Paris, is a narrow sliver of land in the Seine, once covered by the Renault car factory, which is now being redeveloped as a cultural and recreational resource. Shigeru Ban took his cue from the water and the tapered island, designing a low concrete block that evokes a beached liner with stacked decks. A glass bubble enwraps a concert hall, and it is shaded by a photo-voltaic sail that moves with the sun. Adaptive re-use on a heroic scale was the achievement of 5+1AA in renovating and repurposing the former dock buildings of Marseille, employing boldly colored ceramics to animate courtyards and a wall of typography to increase its visibility.

Inserting a new building into the urban fabric is an even greater challenge. In upper Manhattan, Diller Scofidio + Renfrew designed the Vagelos Center for medical education as a hybrid, comprising a reticent stack of laboratories and classrooms to the north, and a transparent complex of social and study spaces that cascade down the south face of the tower, bringing students and teachers together and opening up their activities to the city.

Archi-Tectonics create dynamic buildings that enliven the townscape, notably in the former industrial neighborhood of Tribeca in lower Manhattan. 33 Vestry Street is a new landmark, subtly modeled in its stone and glass street façade, and boldly articulated to the south where the eight stacked townhouses overlook a landscaped courtyard.

Steven Holl's addition to the Glasgow School of Art is a study in contrasts: a light, white minimalist structure soaring over a boldly modeled mass of dark stone, and it has proved as controversial as Charles Rennie Mackintosh's masterpiece was a century ago. In contrast to this audacious approach, 3XN's addition to the Frederiksberg Courthouse in Denmark complements the neo-classical original in scale, section, and buff-brick cladding while creating a distinctive contemporary form. In the Dutch city of Arnhem, Neutlings Riedijk Architects explored the middle ground, exploiting a a narrow site to build a cultural center whose commanding presence makes it a popular destination for a broad public.

Buildings can enhance landscape by establishing a sharp line of demarcation, evoking natural forms, or blending in. At Grace Farms in New Canaan, Connecticut, SANAA explores all three options with a structure that is transparent and organic. Aptly named The River, it comprises a canopy of Douglas fir, supported on slender steel poles, which descends a gentle slope in a series of switchbacks, widening at five points to embrace rounded glass enclosures that seem as insubstantial as soap bubbles.

Half-hidden by trees, the library that Li Xiaogong created for a village near Beijing is a masterpiece of understatement: a steel frame clad with twigs that filter light and reference the rural vernacular. Equally at home in its setting is an interpretation center by Peter Rich Architects for a national park in South Africa. It employs locally sourced materials and building techniques to create arched vaults which seem to rise like rock formations from the land.

The four wood cabins that Rodrigo Duque Motta added to a resort at the foot of the Andes have windows that are tilted up for star-gazing, but they merge into the rugged landscape. And in the misty northwest of the United States, Kengo Kuma has distilled the essence of traditional Japanese architecture and its harmony with nature in the pavilions and courtyards he has added to the garden modeled on those of his homeland.

Then, there are projects that are designed to enrich the quality of life in impoverished communities, alleviating the squalor, and offering hope of a brighter future. SelgasCano designed a summer pavilion for Louisiana, the Danish art museum, as a lightweight, prefabricated structure that could afterwards be shipped to Kenya, and re-assembled to serve as a school in a Nairobi slum. Working with a team of collaborators, they have used their improvisatory skills to transform lives.

Giancarlo Mazzanti designed the Parque Biblioteca España in a mountainside favela overlooking the Colombian city of Medellin. The three faceted blocks, clad in black stone, are a beacon of hope for the community and have become a symbol of regeneration for the whole city.

Michael Webb

EXPANSION OF PORTLAND JAPANESE GARDEN

PORTLAND, OREGON, USA

KENGO KUMA AND ASSOCIATES

Kengo Kuma's architecture is noteworthy for its attention to natural phenomena - in particular, light - and its geometric coordination of multiple building components. His best work, as at the Portland Japanese Garden in Oregon, USA, captures views of sky and plants and satellite architectural elements with grace and wit. To assist this spatial elegance, the architect attends to such details as paving slabs and ceiling soffits, fenestration and sliding screens as an exquisite kit-of-parts, components that are refined in-and-of themselves and, most characteristic of Kuma's *modus operandi*, in the many ways they are arranged to make a complete and integrated tectonic *ensemble*.

The Portland Japanese Garden was established in the aftermath of World War Two as a living symbol of constructive collaboration between Japan and the United States. The Garden inhabits a hilly and forested site, part of a natural amenity of great intrinsic beauty and civic benefit close to the flat, gridded layout of downtown Portland. The narrow public road rises and curves between flanks of sun-dappled forest. Then we encounter a modestly-scaled parking lot and the first new structure, the ticket pavilion for the Garden. It immediately sets the palette and tone of Kuma's intervention with its almost blade-like, low pitched roofs and clever orthogonal planning immediately adjacent to an ornamental pool.

Ahead of us is a traditional Japanese gate or portal. It sits at the base of a small valley, with wooded slopes to either side. We hear the gurgling and splash of water and naturally follow the path upstream into the trees. The path switches back-and-forth as it ascends. Elegant stones underfoot lead to a slender bridge with skinny balustrades. On a warm summer's day, splashes of sunlight mix with light falling on the rushing brook below the soaring canopy of firs and cedars. Then we glimpse the almost floating eaves and soffits of the architectural intervention above, as we approach, with precise lines against the sky. We notice that the upper roofs are planted - a bespoke, miniature meadow - and that glass underneath these roofs reflects the sylvan scene in horizontal, butt-jointed bands.

The massing of Kuma's intervention in this unique natural context is almost an act of stealth. The approach on foot, through the trees and in close proximity to the stream, is reminiscent of that at Frank Lloyd Wright's Fallingwater in Pennsylvania where the visitor, distracted perhaps by the beauty and variation of nature, comes across the architectural object as if by chance. In Portland, Kuma's upper pavilions, his principal contribution to this impressive site, are almost secondary to the artefacts, natural and manmade, about them. There is a sense of refined camouflage (planted roofs, vertical timber screens) as if the new architecture is imitating its surroundings. As we climb the final set of steps, we discover a generous stone plateau, a tautly-paved terrace between the upper pavilions and extending directly into their interiors.

1

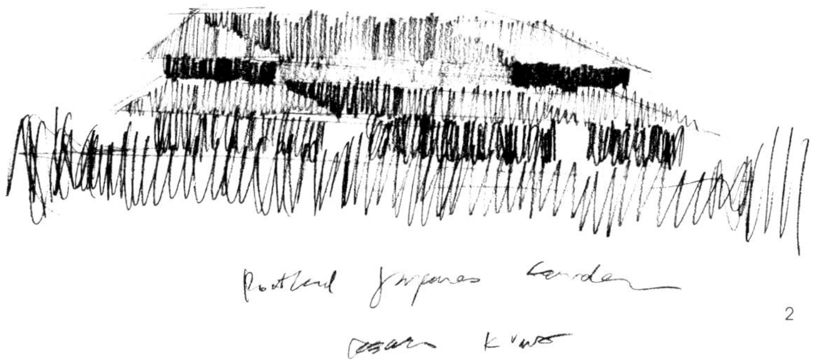

2

3

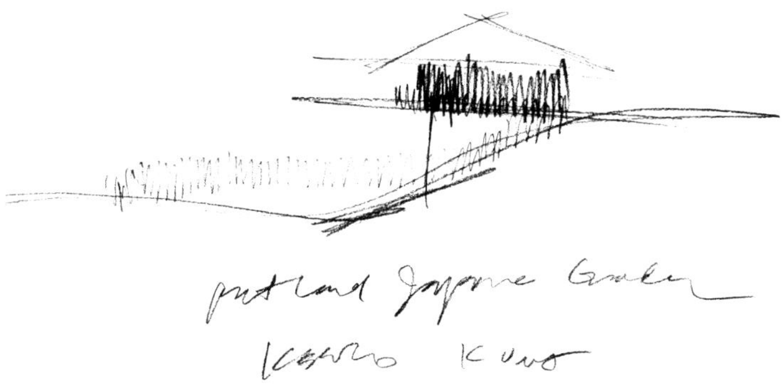

4

■ 1/4 Concept sketches
© Kengo Kuma
1. Competition phase. Initial idea for the complex
2/4 Investigation of construction systems
2. Cultural village seen from inner court
3. Entrance pavilion
4. Cross-sectional and perspective view of the Tea House

This terrace could be considered the primary room of Kuma's intervention. It is of course not a room in any orthodox sense, rather a courtyard open to views and to the sky, bounded by three distinct pavilions. The two more extensive pavilions zigzag in plan to gently embrace the new exterior space; they are both double-story with a sophisticated section stepping back from the courtyard to recede against the sky and surrounding vegetation. The third pavilion is a smaller, freestanding structure, square in plan. It is designed to accommodate a Japanese Tea House with an external terrace wrapping the glazed interior volume - another horizontal stratum and void between the manmade and organic worlds. It is this third pavilion that cantilevers out above the brook and the picturesque path up from the valley below.

In the early 1940s, the curious Italian writer Curzio Malaparte contradicted Field Marshal Rommel's praise of how well his new villa complemented the natural beauty of Capri by claiming that the villa had already existed and that he, Malaparte, had instead designed the landscape. In Portland, both the architecture and the landscape are more subtle. Nevertheless, there is a synergy between Kuma's built form and the landscape in which it is so skillfully sited. The buildings attract the visitor yet also recede. It's difficult to understand the precise plan. Indeed, the same visitor will most likely want to explore, ascend further inside the pavilion known as the Village House via a generous flight of steps that double as an interior theater, or linger in the gently corralled bonsai garden extending from the other pavilion, the Garden House.

Kuma is now an international star, with several projects in France as well the new Victoria & Albert Museum under construction in the Scottish port of Dundee. Some of his larger projects allude to nature in their geological or topographical quality. Some of his smaller projects - the temporary pavilions and installations, for instance, of which he is fond - suggest nature more in their vegetal or frond-like character. Even in his earliest works, in the waning days of postmodernism, these is a tendency to allow different component parts their own identity or expression. This sense almost of delamination seems more akin to Scarpa in its delicacy and eclecticism than the weightier singularity of Zumthor.

Kuma is also of course unmistakably Japanese. His sense of craft, of working with wood and metal, and of harmony with nature derive surely from his native culture and the history of Japanese architecture, both recent and traditional. At times, at least to this non-Japanese observer, his work seems almost to be playing with our preconceptions of Japanese culture. In Portland, however, as at the splendid Nezu Museum in Tokyo, the complex of buildings, their spatial relationships and the resolution of both construction and finish, achieve a seductive tectonic totality. This totality allows, in a very Japanese way, for the inclusion of a mini-garden to interrupt the geometric purity of the courtyard, and opens up to the many other delights of this wonderful re-presentation of Japan in America's Pacific Northwest.

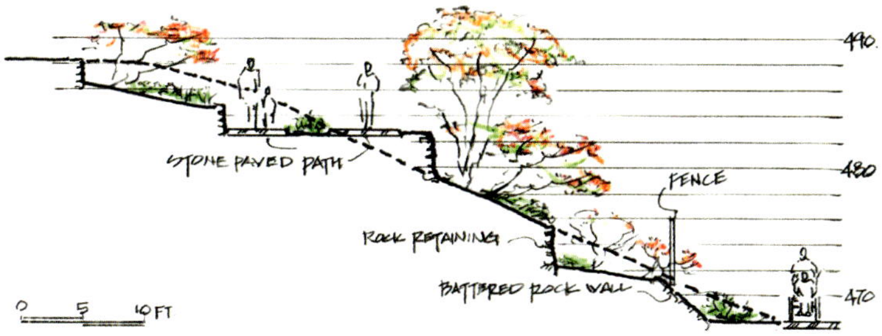

5

6

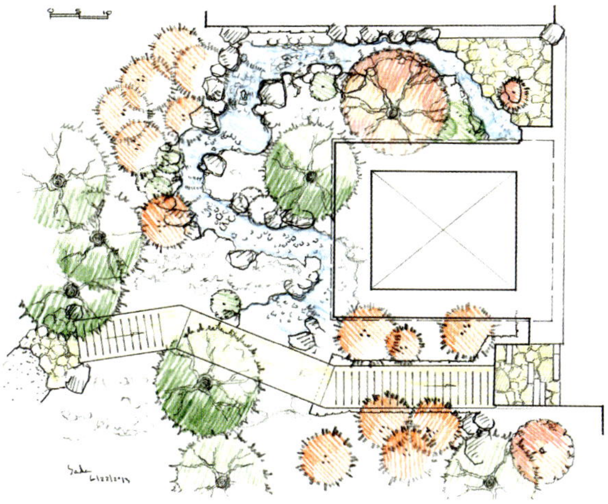

7

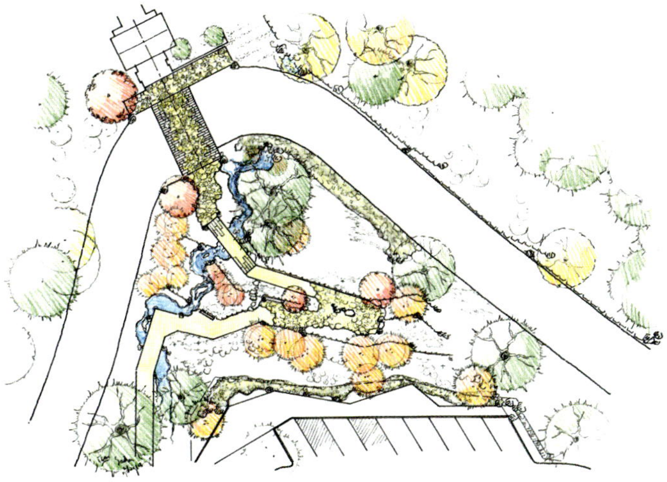

8

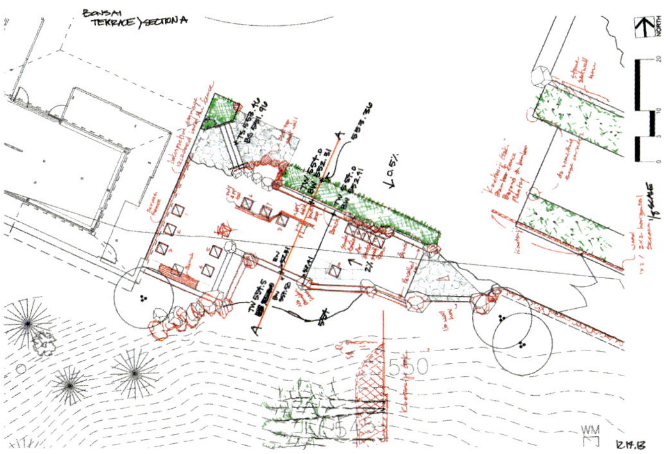

9

10

11

■ 5/11 Study sketches
© Sadafumi Uchiyama
5. Cross-sectional view through the lower garden
6. Perspective view of restored garden. In the background, the old entrance to the park
7/9 Plans
7. Area round the Tea House
8. Lower garden
9. Bonsai garden layout
10. View of the main building: the gardens are an integral part of the building
11. Perspective view of the stone plateau and landscaping around the Tea House

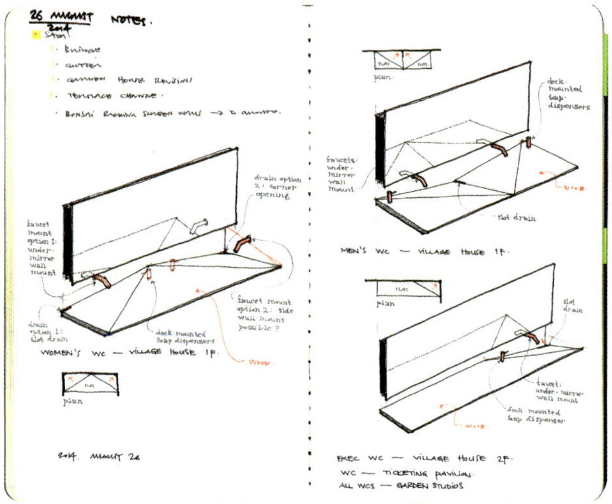

13

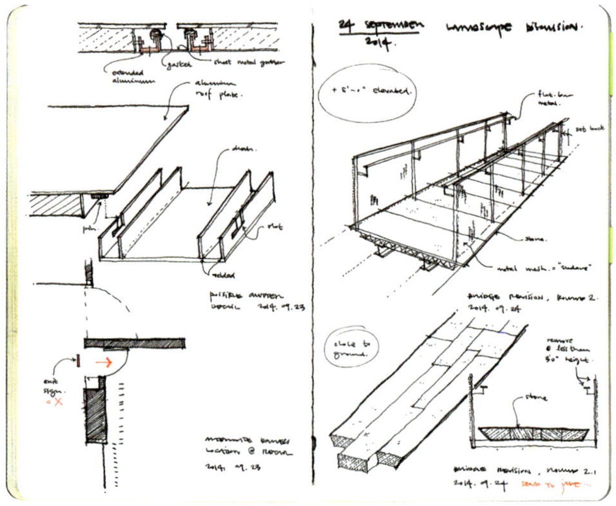

14

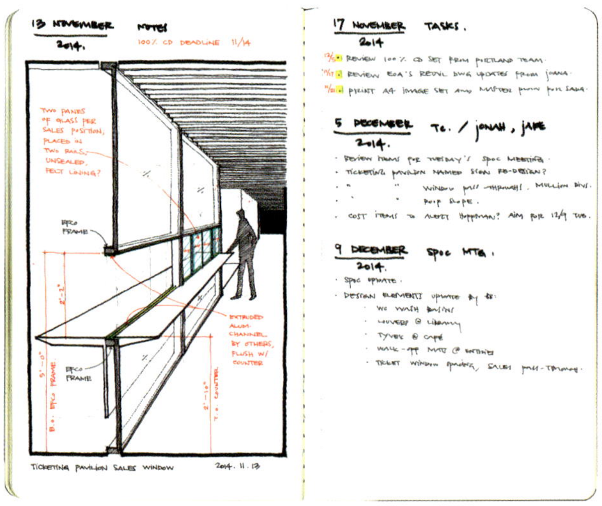

15

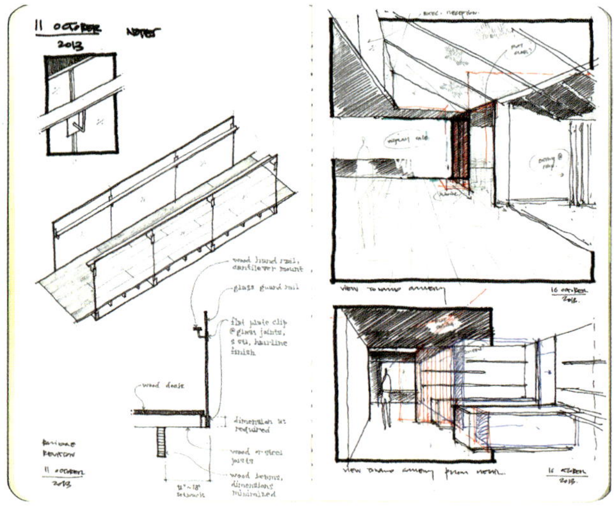

16

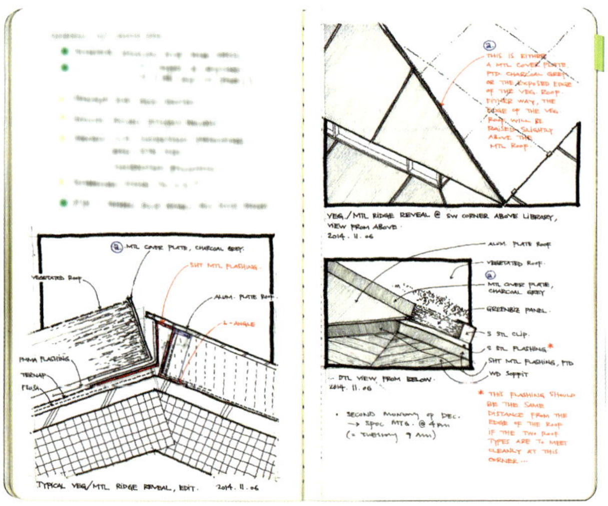

17

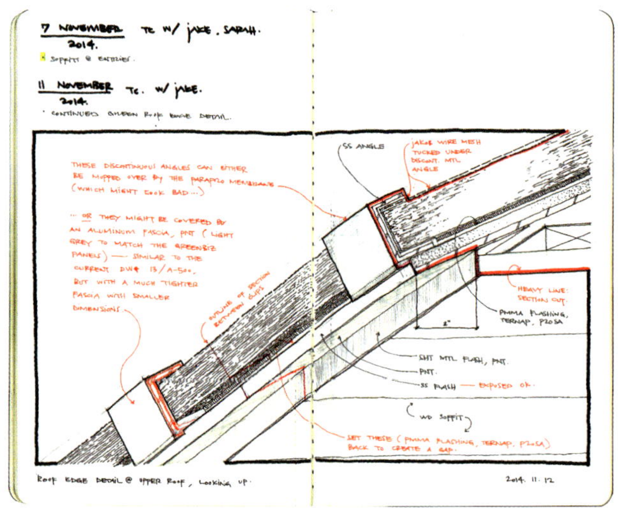

18

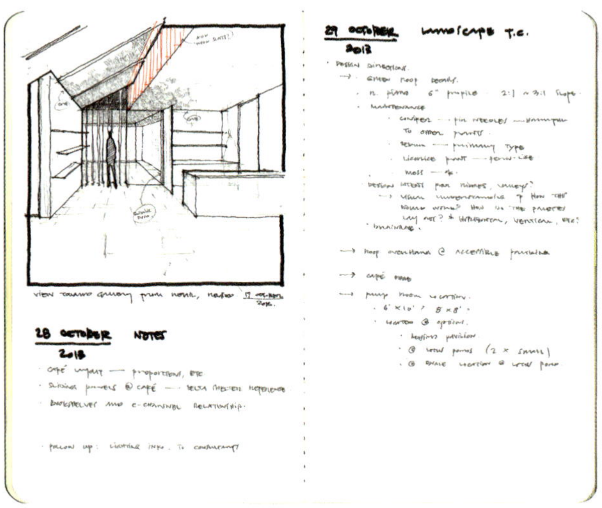

19

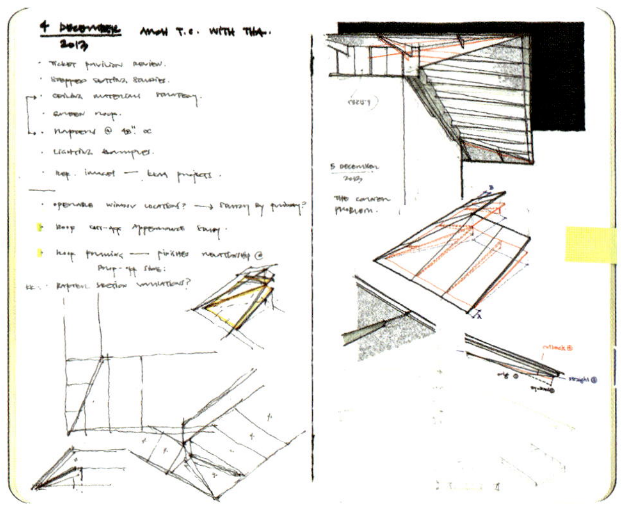

20

■ 13/21 Sketches of technological details taken from Balazs Bognar's study sketchbook
© Balazs Bognar,
Project architect at Kengo Kuma and Associates

13. Various sink design proposals. The aesthetic recalls the art and technique of origami
14. Roof gutters incorporated into the roof panels; proposed pedestrian bridge designs
15. Ticketcounter in the entrance pavilion
16. Views of pedestrian bridge and layout of gallery and shop
17. Detail of design at points where the planted roof connects with the metal facing
18. Study sketches of edges of the planted roof structure
19. Perspective view of shop
20. Study of roof line
21. Study of handles incorporated into wooden doors

21

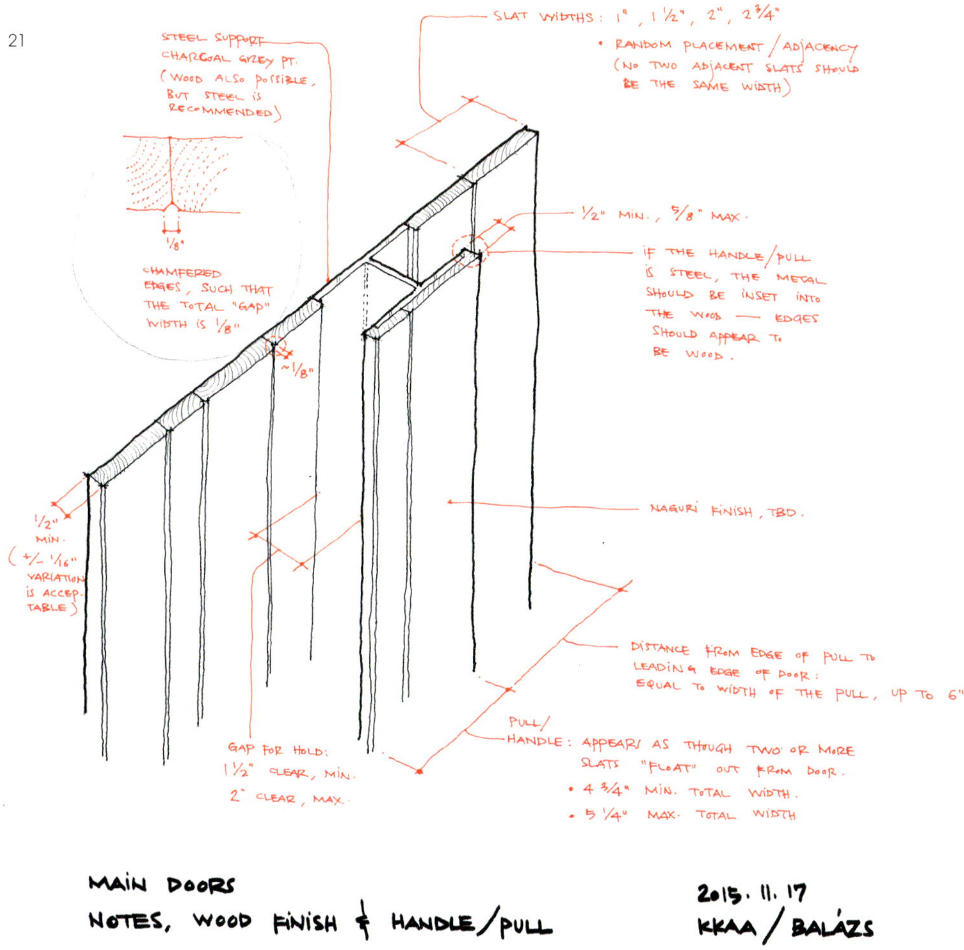

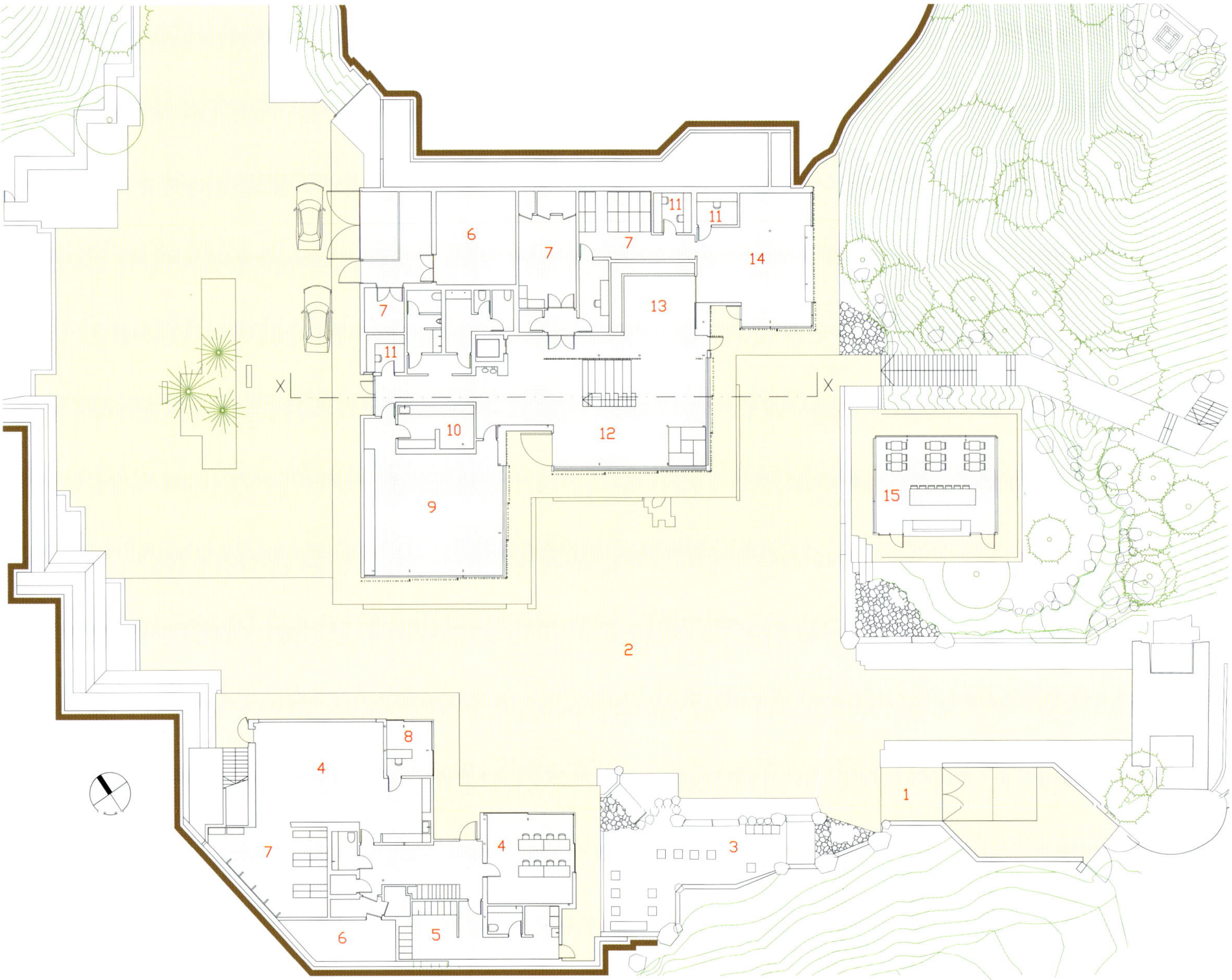

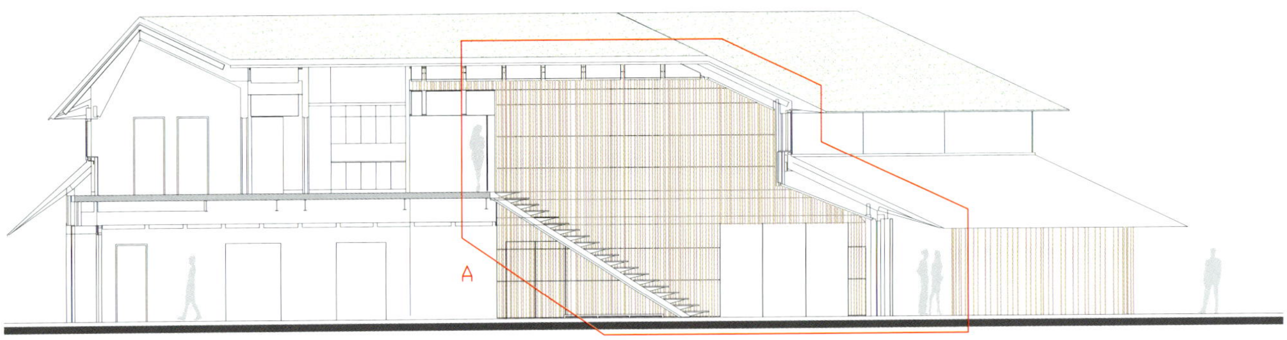

XX Section - Scale 1:200

- 1st level plan - Scale 1:400

1. Main entrance	9. Multipurpose room
2. Courtyard	10. Kitchen
3. Bonsai garden	11. Office
4. Workshop	12. Hall
5. Locker room	13. Gallery
6. Mechanical room	14. Shop
7. Storage	15. Tea House
8. Info point	

- 22.26 Study models from the initial project phases of the architecture in its setting
  23/25 Preliminary study drawing of site plan
  23. Site as found with parking and accessibility proposal
  24. Competition proposal
  25. Project status

22

23

24

25

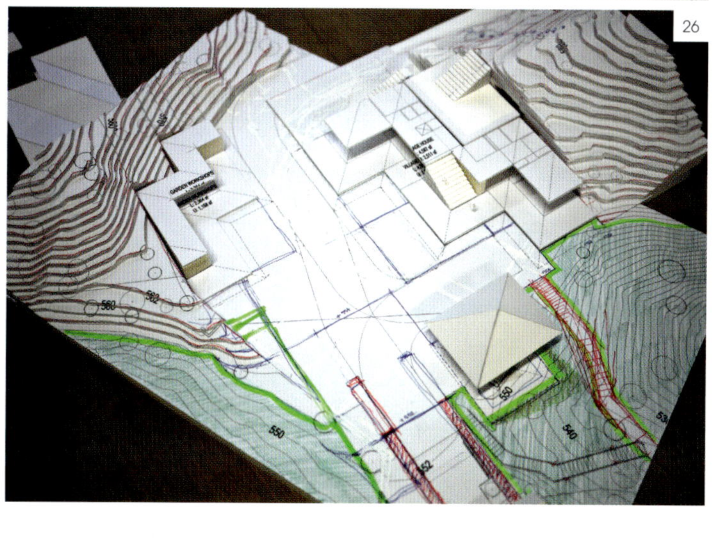

26

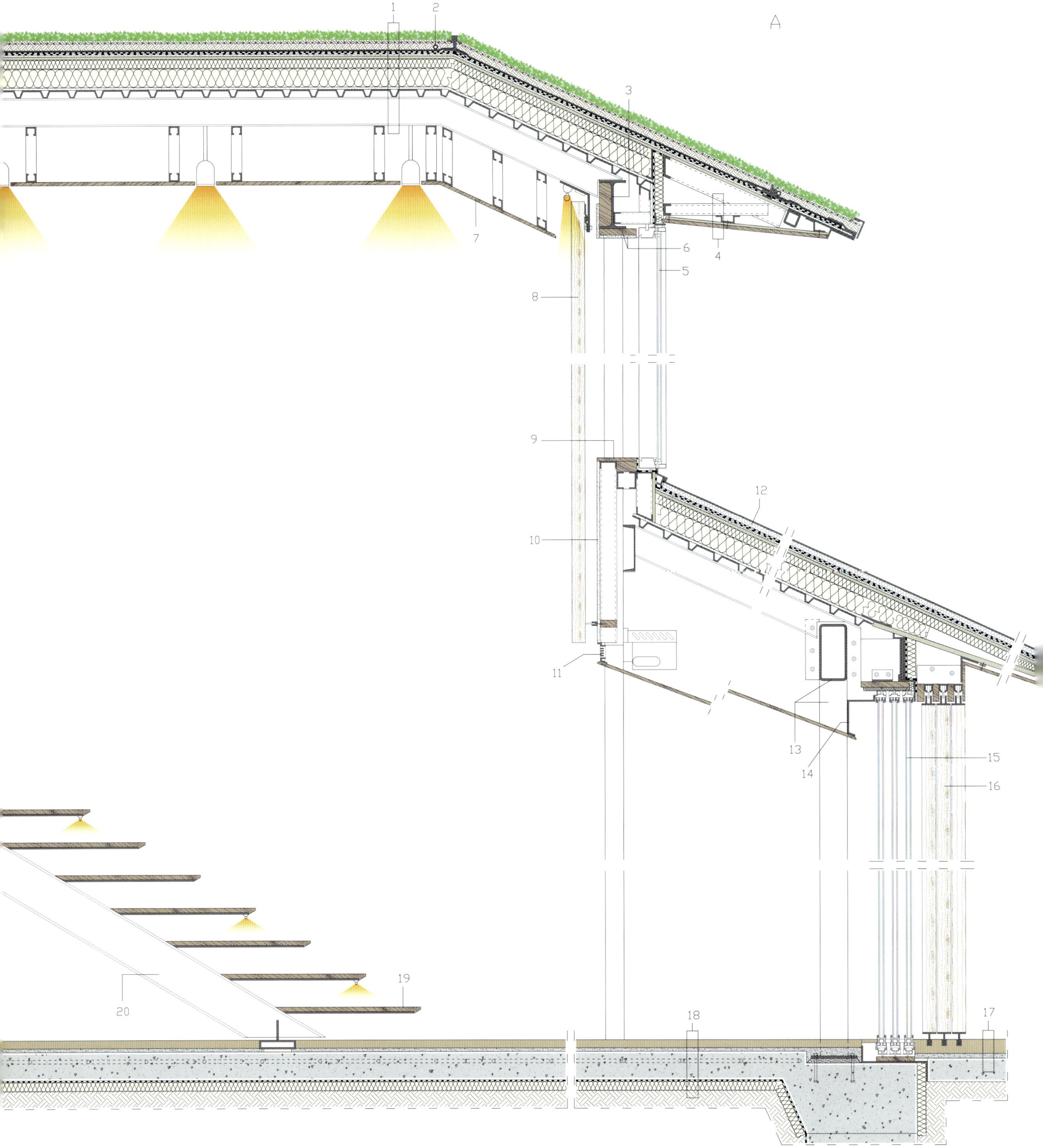
A
1
2
3
4
5
6
7
8
9
10
11
12
13
14
15
16
17
18
19
20

DETAIL A: CONSTRUCTION SYSTEM
VERTICAL SECTION - SCALE 1:25

1. Green roof comprising grass, soil with steel retaining mesh, root membrane, double waterproofing membrane, 1/4" (6 mm) plywood panel, 5/8" (16 mm) plywood panel, 2 x 4" (50+100 mm) rigid insulation, 1/2" (13 mm) drywall panel, 1 3/4" (45 mm) corrugated sheeting, 6 1/8" (155 mm) steel I-beam (parallel to plane of section)
2. Watering pipe
3. 21 5/8 x 11 7/8" (260x145 mm) steel I-beam
4. False ceiling comprising 3/4" (20 mm) Alaskan yellow cedar, 1/2" (13 mm) plywood panel, steel omega profiles, steel C-profile framing
5. Curtain wall comprising aluminum frame and 1/4 - 5/8 - 1/4" (6/16/6 mm) aluminum glazing units
6. Window trim comprising 5/8" (16 mm) drywall panel on wood blocking
7. False ceiling comprising micro-perforated bamboo panels on aluminum profile framing
8. Sunshading comprising wood battens on steel profiles with pin fasteners
9. Wood window trim
10. Bulkhead comprising 5/8" (16 mm) drywall panel on C-profile framing
11. Ventilation grille
12. Roof comprising aluminum panels with honeycomb core
13. Structural frame of 12 x 6 1/8" (305x155 mm) steel box profiles
14. Metal plate trim
15. Sliding aluminum door with 1/4 - 3/4 - 1/4" (6/18/6 mm) glazing unit
16. Sliding wood sunshading
17. 3" (75 mm) stone pavers, 1" (25 mm) screed, 5 1/8" (130 mm) reinforced concrete slab
18. 1 3/4" (44 mm) stone flooring, screed, 6 1/8" (155 mm) reinforced concrete slab with embedded radiant heating, waterproofing membrane, 2" (50 mm) rigid insulation, earth

ELBPHILHARMONIE HAMBURG, GERMANY

HERZOG & DE MEURON

The Free and Hanseatic City of Hamburg has a new landmark to join the Speicherstadt, an island complex of bonded warehouses, and Fritz Höger's Chilehaus - both of which are UNESCO World Heritage Sites. The Elbphilharmonie is a Stadtkrone that dominates the skyline as a cathedral does in older cities. Like the Sydney Opera House it stands apart on a site that juts into the harbor and captures the spirit of the water in its wave-like profile. Both buildings were engineered by Arup. As in Sydney, Hamburg's new icon will pay for itself many times over, making the overruns of cost and scheduling quite forgettable. There are also significant differences. In 1957, when juror Eero Saarinen plucked Jørn Utzon's competition entry from the reject pile, there was no software to translate his vision into reality. It took years to develop shapes that could be built, and Utzon was blamed and banished for problems caused by managerial incompetence and the contractor's shortcomings. Locals derided the project - "copulating turtles" was one sneer - and it destroyed the architect's career.

In contrast, Herzog & de Meuron's concept was acclaimed from the start - by public and planners - and it has retained its integrity through 13 years of design development and stop-go construction. In 2002, architect-developer Alexander Gérard proposed a new concert hall inside the Kaispeicher A warehouse. An austere brick wedge, it was constructed in 1963 to replace a war-devastated storage facility - just before Hamburg's port moved to a deeper stretch of the Elbe to accommodate container ships. Gérard met with Jacques Herzog and Pierre de Meuron, former classmates at the ETH in Zurich, and they quickly sketched a glass-clad complex extruded from the warehouse, treating it as a plinth. Apartments and a hotel would wrap around two centrally located auditoriums; parking, support spaces, public amenities and mechanical services would be accommodated in the warehouse. The city authorities approved the design, waiving height limits and the mandate to hold a competition for public buildings, and later took over as the client.

The Elbphilharmonie anchors HafenCity, an ambitious redevelopment of the former port area. Like many European cities, from Copenhagen to Barcelona, Hamburg has transformed its former industrial waterfront, creating a popular promenade, but the quality of

the buildings is uneven, and the project inevitably lacks the coherence of the old city, which was built up over centuries. At least the authorities are trying their best, with a thoughtful master plan and a requirement that developers hire talented architects. Much remains to be done before HafenCity is completed in the late 2020s, but Herzog & de Meuron have raised the bar.

The cost of construction was initially estimated at 77 million Euros - "a figure that no schoolchild would believe," says Herzog. It rose seven-fold as the program was enlarged to include a third hall and more apartments, and as the complexity of the new structure grew. Six hundred steel piles had to be added to the existing 1,100. The grid of columns that supported the six upper floors of the warehouse were removed to accommodate more cars on the lower levels, and three service cores provide support for the entire complex. The main auditorium, seating 2,150, had to be isolated from the noise and vibration of passing ships, which required a double concrete shell suspended from cable trusses and mounted on 360 springs. Project director Jan-Christoph Lindert likens it to the yolk in an egg. A 550-seat multipurpose hall is separately isolated.

The new structure, rising to a peak of 29 stories, is clad in a double layer of warped glass panels printed with 500 different dot patterns to provide thermal insulation, frame views, enrich the façades, and provide a point of reference for ships' radar. Surface patterns have long been a signature feature of this firm, and here they've created a sparkling crystal, which changes shape as you move around it, and goes from dark to reflective as shifts of light illuminate its facets. The bottom floor, containing a public plaza, is recessed and opens onto terraces with arches that frame views of city and harbor to east and west. Scooped out apartment balconies add depth to the harbor frontages. The roof is a fifth façade of eight concave surfaces.

A curved escalator slices through the warehouse, launching concertgoers and visitors on an architectural promenade that continues to the upper levels of the main auditorium. Hotel and apartments can also be accessed from this multi-level plaza or from separate ground-level entrances. Brick gives way to oak, exposed concrete to Venetian plaster, and strip to rounded ceiling lights as one ascends stairs whose angular complexity evokes the drawings of Maurits Cornelis Escher.

A glass-capped lightwell provides vistas up and down. All this builds anticipation for the main event: a four-level concert hall of dazzling virtuosity. The vineyard plan of Scharoun's Berlin Philharmonie was a point of departure but the architects looked to earlier models to create a new typology. "We were inspired by the Greek theater, which is carved from stone, to give gravity to a concert hall that is up in the air," says Herzog. "Another important ingredient is the soccer stadium with its steep tiers to create a strong interaction between audience and players. And third is the tent-like roof that you find in the Bayreuth Festspielhaus - the notion of a suspended fabric canopy, rather than a dome or acoustic panels."

Working with acoustician Yasuhisa Toyota, the architects lined the hall with high-density gypsum fiberboard panels, milled into a relief pattern that evokes the volcanic rock of Lanzarote. The depth and scale of the relief was determined by an algorithm, to diffuse the sound as needed and to ensure a consistency of surface texture in places where no diffusion is needed. A trumpet like form descends from the peak of the canopy to provide a sound reflector 15 meters above the central performance area, which employs Oregon cedar for added resonance. The art and science of acoustics has advanced since Toyota's predecessor advised Frank O. Gehry to abandon his vineyard plan for Walt Disney Concert Hall and put everything in a shoebox. The architect created a wooden ship within the rectilinear concrete container, turning constraints to advantage; Herzog & de Meuron were able to shape the hall as they pleased with no compromise in the quality of the sound. Some things are slow to change. Though acoustics can be precisely plotted with software, the architects constructed a 1:10 model for additional testing, as Gehry did.

The auditorium can best be appreciated from the top level, where its verticality is most evident, and the blocks of seating are spaced out by the richly textured walls and sculptured oak balustrades. Blocky gray seats are designed to absorb sound in the unlikely event that any remain unoccupied. Three internal circulation routes spiral down from the stacked lobbies, linking seating areas and bringing concertgoers together. The three-level organ pipes shimmer in a soft light and enrich this visual expression of the profundity and excitement of classical music at its best. Sight and sound are fused and achieve the sublime.

16th level plan - Scale 1:1000

1. Main concert hall
2. Organ
3. Foyer
4. Residential
5. Hotel

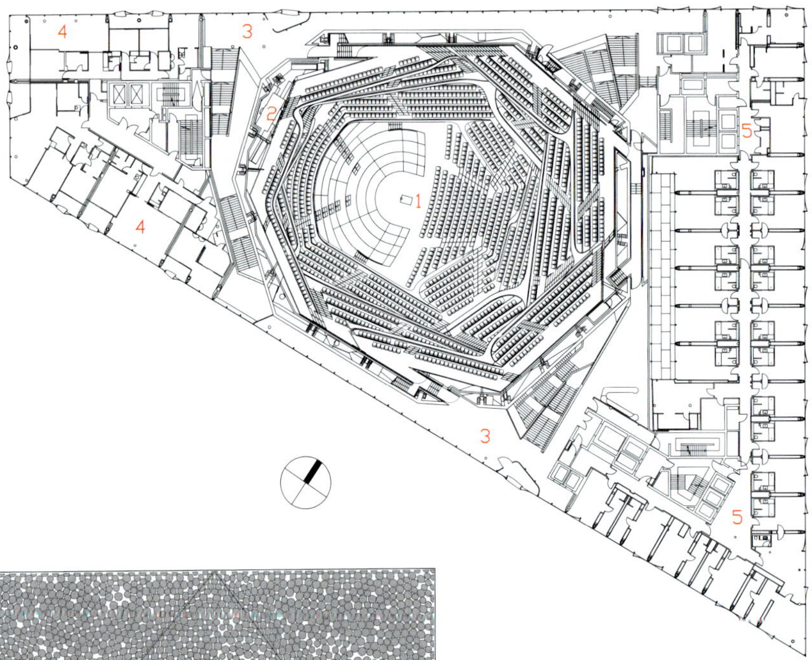

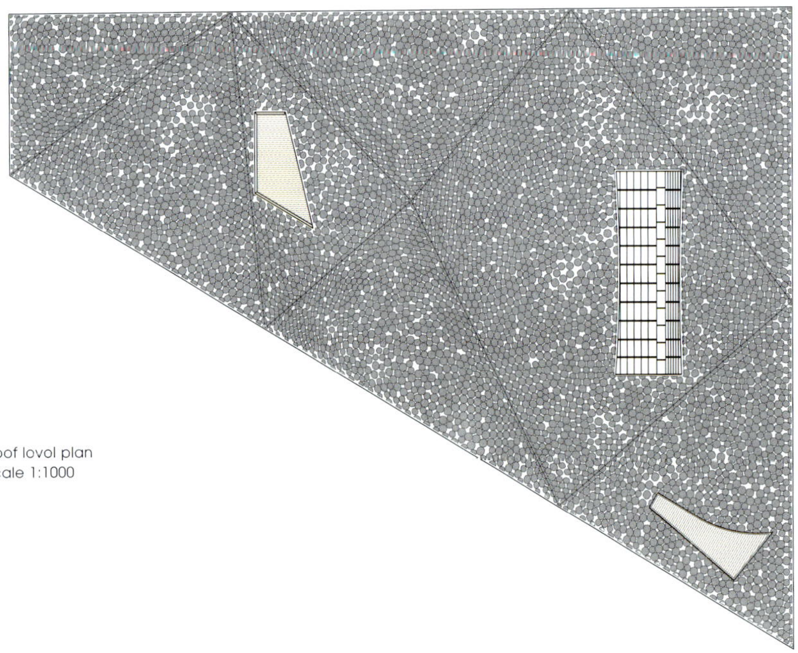

Roof lovol plan
Scale 1:1000

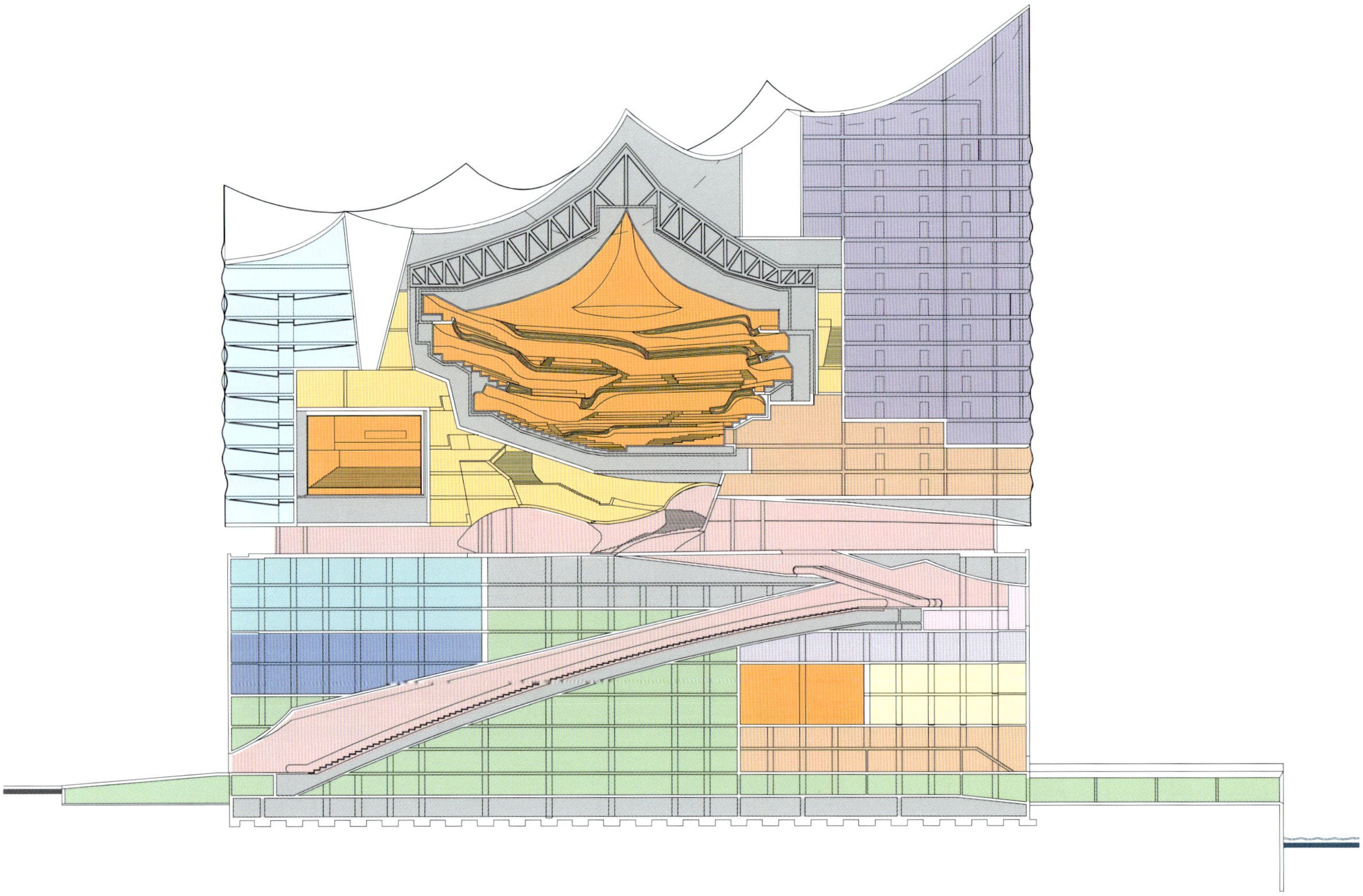

■ Longitudinal cross-section showing functional distribution

Philharmonie

- Music hall
- Foyer
- Music education area
- Backstage

Hotel

- Rooms
- Conference area, restaurant, wellness and fitness
- Facilities management, hotel administration

Residential

- Apartments
- Storage

Services

- Parking
- Technical room

Plaza

- Escalator, plaza
- Cafeteria

■ Cutaway view showing concert halls and distribution spaces. Rendering

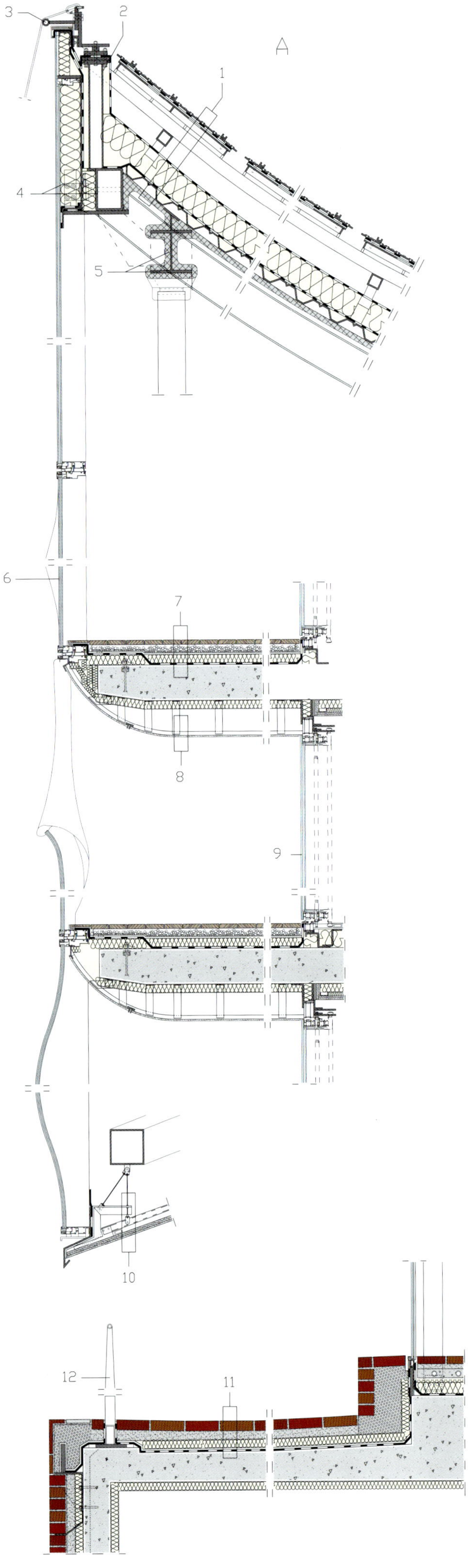

DETAIL A:
ROOF AND EASTERN FAÇADE
VERTICAL SECTION
SCALE 1:40

1. Roof comprising circular micro-perforated aluminum "sequins" of different diameters, sub-structure of Ø 3 1/2" (90 mm) steel pipe profiles, 3 1/2 x 3 1/2" (90x90 mm) steel box beams, steel pedestals, waterproofing membrane, 7 1/8" (180 mm) impact-resistant rigid insulation, vapor barrier, insulated corrugated sheeting
2. Roof edging consisting of bolted 2 x 4" (50x100 mm) steel box profiles
3. Steel profile anchoring maintenance safety cables
4. 7 7/8 x 11 3/4" (200x300 mm) steel box beam upright connected to glazed curtain wall by bolted steel plates and profiles
5. Supporting structure comprising 11 3/4" (300 mm) h and 10 5/8" (270 mm) h steel I-beams fixed to roof by steel point fasteners
6. Glazed curtain wall with aluminum frame and double glazing units comprising curved laminated glass printed with dots with different diameters
7. Loggia flooring comprising 1 1/4" (30 mm) European oak floorboards, aluminum sub-structure, 2" (50 mm) gravel fire protection, protective membrane, 2 3/8" (60 mm) insulation layer, waterproofing membrane, cantilevered 9 7/8" (250 mm) reinforced concrete slab, 2 3/8" (60 mm) rigid insulation
8. Loggia soffit comprising 1/2" (12 mm) eco-friendly gypsum board with smooth finish, plates with different dimensions anchored to slab
9. Operable full-height glazed façade with 3/8 x 5/8 x 1/4" (9/16/6 mm) aluminum glazing units
10. Plaza ceiling with plaster finish painted white, double 1/2" (12.5 mm) fiber cement panel, 1 1/16" (27 mm) steel C-profile supports, 2" (50 mm) steel plate, folded steel profile with tie rods suspended from supporting structure
11. Plaza paving comprising 3" (75 mm) clinker bricks, 3" (75 mm) screed, waterproofing membrane, 2 3/8" (60 mm) rigid insulation, protective membrane, waterproofing membrane, reinforced concrete slab
12. Railing comprising black steel profiles

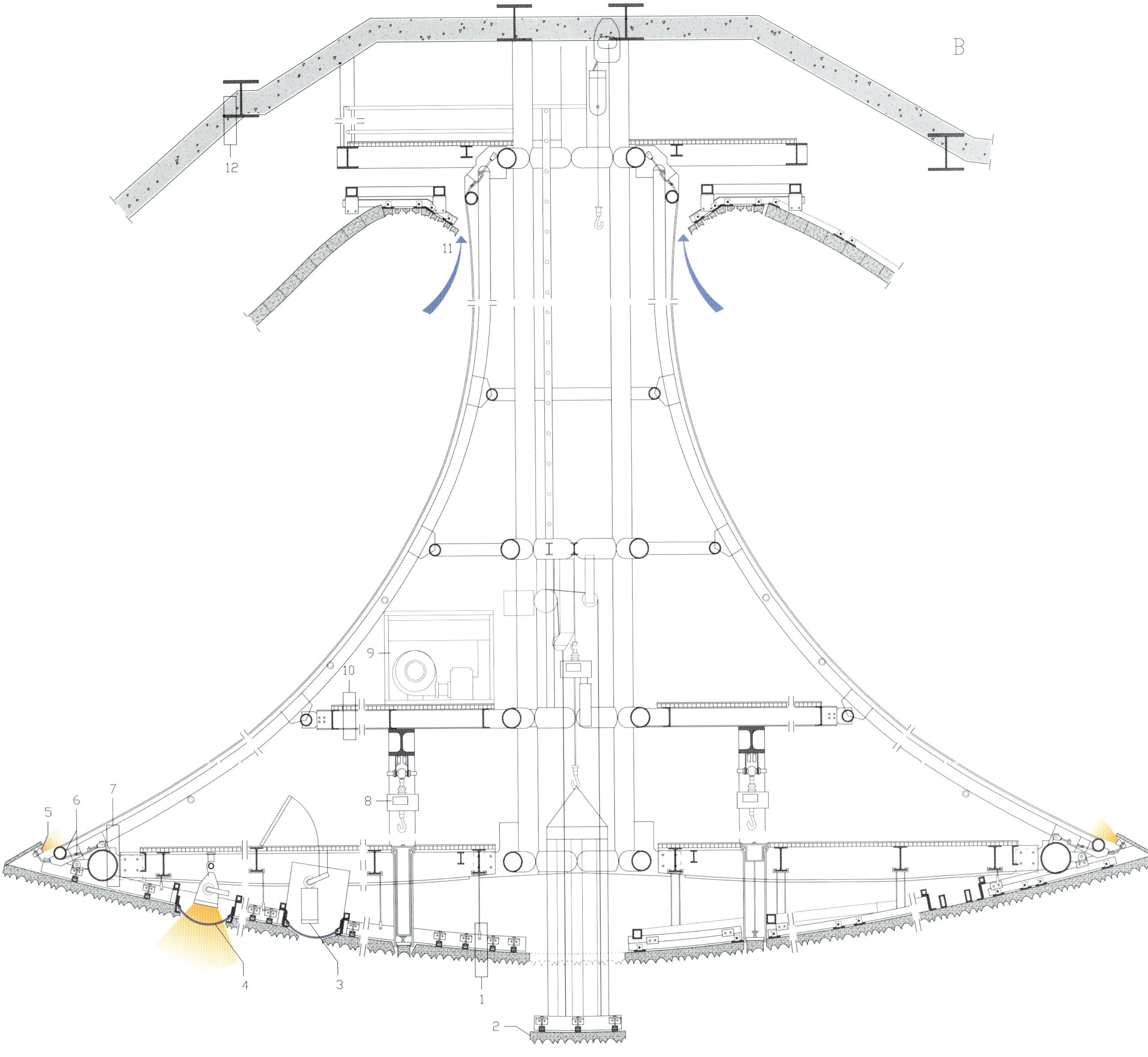

DETAIL B: SOUND REFLECTOR
VERTICAL SECTION - SCALE 1:40

1. Acoustic ceiling comprising 4″ (100 mm) irregularly potholed gypsum fiberglass panels, fastening system comprising steel C- and L-profiles bolted to steel plates, tie rods suspended from structure
2. Recessed speaker with system of pulleys and steel cables for adjusting height
3. Camera
4. Adjustable spotlight for scene lighting
5. Spotlights for illuminating reflector
6. Transparent fiberglass fabric skin tensioned on Ø 4″ (100 mm) steel pipe profiles and attached by steel fasteners
7. Concentric frame of Ø 3 3/4″ (95 mm) steel pipe profiles, Ø 9 5/8″ (245 mm) steel pipe profile around perimeter, connecting radial Ø 4 1/8″ (105 mm) steel pipe profiles
8. System of pulleys and steel cables for moving stage equipment
9. Organ echo division
10. Operator platform consisting of steel grating on IPE 160 beams and steel C-profiles
11. Opening for expulsion of exhaust fumes
12. 7 7/8″ (200 mm) reinforced concrete shell with 11 3/8″ (290 mm) steel I-beams

DETAIL C: BALCONY
VERTICAL SECTION - SCALE 1:40

1. Balcony finish comprising gypsum fiberglass panels irregularly potholed to increase acoustic modulation
2. Steel plate anchoring railing to structure
3. Inside finish of railing comprising cut and polished oak
4. Steel profile handrail painted black
5. 5/8″ (15 mm) oak flooring, glue, acoustical insulating mat, 3/4 + 1 1/4″ (18+32 mm) plaster fiber panels, 1″ (25 mm) flame-retardant panel, 7 7/8 x 7 7/8″ (200x200 mm) box edge beam
6. Spotlights providing walkway lighting
7. Structural frame of 11 7/8″ (300 mm) h steel I-beams with 1″ (25 mm) thick flameproof insulation
8. Adjustable acoustic baffles with mechanical winding system recessed in floor

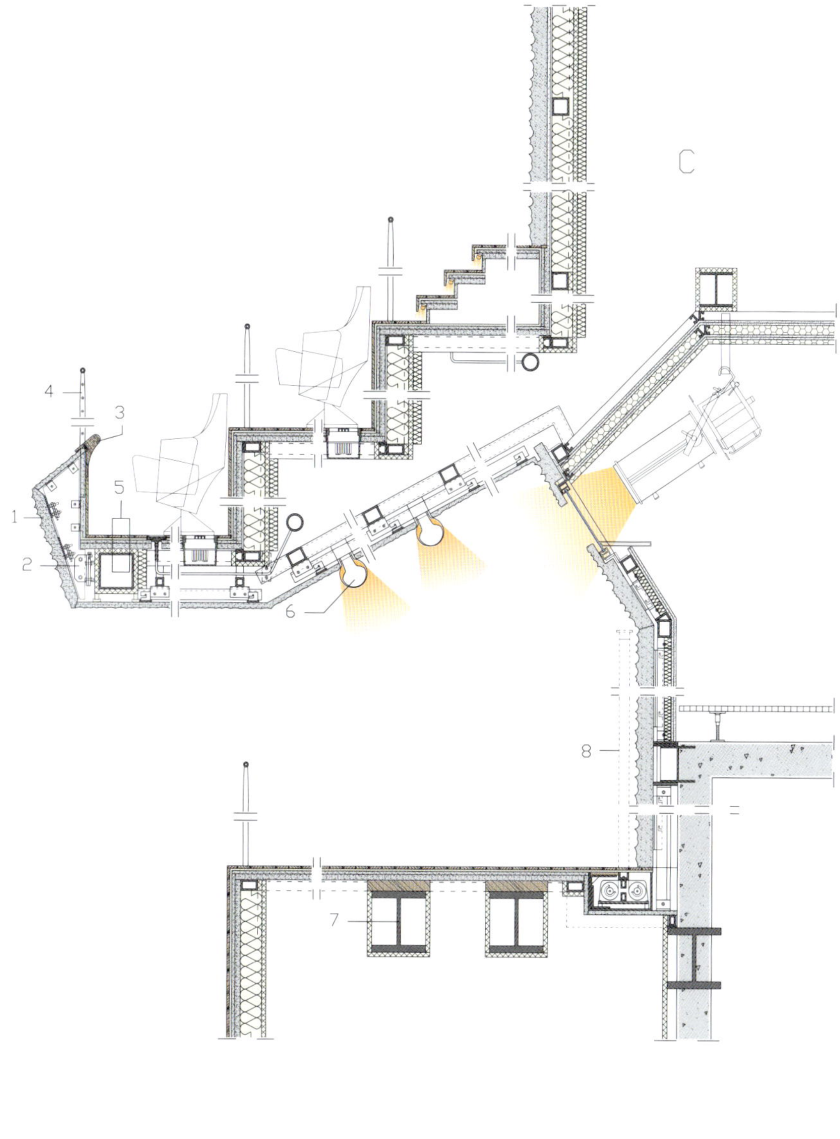

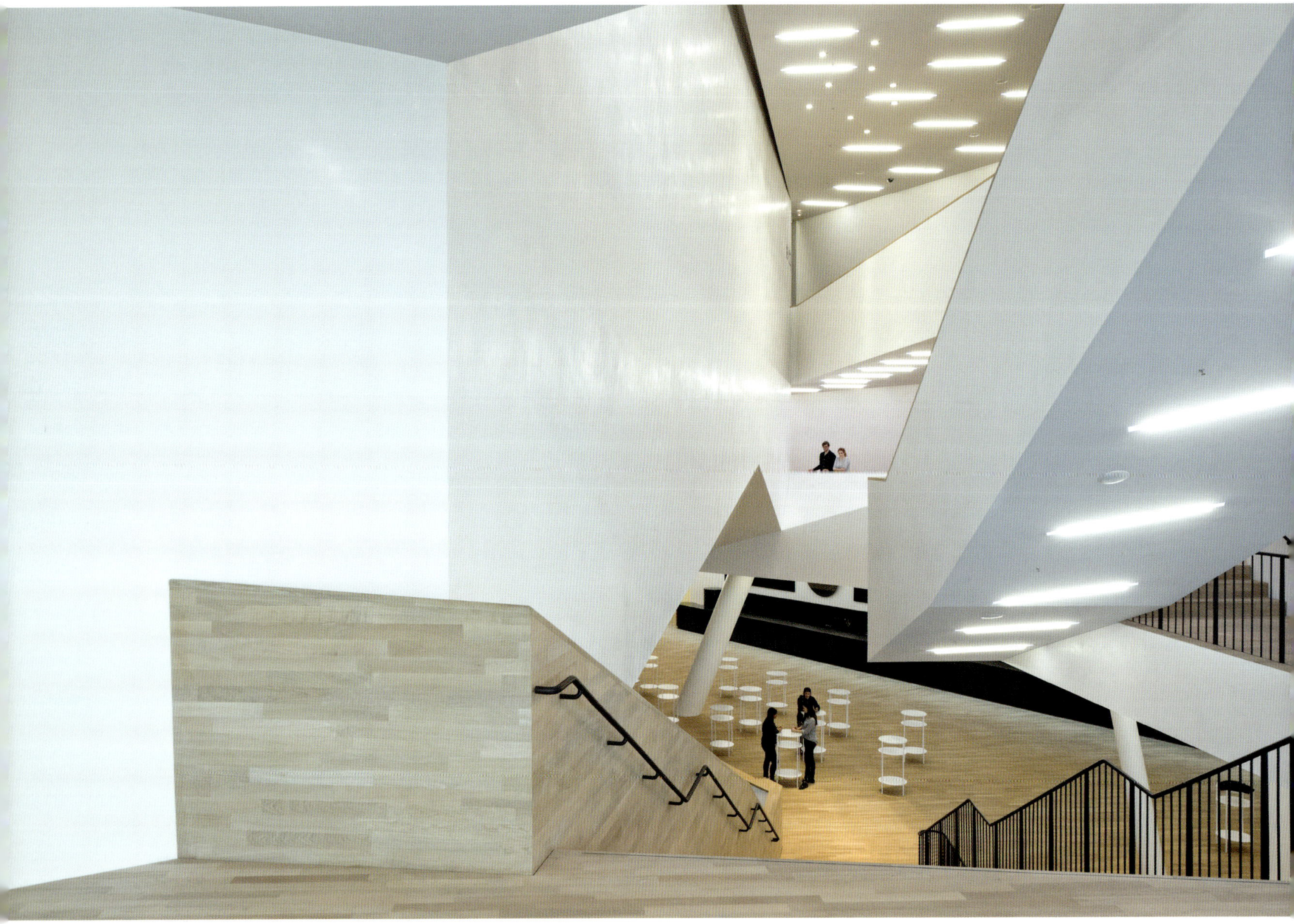

TEOPANZOLCO AUDITORIUM, CUERNAVACA
CULTURAL CENTER, TEOTITLÁN DEL VALLE
MEXICO
PRODUCTORA

The community cultural center in the small town of Teotitlán del Valle is nimble and assured. In the southern state of Oaxaca, Teotitlán is famous for its tapestries, carpets and weaving; with a wonderful urban structure, the town has however few recent buildings of note. The architects for the project, Productora, are known for intellect and cultural finesse. While the community cultural center has still to be fully occupied, it nevertheless shows Productora's adroitness at conceptualizing a civic institution in tune with context. Similar traits are evident at the Teopanzolco auditorium, recently completed by Productora in Cuernavaca in collaboration with Isaac Broid, also from Mexico City.

Different in form and scale, the two projects share a sense of strategic thinking characteristic of Productora. Each has a distinct and distinctive morphology in reciprocity with its urban and topographic setting. The Teotitlán project is a linear bar, cranking in plan to reinforce its site and split to create a portico that shelters entrances and a generous flight of steps descending to the village stream. In Cuernavaca, the auditorium is planned as a giant triangle rising above the principal performance space with a higher, supplementary triangle above the foyer. This is an architecture of emphatic geometry. In the case of Cuernavaca, such boldness is in response to adjacent temple ruins dating from the 14th and 15th Centuries.

In Teotitlán the new architecture works with an urban fabric at once vernacular and classical; in fact, the sequential gardens and terraces of the town also date from pre-Columbian times. The new structure stitches together older, stoa-like buildings (housing weavers) that face a long rectangular plaza, reinforcing one corner of this outdoor public room. The roof of Productora's insertion continues as a unifying element across the entry void with its grand staircase. The Cuernavaca building is a more direct response to landscape - there, the institution functions as a contemporary earthwork. Visitors can clamber across the roof of the auditorium, then turn to ascend to the building's prow and look out across the ancient ruins.

The difference is a matter of scale and place: the auditorium is bigger, its site simultaneously suburban and next to an archeological precinct. Nevertheless, there are echoes of one project in the other, and vice versa.

With its giant sloping roof, the auditorium is akin to such recent iconic projects as Mecanoo's library for TU Delft (1995) and Snøhetta's opera house emerging out of the Oslo fjord (2008). All three subsume the given program and many necessary constituents of the interior beneath an artificial ground plane, a scenographic marker that serves as a generous meeting place, for encounter with each location and each institution. Between sculpture and infrastructure, the roofscape in Cuernavaca may also recall a specifically Mexican modernity of vivid geometry and bravura structure. Witness, for instance, many large seminal projects by Pedro Ramírez Vázquez or by Teodoro González de León in the 1960s and 70s.

1

2

3

4

The Aztec ruins of Teopanzolco are contiguous with the auditorium site. A dozen or so platform buildings survive, rectangular mounds of black basalt set in a sea of deep, preternatural green grass. Their construction is weighty and archaic whereas the auditorium uses modern technology and techniques. However, the idea of platform is common to both - massive and impenetrable-looking, in the case of Teopanzolco; lean and even bony for the auditorium, offering a raked pier or promenade. A half century ago, the Danish architect Jørn Utzon wrote in praise of platform structures he saw in the Yucatán: "They (the Mayans) had from here the sky, the clouds and the breeze" (*Platforms and Plateaus: Ideas of a Danish Architect*, Jørn Utzon, *Zodiac*, no. 10, Milan, 1962). Now visitors to Cuernavaca can enjoy a similar experience.

Both new buildings are constructed of poured-in-place concrete, with horizontal board-marking (to emphasize its topographic allusions) in Cuernavaca, and vertical marking in Teotitlán (in sync with its vertical apertures and the traditional proportions of immediate neighbors). In both projects, the palette is necessarily limited. In Cuernavaca, steel is used to create skeletal handrails on the roof terraces above and unglazed gridded screens allowing for aeration of foyer areas below; from the main foyer, there is a framed panoramic view through such a screen to the great platform of Teopanzolco, once the base for twin Aztec temples. The designers also use minimal steel sections to fabricate witty signage for the auditorium interior.

In section, the auditorium descends gently with the site; interior spaces are lined in cumaru, a Brazilian teak, articulating the linearity of individual lumber elements. To the rear of the auditorium, a flat-roofed extension houses changing rooms, a black box theater, and other auxiliary spaces. This accessible terrace is punctured with small glazed patios, its perimeter wall breached with a portico and flight of stairs reminiscent of those in Teotitlán. If the Teotitlán building is more urbanistic in form, it is also more surprising in section, falling beneath the level of the village stream. Interior spaces include one remarkable, triple-height gallery with a bullnose sculptural stairs and a mysterious service door several meters above the gallery floor.

Productora know form and know strategy. Created a decade ago by two young Mexicans, a Belgian and an Argentinian, all of whom had worked for Fernando Romero at LCM (Laboratorio de la Ciudad de México), Productora first came to attention with their winning yet unrealized proposal for Caracas, Venezuela: a slender cubic tower with hints of Terragni in Como. Soon after, in the northern state of Chihuahua, they interred a residence into a hillside to capitalize on its sloping site and respond to regulations demanding pitched roofs. To compete for the auditorium, they collaborated with Broid, an established member of the Mexico City design scene with a track record of institutional buildings and proposals.

Frequently published and included in exhibitions at home and abroad, Productora have with these projects in Teotitlán and Cuernavaca moved to the next level of professional achievement. They now represent a vivid strand in the evolution of Mexican Modernism.

TEOPANZOLCO AUDITORIUM
PRODUCTORA WITH ISAAC BROID

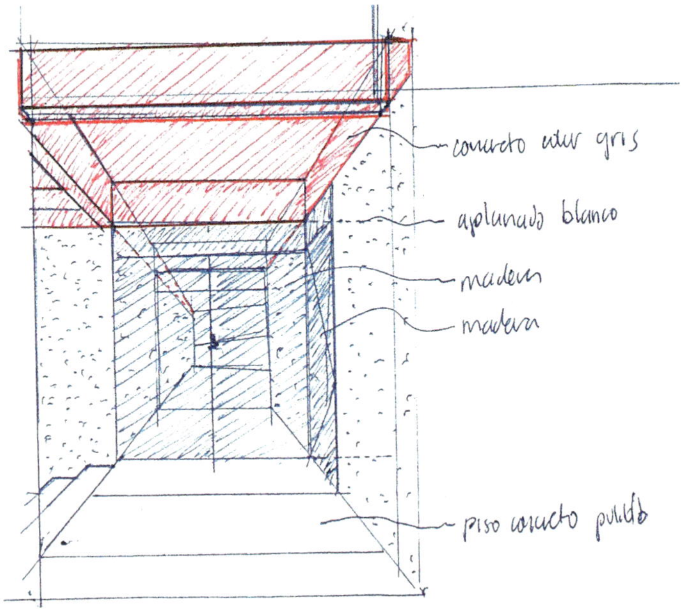

5

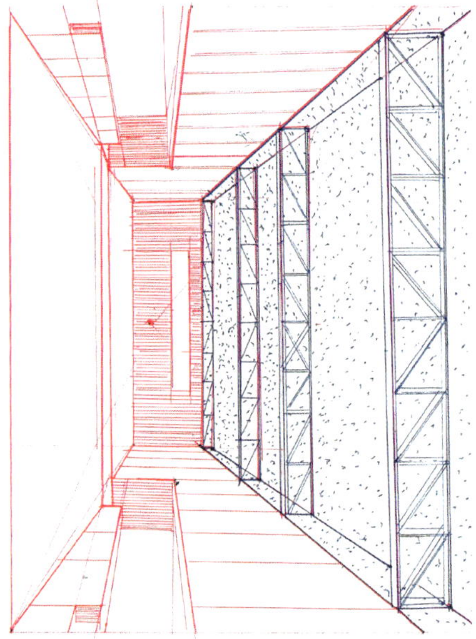

6

■ 5/7 Details of materials employed and study sketches of the façade's geometrical configuration

8/10 Planimetric/volumetric study model showing new building in relation to the nearby archeological site

8

9

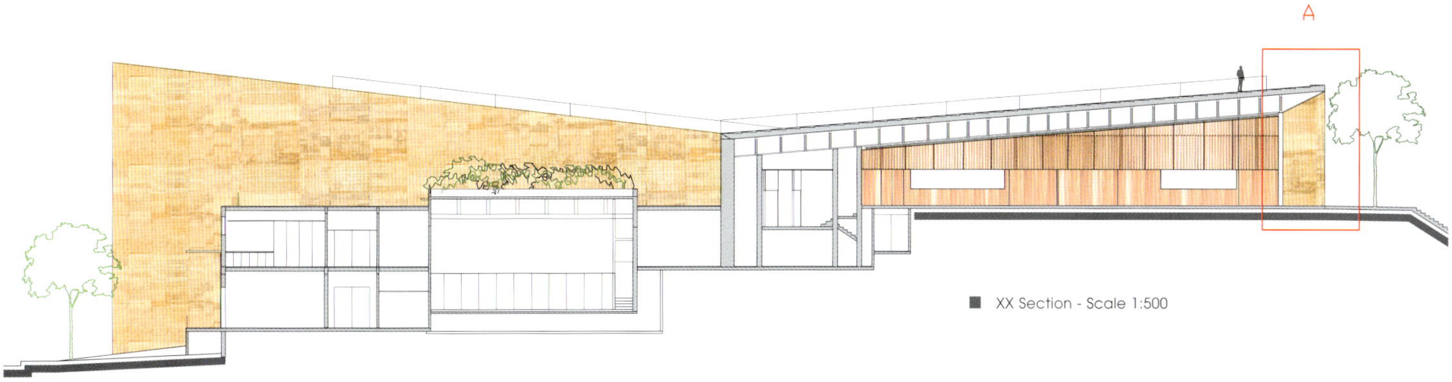

■ XX Section - Scale 1:500

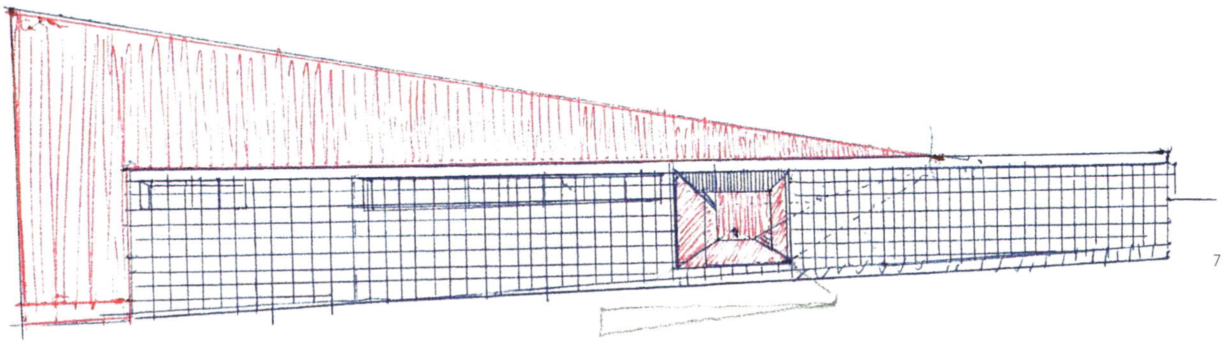

7

■ East elevation - Scale 1:500

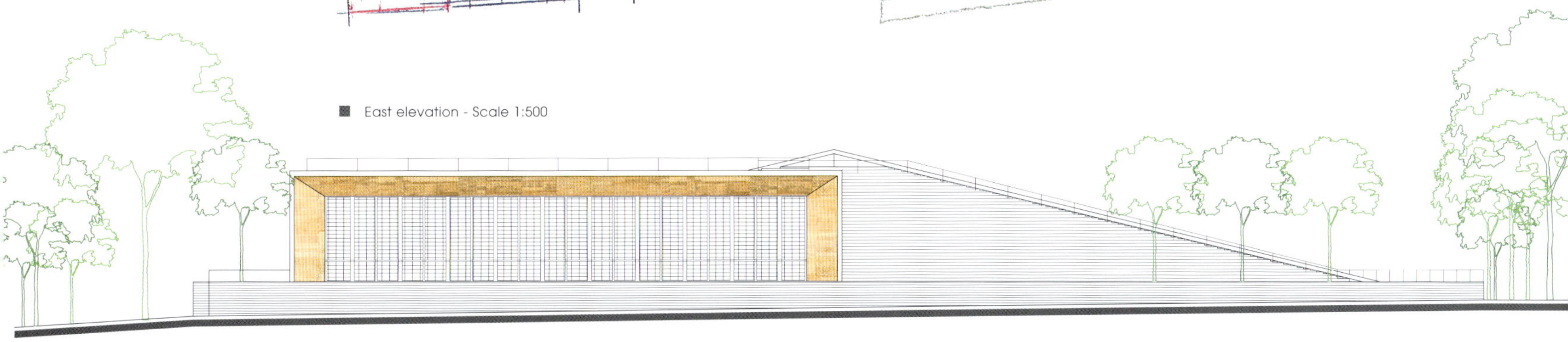

10

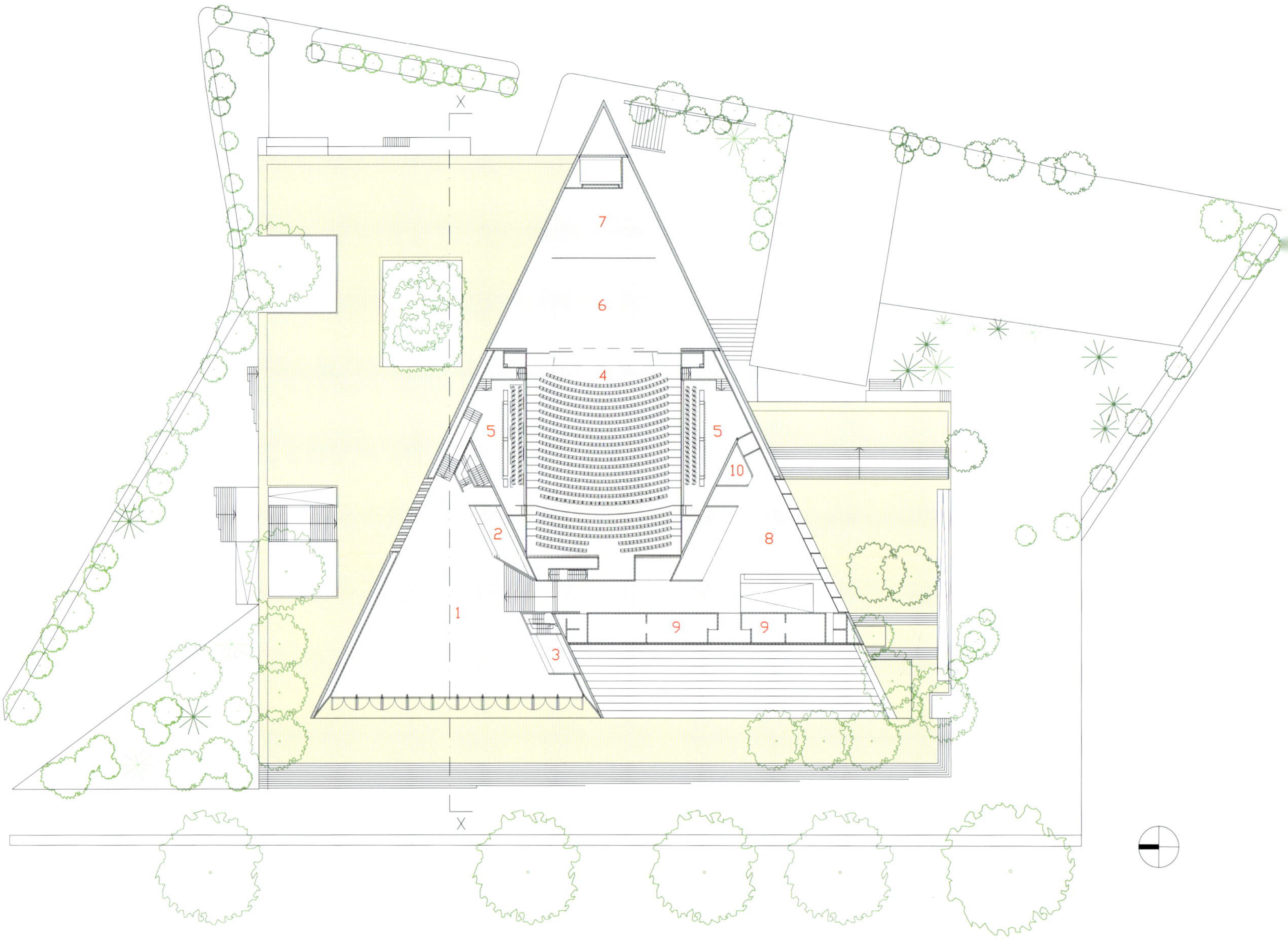

■ 2nd level plan - Scale 1:800

1. Foyer
2. Box office
3. Cafeteria
4. Orchestra seats
5. Box seats
6. Stage
7. Backstage
8. Foyer
9. Restroom
10. First aid

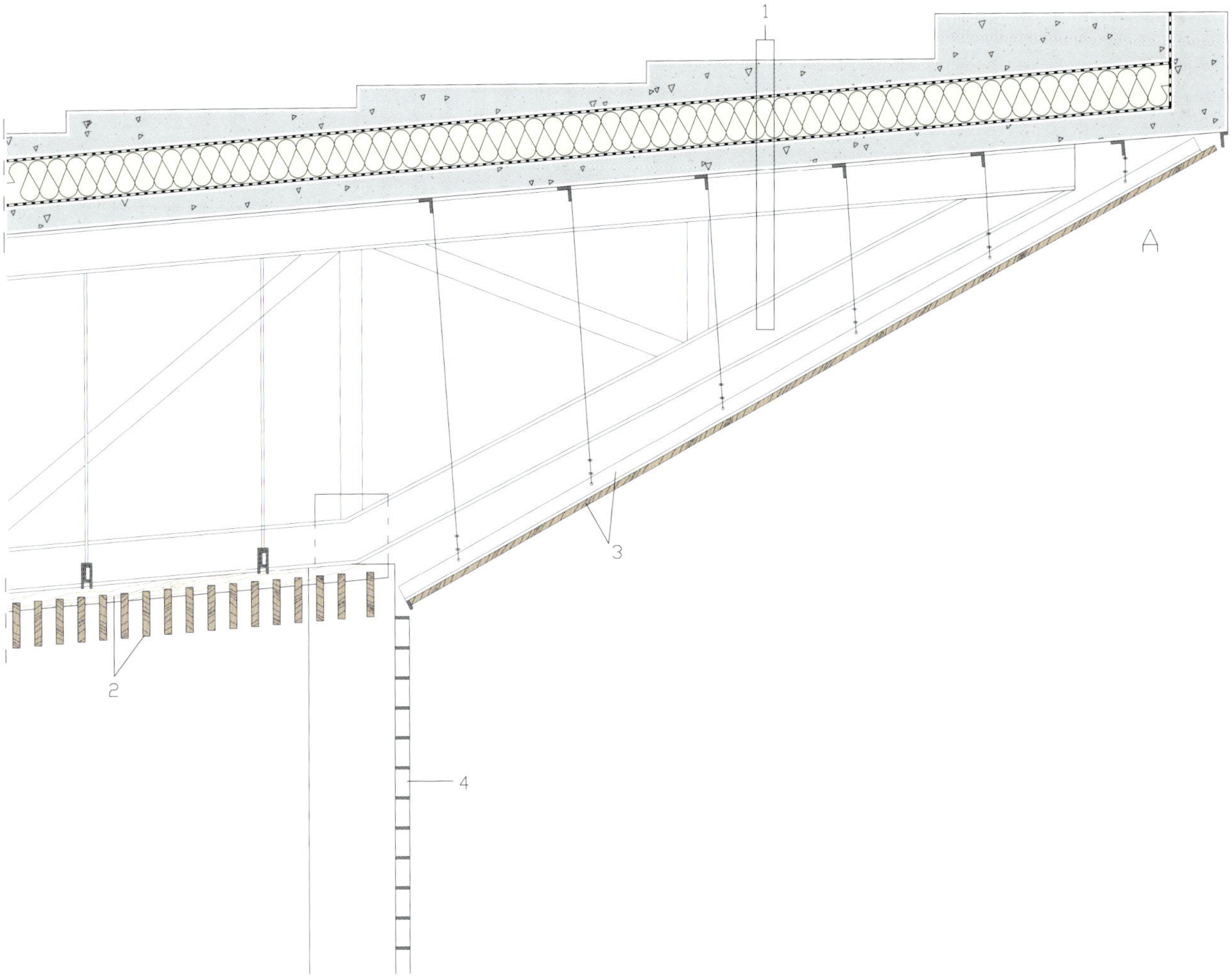

DETAIL A: FAÇADE WITH WINDSCREEN
VERTICAL SECTION - SCALE 1:25

1. Reinforced concrete stepped roof, waterproofing membrane, 5 7/8" (150 mm) polystyrene rigid insulation, 4" (100 mm) reinforced concrete slab, roof truss comprising steel C- and L-profiles
2- False ceiling comprising 5 7/8 x 1" (150x25 mm) on wood beam suspended by tie rods from supporting structure
3- Soffit comprising 3/4" (19 mm) wood on steel angle profiles suspended by tie rods from supporting structure
4- Opening steel grating windscreen
5- 2" (50 mm) polished concrete floor, 5 7/8" (150 mm) reinforced concrete slab, compacted earth layer
6- Waterproofing membrane protecting rainwater guttering
7- 3 1/2 x 3 1/2" (90x90 mm) steel angle profiles

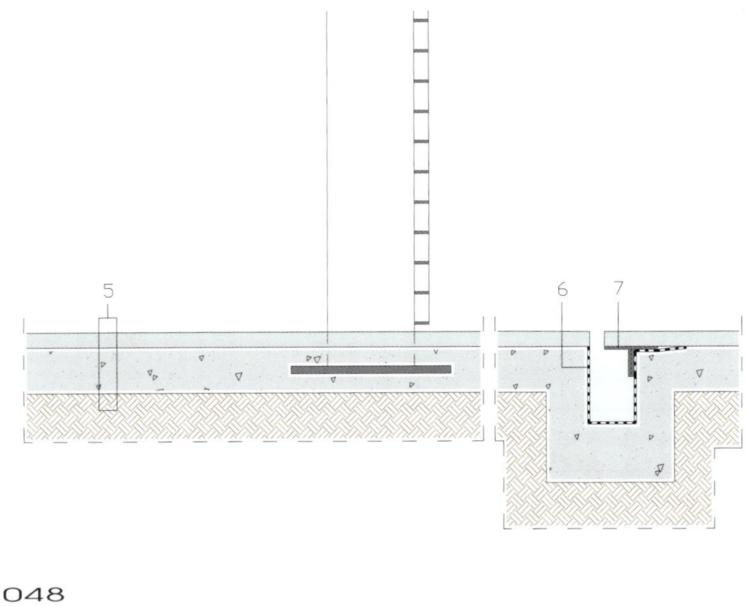

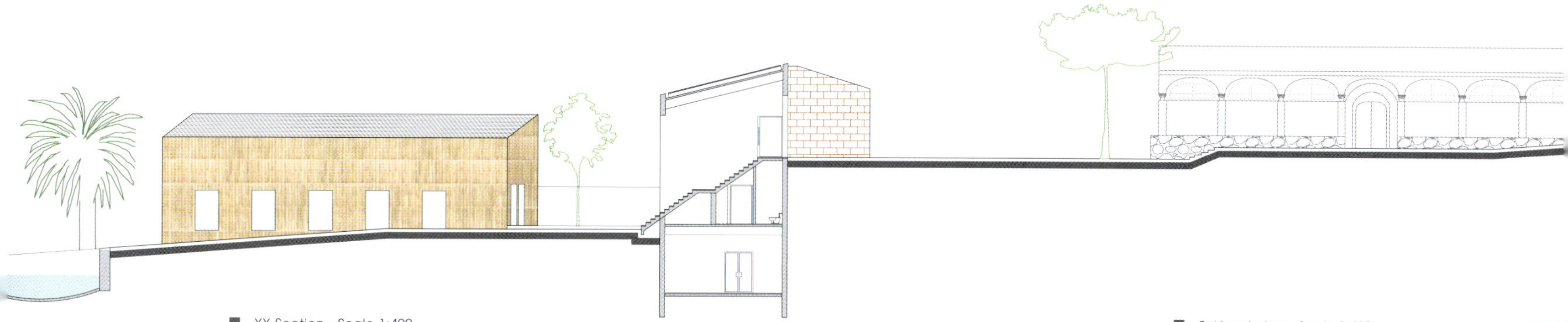

■ XX Section - Scale 1:400

■ 2nd level plan - Scale 1:400

1. Access
2. Reception
3. Office
4. Temporary exhibition room
5. Patio
6. Reading room
7. Children´s reading room
8. Multipurpose room
9. Exhibition room
10. Storage room
11. Computer room

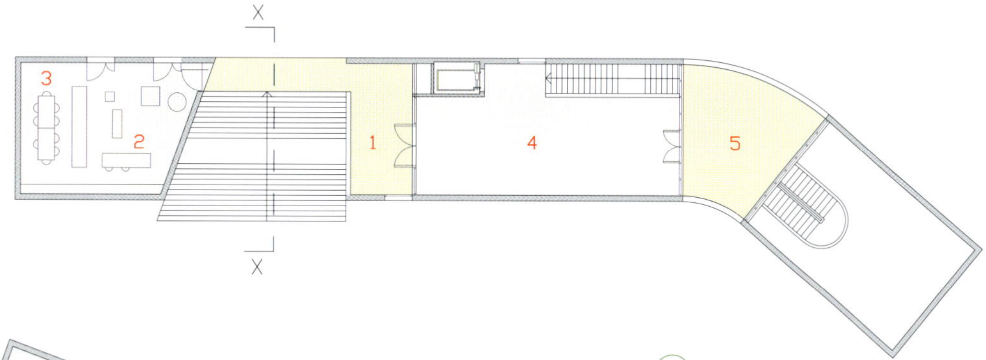

■ 1st level plan - Scale 1:400

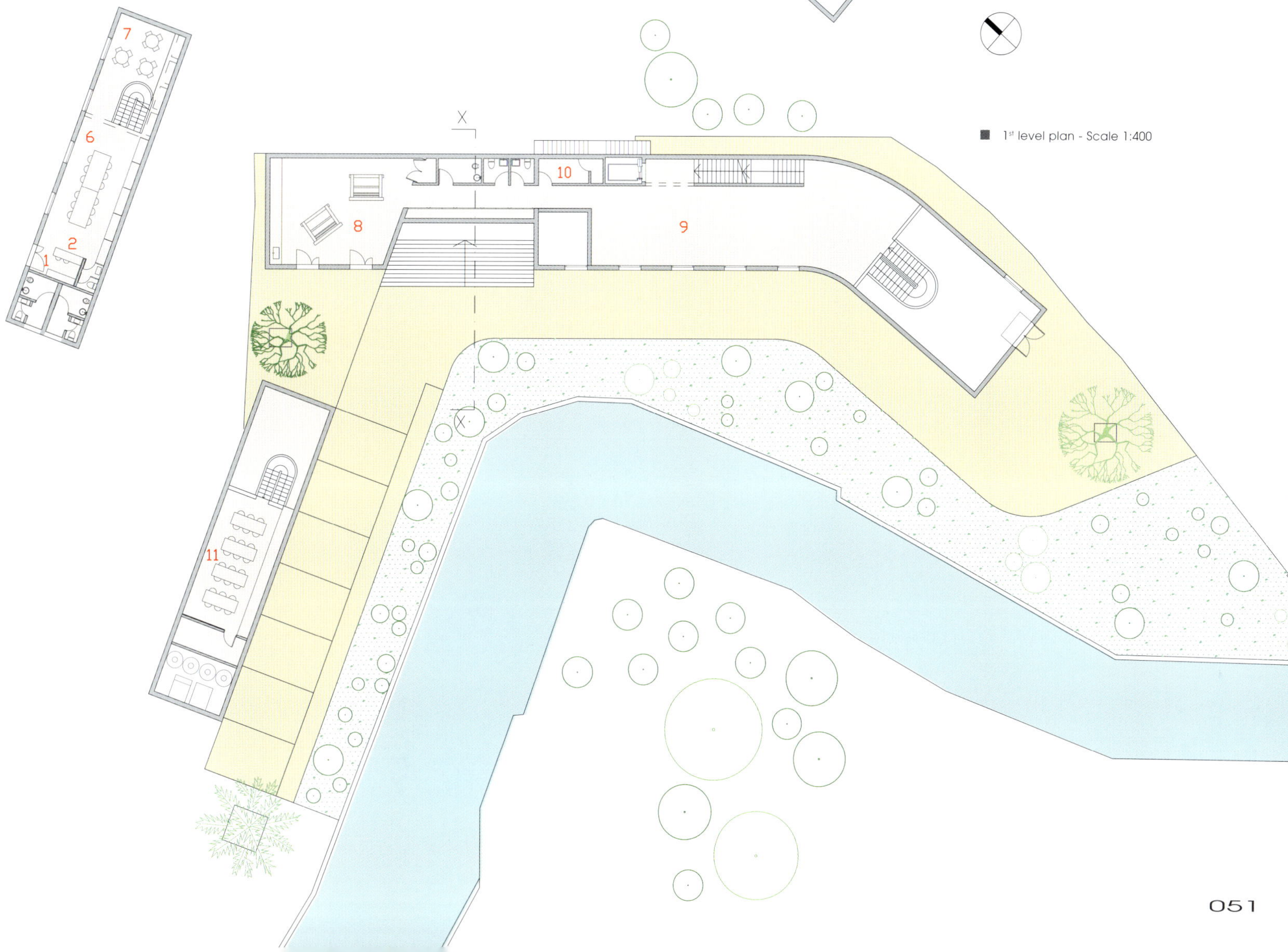

DETAIL A: CONSTRUCTION SYSTEM
VERTICAL SECTION - SCALE 1:25

1. Roof comprising 2" (50 mm) prefabricated concrete panels fastened by steel T-profiles, supporting reinforced concrete beam (parallel to plane of section), waterproofing membrane, 4" (100 mm) reinforced concrete slab, exposed 19 3/4" (500 mm) reinforced concrete beam
2- Screed forming slope
3- 11 3/4" (300 mm) thick exposed reinforced concrete edge structure
4- 1 1/8" (30 mm) terracotta block paving, 1 1/8" (30 mm) sand layer, 7 7/8" (200 mm) compacted bedding layer, earth
5- 2" (50 mm) polished concrete floor, 5 7/8" (150 mm) reinforced concrete slab, 2" (50 mm) lean concrete layer, waterproofing membrane, gravel
6- Linseed oil-treated pine cupboards
7- Linseed oil-treated pine hollow-core door

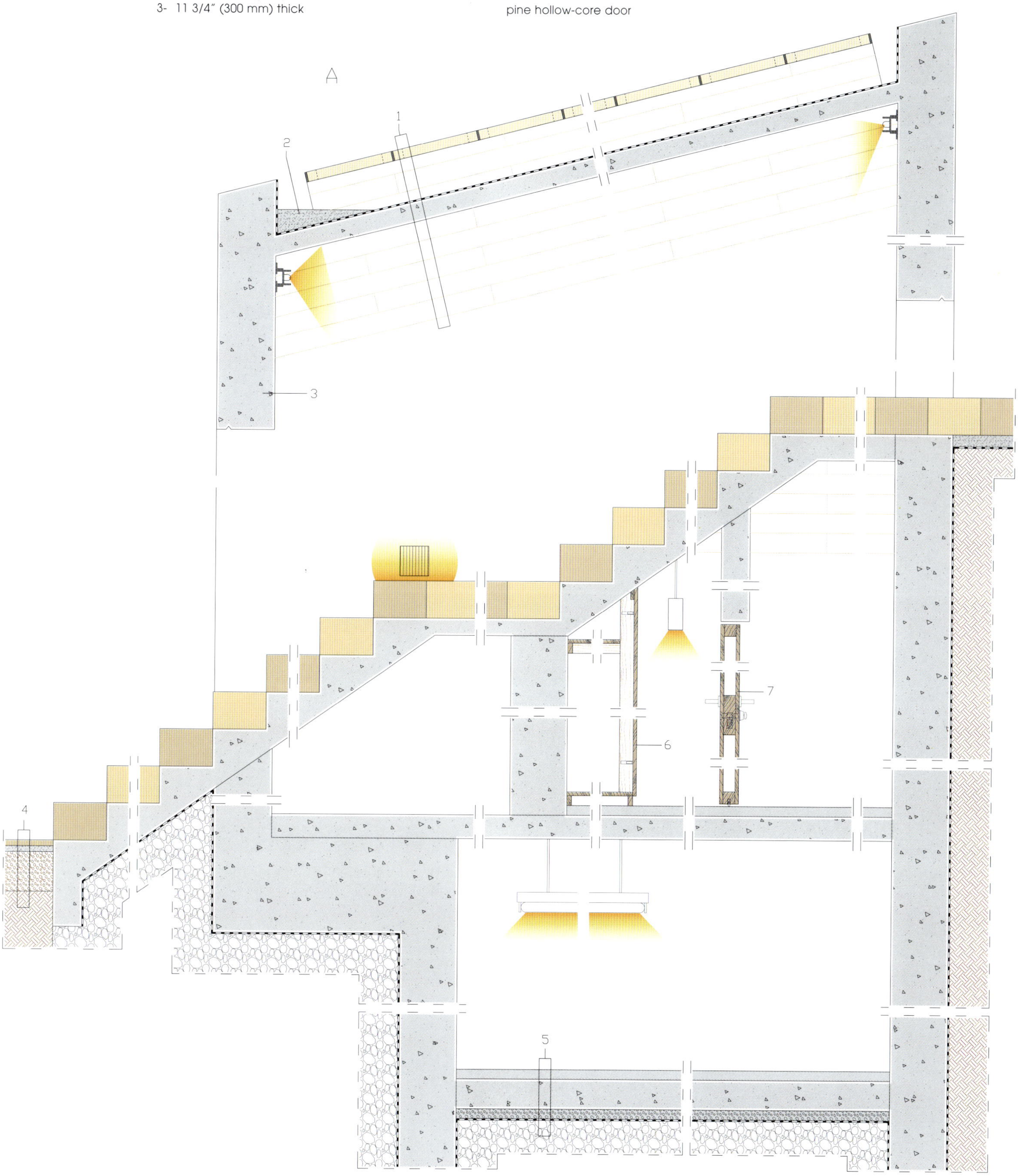

REID BUILDING, GLASGOW SCHOOL OF ART

GLASGOW, UK

STEVEN HOLL ARCHITECTS

It is both rare and difficult to erect a new building next to a much-admired, well-known and beloved masterpiece. Ever since Charles Rennie Mackintosh designed and built the Glasgow School of Art some one hundred years ago, it has never ceased to amaze and attract visitors. Not that it was received with universal acclaim, far from it.

The truly new and original is bound to raise an eyebrow and to provoke outrage and dismay. What was true of Mackintosh then, *mutatis mutandis*, is true of Holl now. Holl's restraint and respect for the old edifice is already taken as a sign of weakness, of lack of beauty. On the contrary, one of the major virtues of the new building is that it shows tremendous respect for the grand old dame opposite. As if the young man who is invited to a dance with an old venerable dancer does everything in his power not to overwhelm her with his own dexterity and charm.

Mackintosh and Holl share moreover the love of watercolor, a predilection that is rooted in the ability to respond to the conditions of light and atmosphere and to be inspired by natural forms. The invitation to Steven Holl, following an international competition, to extend the School with an addition of a new wing, the Reid building, parallel to Mackintosh's original building, must have been a thrill and a challenge. Steven Holl, Chris McVoy and the office understood that none of the conventional methods could suffice: they had to forgo any effect of competing with the existing building. They knew that no mimetic device would match such an invitation. Their response had to be finely calibrated and profound.

Above all, what stood out from the old building was Mackintosh's inspired approach in the use of natural Northern light, which in Glasgow has a distinct quality. If the old building had a thick stone skin, the new answered with thin glass membrane.

Mackintosh's fine bone structure was matched by a thick concrete frame. His sinuous lines were turned into stern edges.

The result is an extremely robust building with an impressive, open and translucent façade, which offers plenty of light to illuminate the interiors of the studios inside while providing an unobstructed view of the Mackintosh building outside and opposite. Above all, in a series of large conic volumes that penetrate vertically the entire 25 m height of the building, light, air and circulation are played against the horizontal

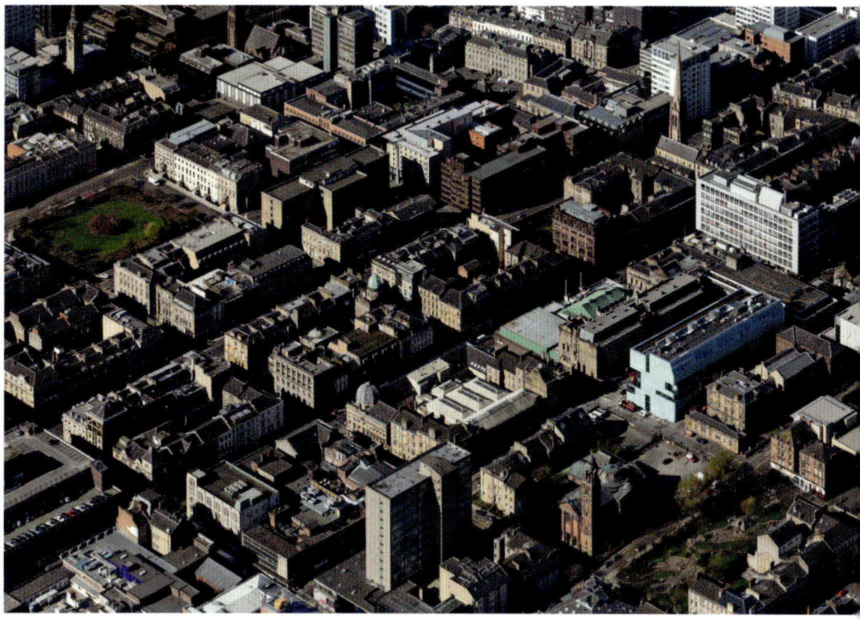

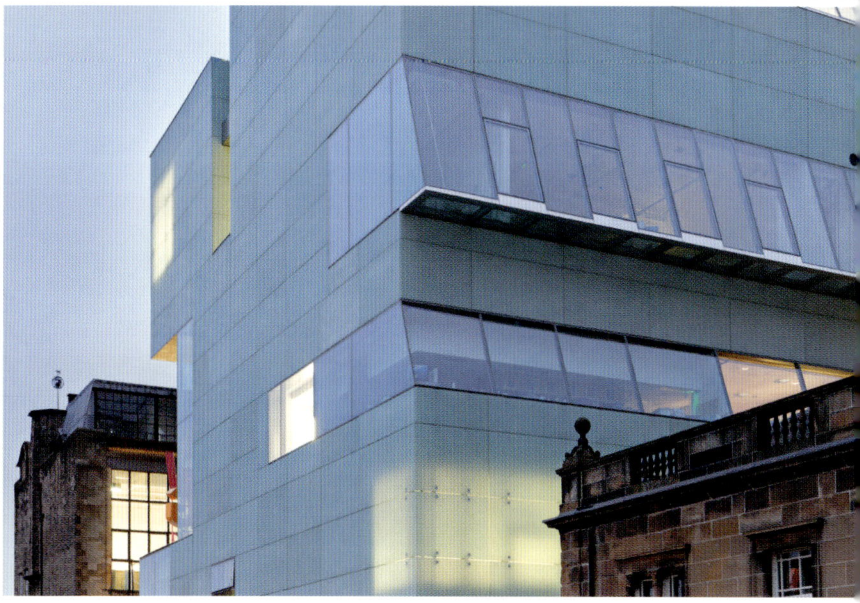

datum of each floor, culminating in the very high ceiling 7.6 m at the top floor.

The greatest works of art during the last century were often conceived and executed in a relatively, modest environment. From Cézanne's studio in Aix to Pollock's studio in Southampton, not to speak of Andy Warhol's factory in Manhattan, this observation encourages us to consider the robustness of these new studios space as it is indeed, the primary condition necessary to provide the young generation with an apt creative environment.

Excellence, as Spinoza thought, is as rare as it is difficult. Here in Glasgow, Steven Holl and his office have been able to study the particular achievement of Charles Rennie Mackintosh, to transcribe it into a new idiom. One cannot visit the new building without admiring it in terms of the old one.

For the two share the most important qualities of light and proportions. The two works share a common rhythm. The light penetrating through the different glass, from above and below; reflected on the different surfaces, including the concrete that is painted white, are reminders of the miracle of being alive. Not only in the here and now, but forever and everywhere. We can only imagine that this insight drove Mackintosh and his wife to the south of France in search of light, only to remain there forever.

On the night of the inauguration, when the sky was filled with artificial lights working their magic above, sitting on the terrace of the Reid building below, facing the Mackintosh building one could not be happier. Observing us from heaven Mackintosh could not be happier.

At last, somebody was directly inspired by him to do something fundamentally different. If the constrains are many, so are the potentials. To embrace the old building at the far corner, to be able to see the Mackintosh façade from just about everywhere in the new building, to be able to accommodate such generous and well-proportioned new studios are among the formidable achievements of the Reid building.

Holl's work is indeed a new addition to the vocabulary of the architecture of our time, highly disciplined and restrained and the same time generous and rich. In short, a masterpiece.

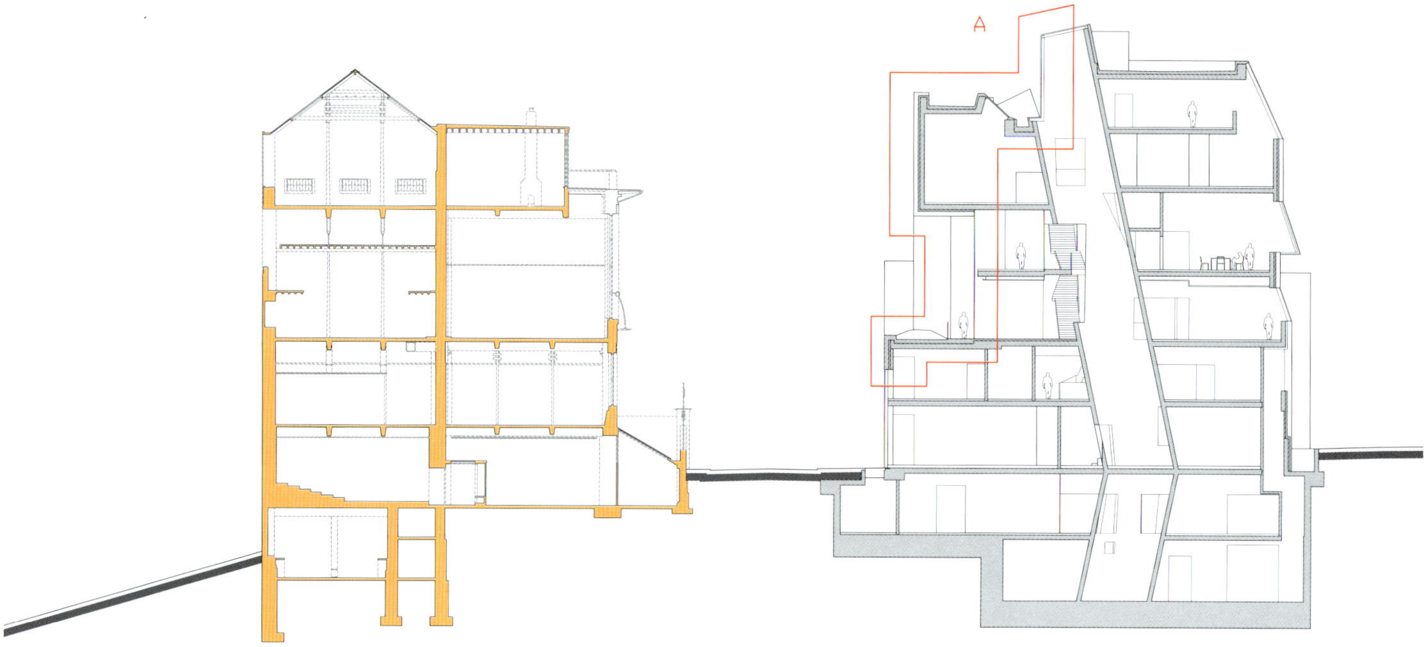

■ XX Section - Scale 1:500

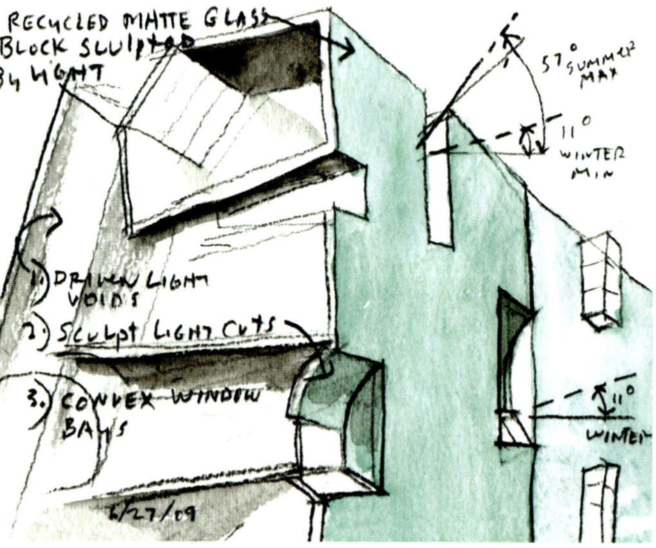

■ Study of building form in relation to natural light
Watercolors

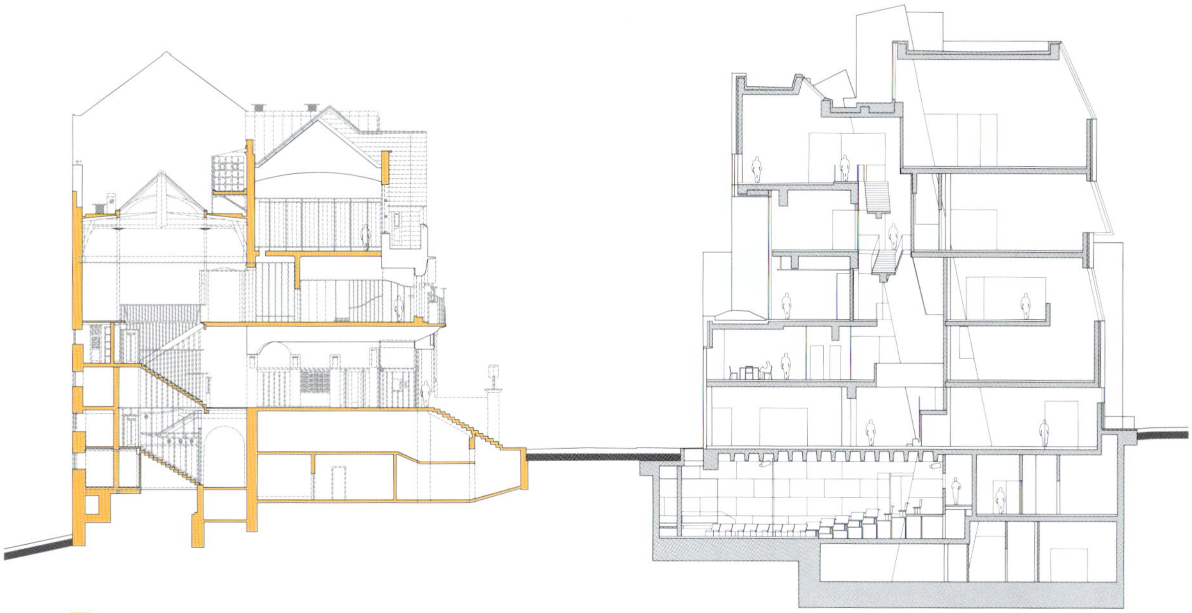

Existing walls

■ YY Section - Scale 1:500

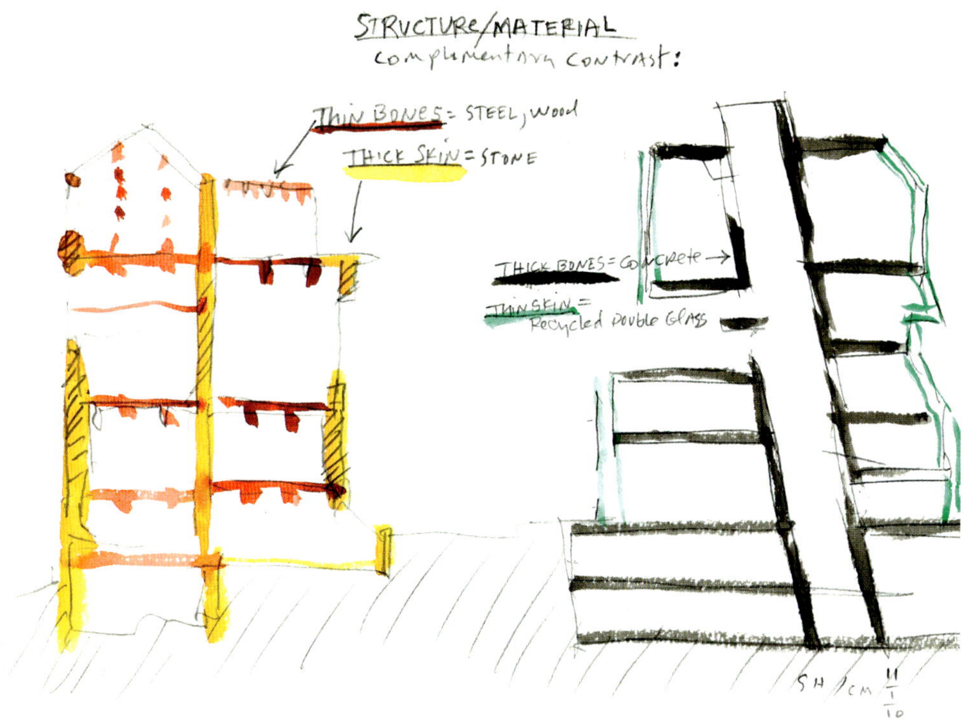

■ Frame and skin. Relationship between the Reid Building and the School of Art
Watercolor

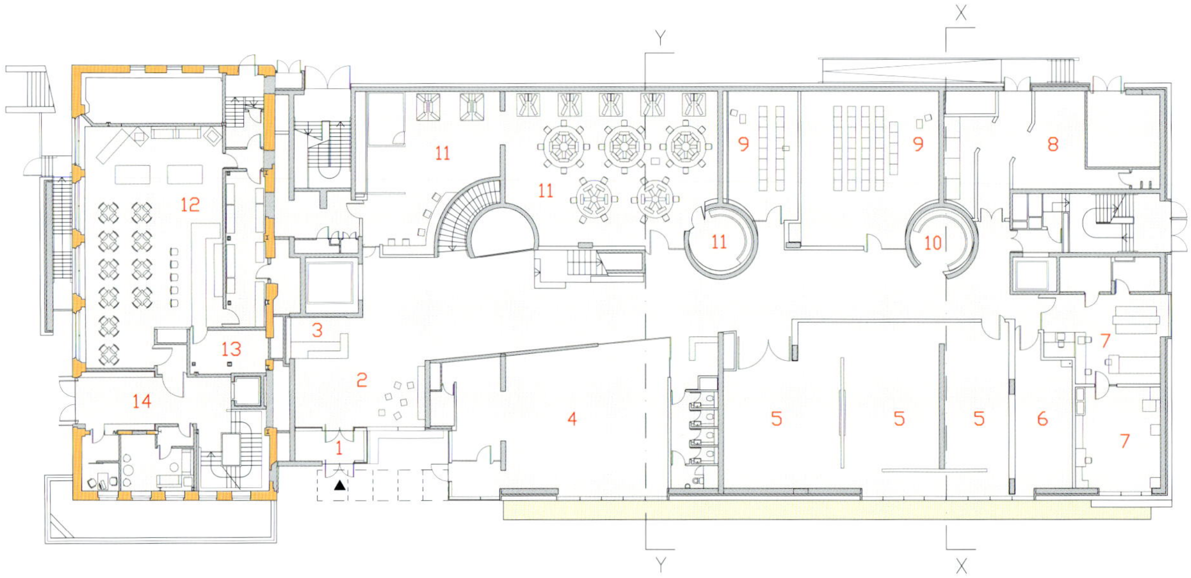

■ Ground floor plan - Scale 1:500

1. Entrance
2. Lobby
3. Reception
4. "Window on Mackintosh" Visitors center
5. Exhibition space
6. Project space
7. Center for advanced textiles
8. Service / storage
9. Seminar room
10. Digital workshop
11. Learning centre
12. Café
13. Kitchen
14. Security
15. Photo studio
16. Auditorium
17. Assembly space
18. Metal workshop
19. Wood workshop
20. Mechanical room

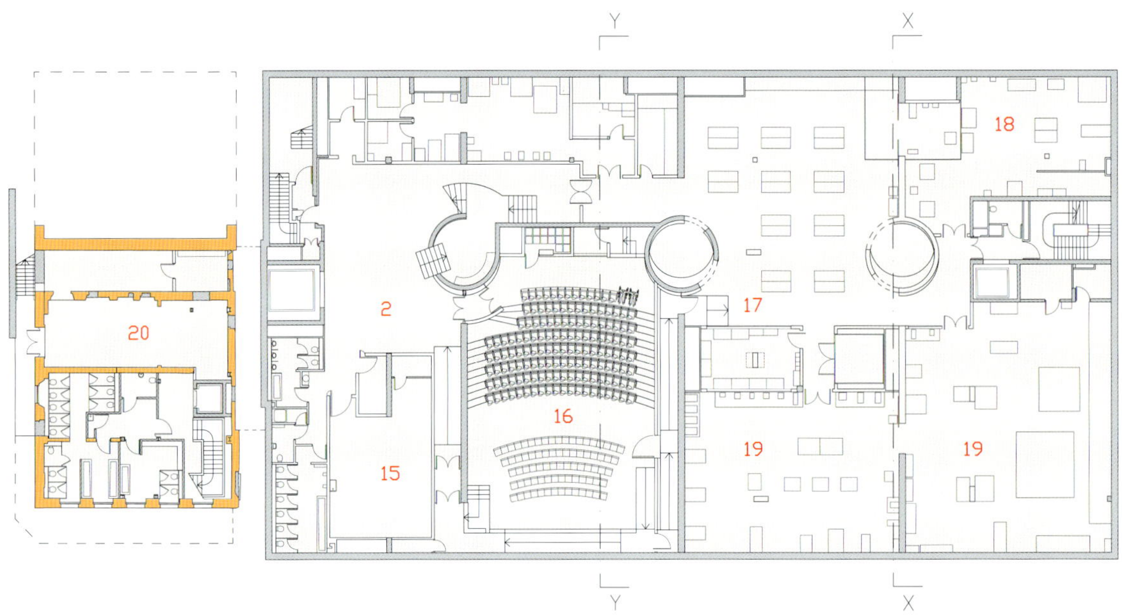

■ Underground floor plan - Scale 1:500

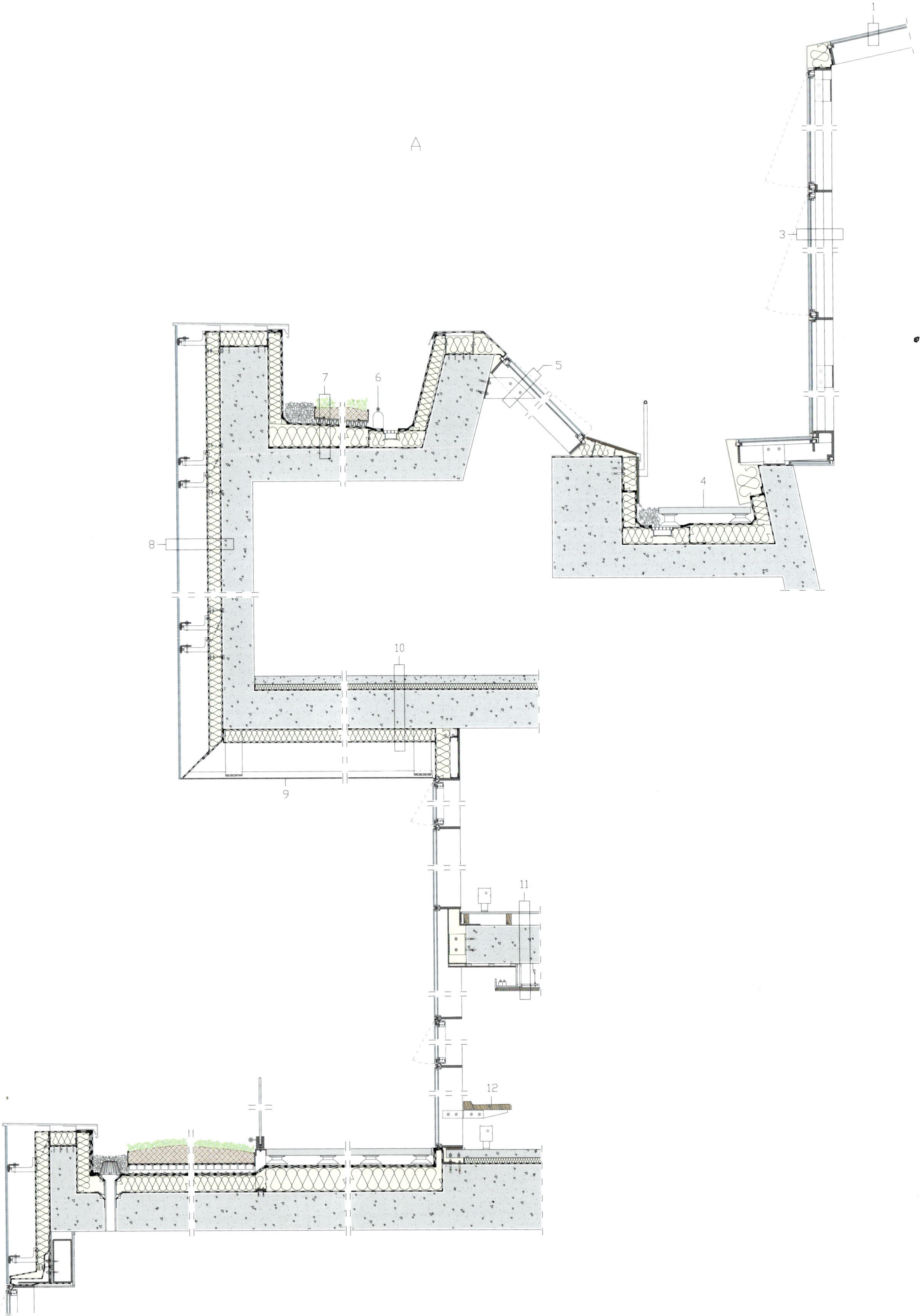

A
1
3
5
7
6
4
8
10
9
11
12

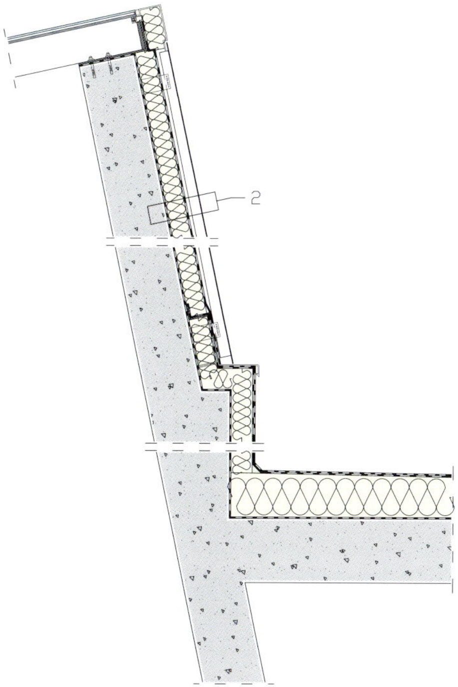

Study of interior layout and distribution
Watercolor

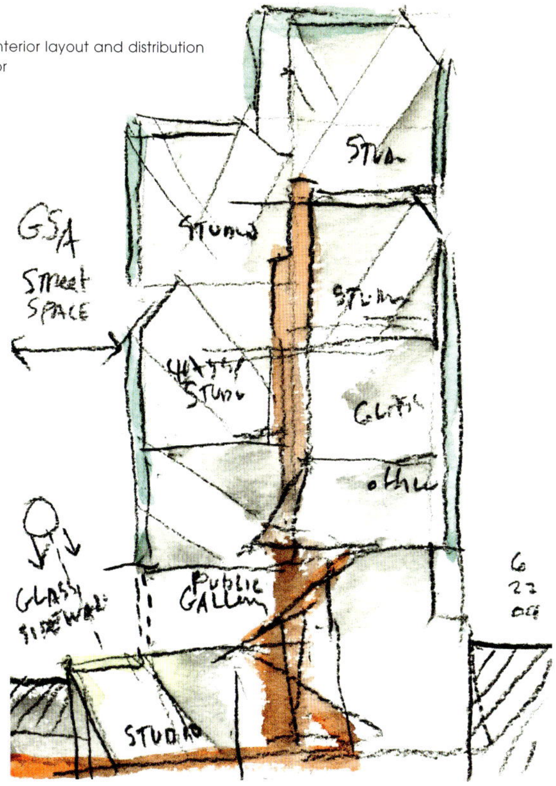

DETAIL A: CONSTRUCTION SYSTEM
VERTICAL SECTION – SCALE 1:40

1. Light shaft with skylight with automated opening system, 3/8 - 1/2 - 1/4 + 1/4″ (10/12/6.5+6.5 mm) aluminum glazing unit in frame of (20x150 mm) steel plates
2. Steel cladding panels on aluminum profile point fasteners, waterproofing sheathing, 4 7/8″ (125 mm) rigid insulation, vapor barrier, curved 12 1/2″ (320 mm) reinforced concrete load-bearing structure
3. Glazed façade of light shaft comprising 3/8 - 1/2 - 1/4 + 1/4″ (10/12/6.5+6.5 mm) aluminum glazing units FW50+ SG by Schüco on frame of 3/4 x 5 7/8″ (20x150 mm) mullions and 2 3/4 x 5 7/8″ (70x150 mm) steel L-profile transoms anchored to curved load-bearing structure by 6 1/8 x 7 7/8″ (155x200 mm) steel L-profiles (parallel to plane of section)
4. Façade maintenance walkway comprising floating floor of concrete sheets on steel pedestals
5. Sloping skylight with 3/8 - 1/2 - 1/4 + 1/4″ (10/12/6.5+6.5 mm) aluminum glazing unit on frame of 3/4 x 5 7/8″ (20x150 mm) steel profiles anchored to structure by bolted steel bracket
6. Fall prevention steel cable
7. Hanging garden comprising 4″ (100 mm) soil, sheet steel edging, geotextile filter, 1 3/4″ (45 mm) polypropylene drainage mat, double waterproofing membrane, 8 1/2″ (215 mm) max h rigid insulation shaped to form slope, double vapor barrier, 11 7/8″ (300 mm) reinforced concrete slab
8. Building envelope consisting of 5/16 + 1/2″ (8+11 mm) opaque laminated glass, 2 3/4 x 4″ (70x100 mm) fasteners and steel brackets fixed to structure by steel cables and anchors, waterproofing membrane, 4 1/2″ (115 mm) rigid insulation, 11 7/8″ (300 mm) reinforced concrete structure
9. Soffit of projecting volume with steel plate finish on aluminum profile point fasteners
10. 2 7/8″ (75 mm) polished concrete flooring, 2″ (50 mm) rigid insulation, vapor barrier, 13 3/4″ (350 mm) reinforced concrete slab, waterproofing membrane, 4 3/8″ (110 mm) rigid insulation, waterproofing membrane
11. Floating floor comprising 3/4″ (18 mm) concrete panels, 2 x 4″ (50x100 mm) joists on soundproofing base, 13 3/4″ (350 mm) reinforced concrete slab, false ceiling comprising perforated 3/4″ (18 mm) birch panels with 5/8″ (15 mm) acoustic panel and steel bars suspended from slab by steel cable and 1 x 2 3/8″ (25x60 mm) steel Z-profiles

MAPUNGUBWE INTERPRETATION CENTRE

LIMPOPO, SOUTH AFRICA

PETER RICH ARCHITECTS

Designed by Peter Rich Architects, the Mapungubwe Interpretation Centre is the physical and symbolic entrance to the Mapungubwe National Park located in north-eastern South Africa near the borders with Zimbabwe and Botswana at the confluence of the Shashi and Limpopo rivers.

In past centuries a major trading hub and cultural melting pot on the vast, undulating savannah, the site is a unique archaeological, cultural and natural location. The modulated architecture of the Mapungubwe Interpretation Centre reflects this long history while asserting its contemporary relevance.

Traditional building techniques have made use of locally produced brick, stone from local quarries and wooden secondary sun-shading structures. More contemporary features include the overall project design, the way the timbrel-vault forces have been distributed, the particular concrete mix, and the use of metal uprights and glazed lights with a web of organic decorative motifs.

The result is a strong architectural experience yet one that fits seamlessly into its earthy landscape. The timbrel vaults (made of layers of slender bricks on a bed of rapid-set concrete) of the various pavilions rise from the land like natural elements. The slightly sloping ground makes them look even more like natural outcrops. The sloping terrain is an integral part of the architectural design providing a series of viewpoints along the paved route set between dry-stone walls and from the terraced seating carved out of the hillside.

The stone cladding of the roofs and most of the walls echoes the colours of the surrounding savannah. It provides a materiality that somehow reinforces the conceptual program of the whole complex.

Light plays a key role: filtering through the glazing on the sidewalls of the domed volumes, streaming dramatically down from the centrer oculus into the spacious interior of the main timbrel-vaulted pavilion, and creating dappled patterns as it filters through the natural timber slats of metal framed pergolas.

This geometrically composite architecture combines vaulted spaces, the regular patterns of closely set stone cladding, the opus incertum aspect of roofs and some flooring, and the smooth, regular finish of the brick-lined interior walls. References to vernacular and traditional african architecture blend here perfectly with contemporary design and materials.

■ Site plan - Scale 1:300

1. Arrival
2. Bridge
3. Offices
4. Reception
5. Court
6. Restaurant
7. Shop
8. Walkway
9. Classroom
10. Exhibition space
11. Cairn

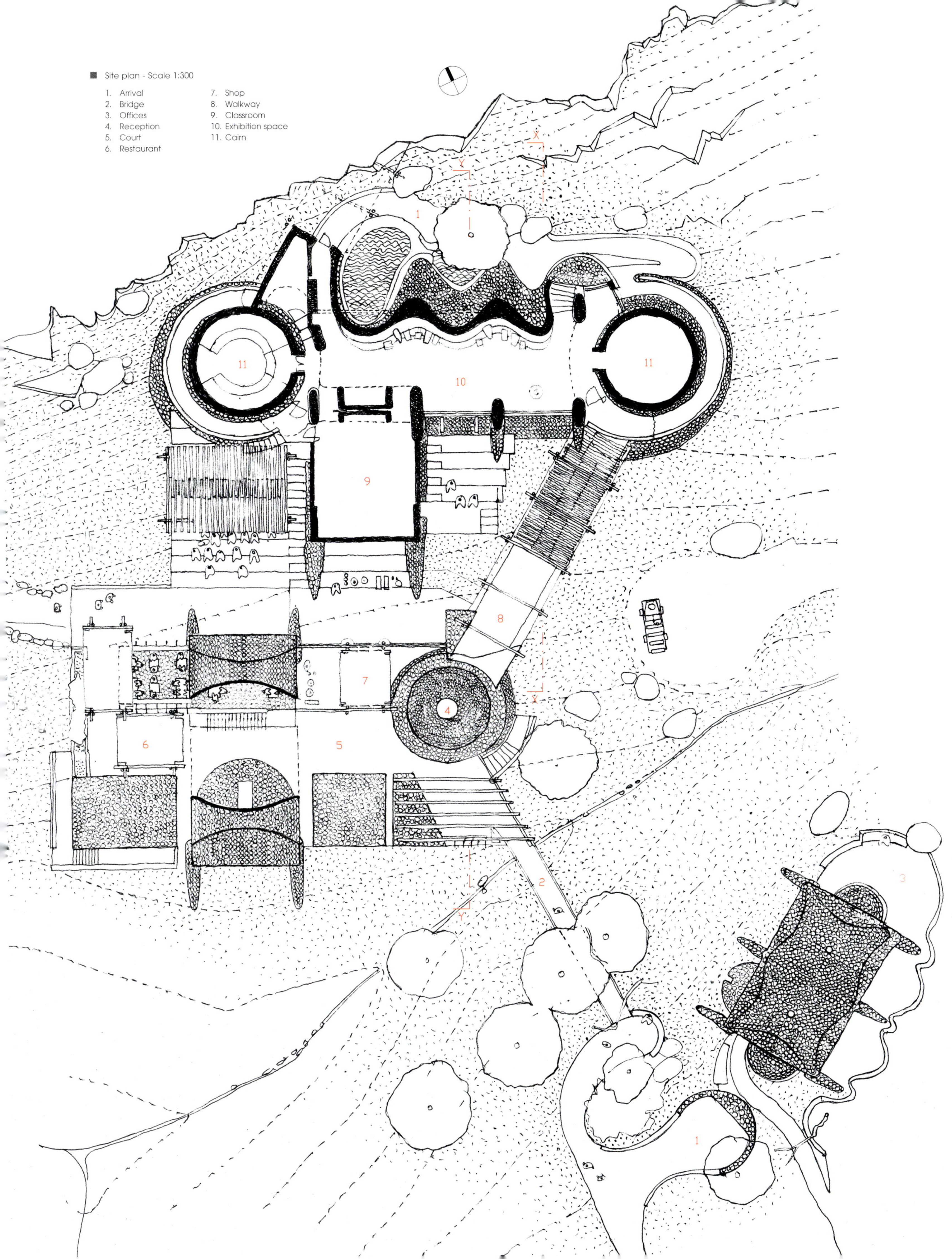

■ XX Section - Scale 1:300

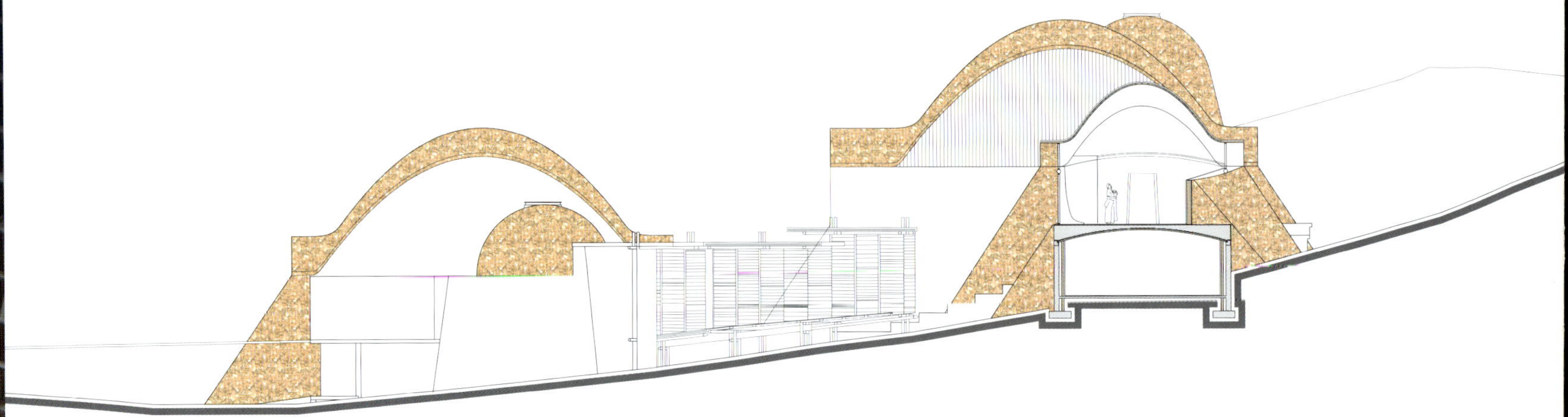

■ YY Section - Scale 1:300

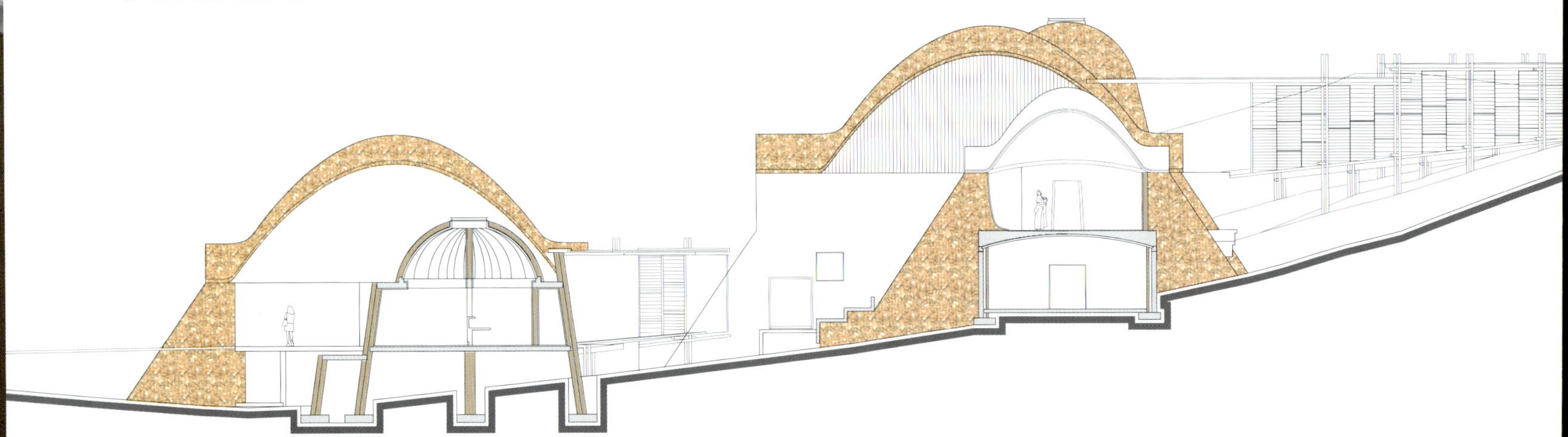

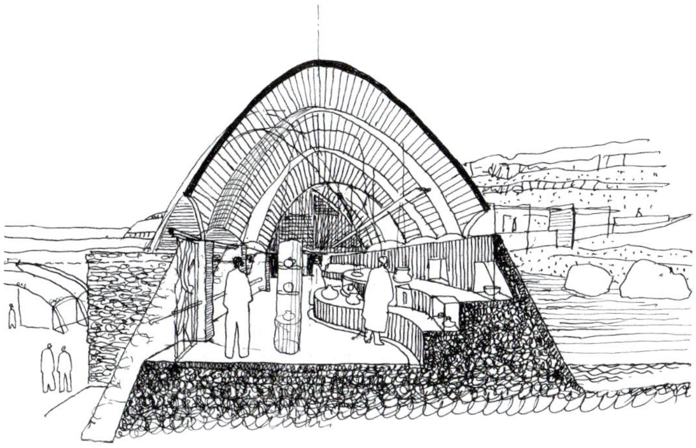
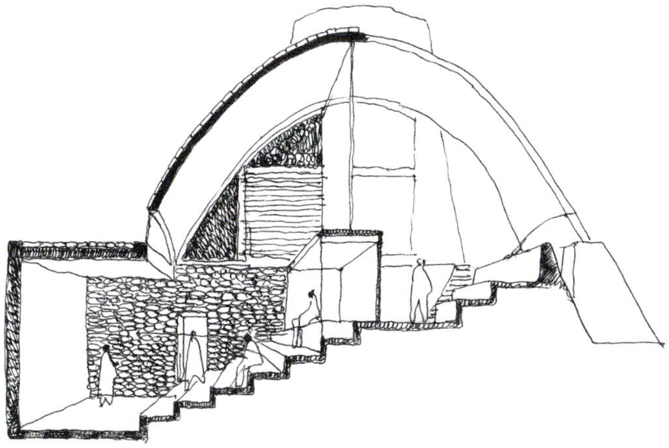

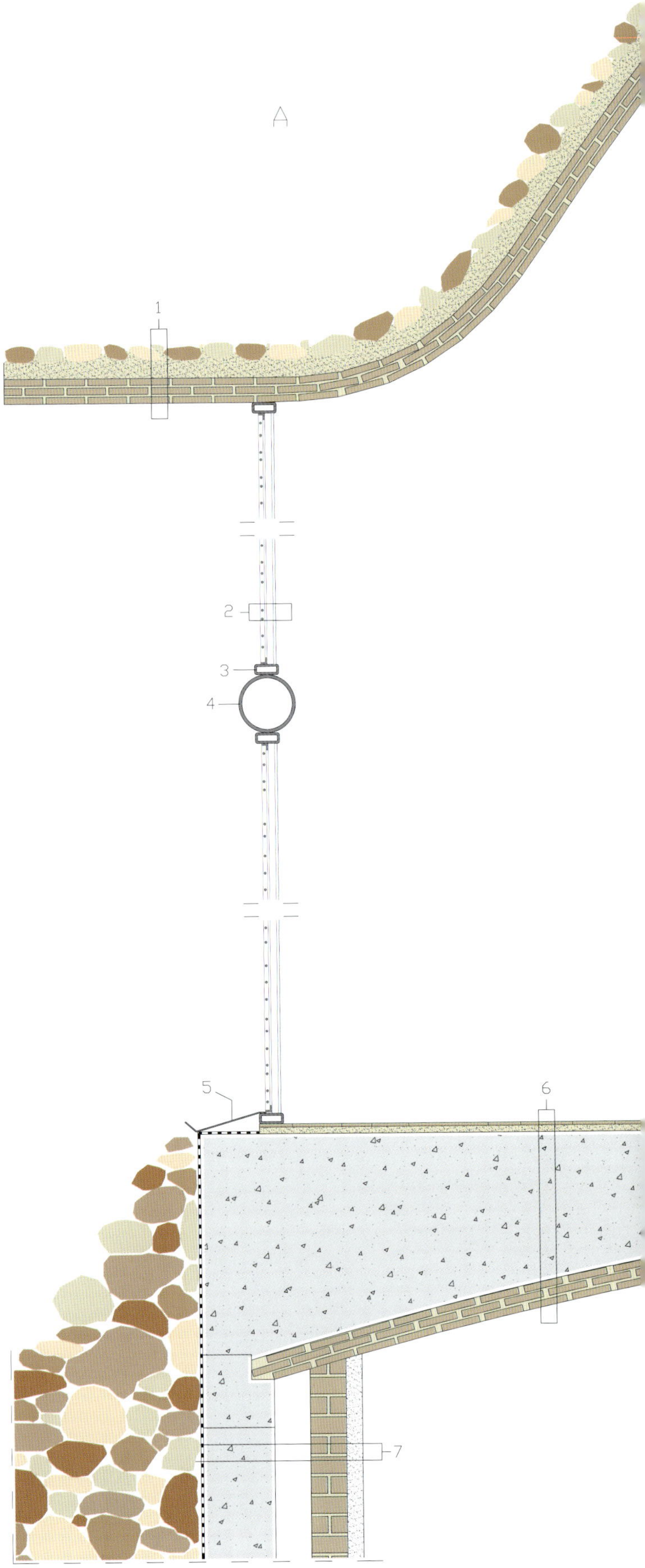

DETAIL A: EXHIBITION ROOM
VERTICAL SECTION - SCALE 1:20

1. Exhibition room roof in sandstone, 2″ (50 mm) screed, 2 7/8″ (75 mm) slab comprising triple layer of bricks on ribbing and mortar
2- Transparent façade with external security grating consisting of steel pipe profiles with floral decorations and corrugated polycarbonate panel
3- 2 7/8 x 1 1/4″ (75x30 mm) steel box profile frame
4- Façade Ø 6 7/8″ (175 mm) structural steel pipe beam
5- Steel flashing
6- Floor in 3/8″ (10 mm) quartzite blocks, 3/4″ (20 mm) screed, vaulted reinforced concrete slab, 2 7/8″ (75 mm) triple layer of bricks on ribbing and mortar
7- 2″ (50 mm) render, 4 3/8″ (110 mm) brick wall, 4 3/8″ (110 mm) air space, 8 5/8″ (220 mm) reinforced concrete structure, waterproofing membrane, sandstone fill
8- 2″ (50 mm) render, 8 5/8″ (220 mm) brick wall, sandstone fill
9- Steel L-profile connecting façade to load-bearing structure

9
8

COMMUNITY CENTER GRACE FARMS NEW CANAAN, USA

SANAA, KAZUYO SEJIMA + RYUE NISHIZAWA

This is the name of the recent project by Kazuyo Sejima and Ryue Nishizawa in New Canaan, Connecticut, USA. From the name, the reader will already understand that the initiative has the flavor of a community center, somewhat Christian in spirit, and with enough economic clout to acquire 80 acres in one of the wealthiest communities on Earth. Programmed in the most general terms to meet almost minimal requirements, the large landscaping project included shaping the earth, containing a body of water, and planting trees and vegetation. In comparison with earlier SANAA projects in North America such as the Toledo Museum of Art's Glass Pavilion in Toledo, Ohio, and the New Museum of Contemporary Art in New York, this one is far more accomplished.

Unlike some of their teachers and mentors such as Shinohara and Toyo Ito, the SANAA architecture firm has developed a vocabulary far closer to Western sensibilities and the dominant tastes of Western countries. The conversion seems subliminal. To what extent they are aware of their accommodation is hard to tell. When asked about East and West, Sejima used her two hands to demonstrate the differences in the thickness of the walls. Yet, as a rule, her projects have no walls as such. It was Alberti who drew the distinction between architecture of walls and architecture of columns; this office is certainly in the realm of columns, not walls. "The River" is a glass pavilion that meanders from the top of a modest hill to the bottom. On its way it provides a sports hall - under grade at the lower part - passing through a tea-serving kiosk, a very large dining hall and a kitchen (hidden by a wall), a library/bookshop, to end in a beautiful assembly place, a cavity in the upper most level. Curtains provide protection from the daylight when needed.

Of course the etymology of the word pavilion is papillon (French for butterfly).

A pavilion thus requires lightness, above all in its contact with the ground. Here, at Grace Farms SANAA has made the roof entirely parallel with the ground, its thickness and color emphasizing the similarity. The overall result is a structure resembling a ribbon for wrapping a gift. Or a Dan Graham sculpture. Two-Way Mirror Cylinder Inside Cube and Video Salon (1981-1991). The gift is surely the tension, or invisible thread between Earth and heaven.

The building presents as another natural layer on the land's surface, its resistance to gravity modest - enhancing the ribbon metaphor. It rests flat, embracing the earth, with the exception of the highest level that needs an additional staircase and alternative elevator.

The still columns are all equal to each other and distributed in equal measure in pairs. Uniformity seems to be of the essence in this project. Does it enhance a sense of community? It certainly does emphasize the parallel "horizontals": ground and roof running together.

It is hard not to think of Philip Johnson's Glass House, not far down the road. Nor is it possible not to think of *Transparency: Literal and Phenomenal* by Colin Rowe and Robert Slutzky. Here, of course, transparency is absolute and literal. The pleasure of seeing, simultaneously, the interior from the exterior and the exterior from other side layered by our own, and everybody else's reflections in the glass, is ambiguous. Clear ambiguity is the outcome. The continuous wrapping of glass in time creates an almost giddy sense of imbalance and disorientation. It contrasts sharply to the subtle layers of membranes, shaded by transparency and chiaroscuro that we find in classical Japanese architecture. In the absence of any framing devices, shadows are here systematically avoided. Our confrontation with the uninterrupted glass façade creates a sense of unreality, as opposed to a sense of place. Johnson's Glass House appears to announce a comparable extreme. Here at Grace Farms the scale and fluency of the undulating curves of the glass curtain wall give it an incomparable quality.

One cannot but admire the singularity of the project; the magic of this glass carpet has the quality of a fairy tale. Will our Little Prince find his flower in spite of his reflection in the glass screen speaking back to him? Could we savor our meal surrounded by endless reflections? Not always.

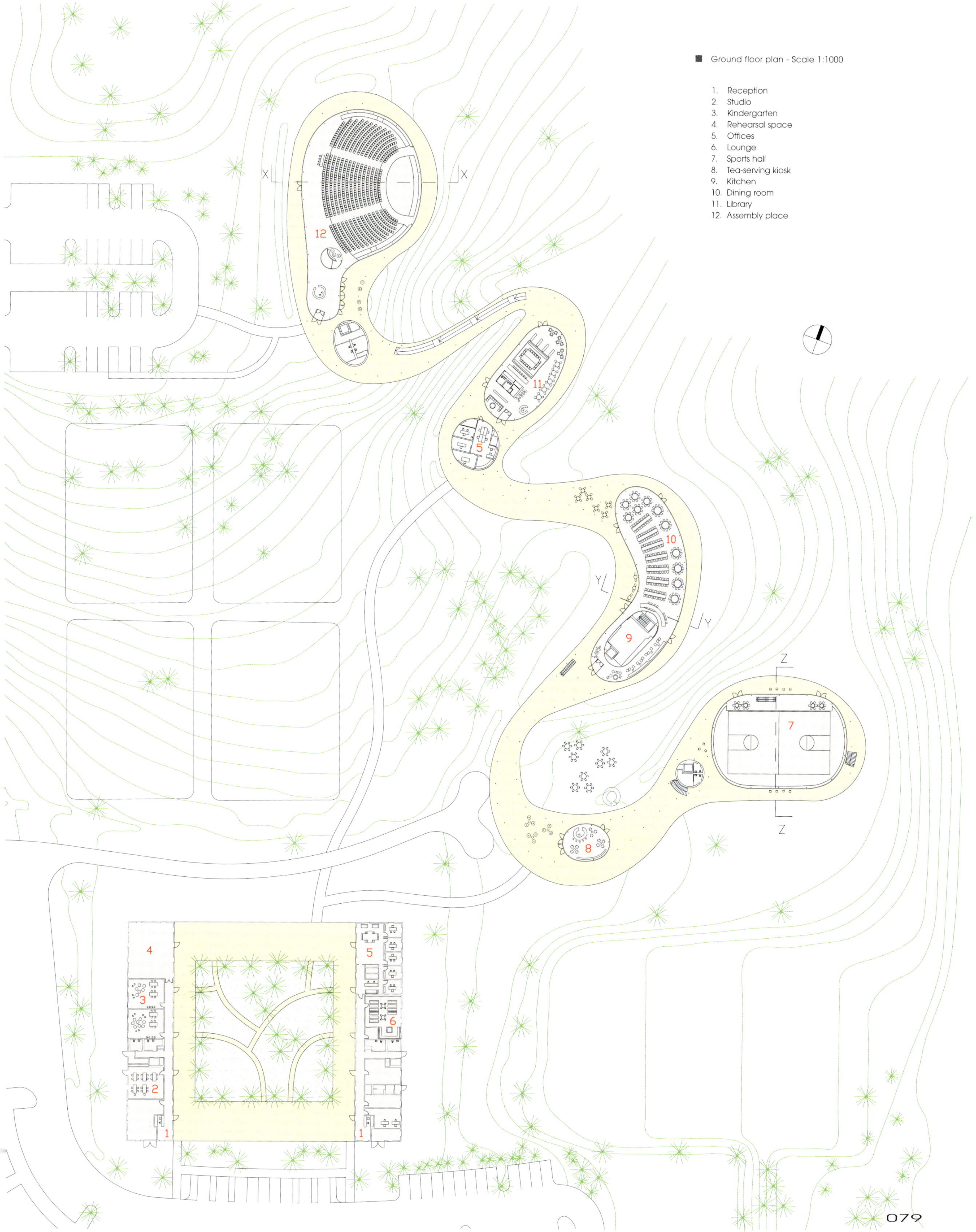

■ Ground floor plan - Scale 1:1000

1. Reception
2. Studio
3. Kindergarten
4. Rehearsal space
5. Offices
6. Lounge
7. Sports hall
8. Tea-serving kiosk
9. Kitchen
10. Dining room
11. Library
12. Assembly place

1

2

3

■ 1-2 Building as it sits in the natural gradients

3/5 Timber roof structure and weight-bearing columns

4

5

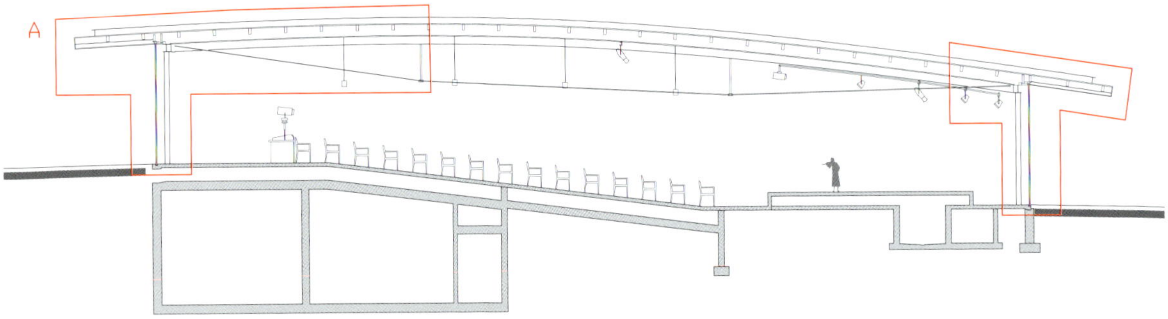

XX Section - Scale 1:250

South-west elevation - Scale 1:500

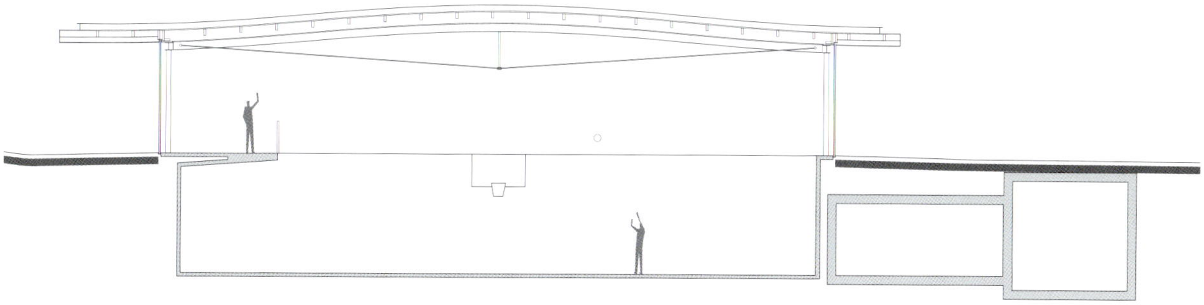

■ ZZ Section - Scale 1:250

■ YY Section - Scale 1:250

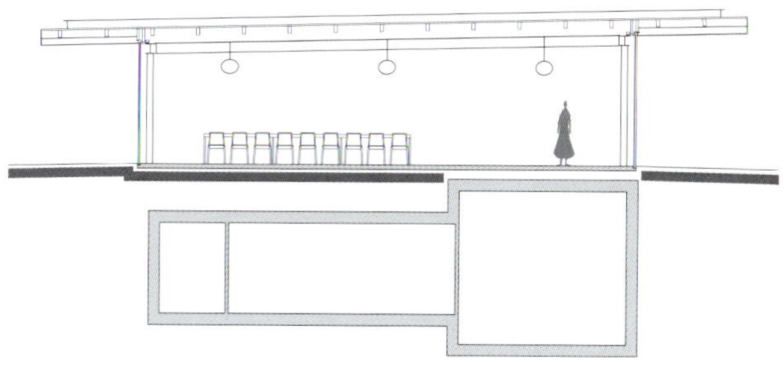

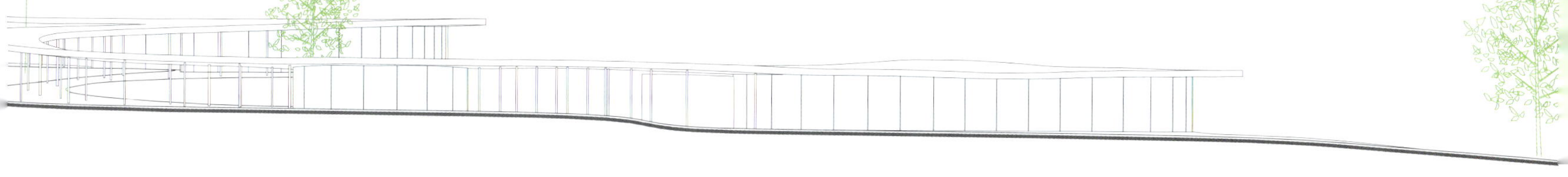

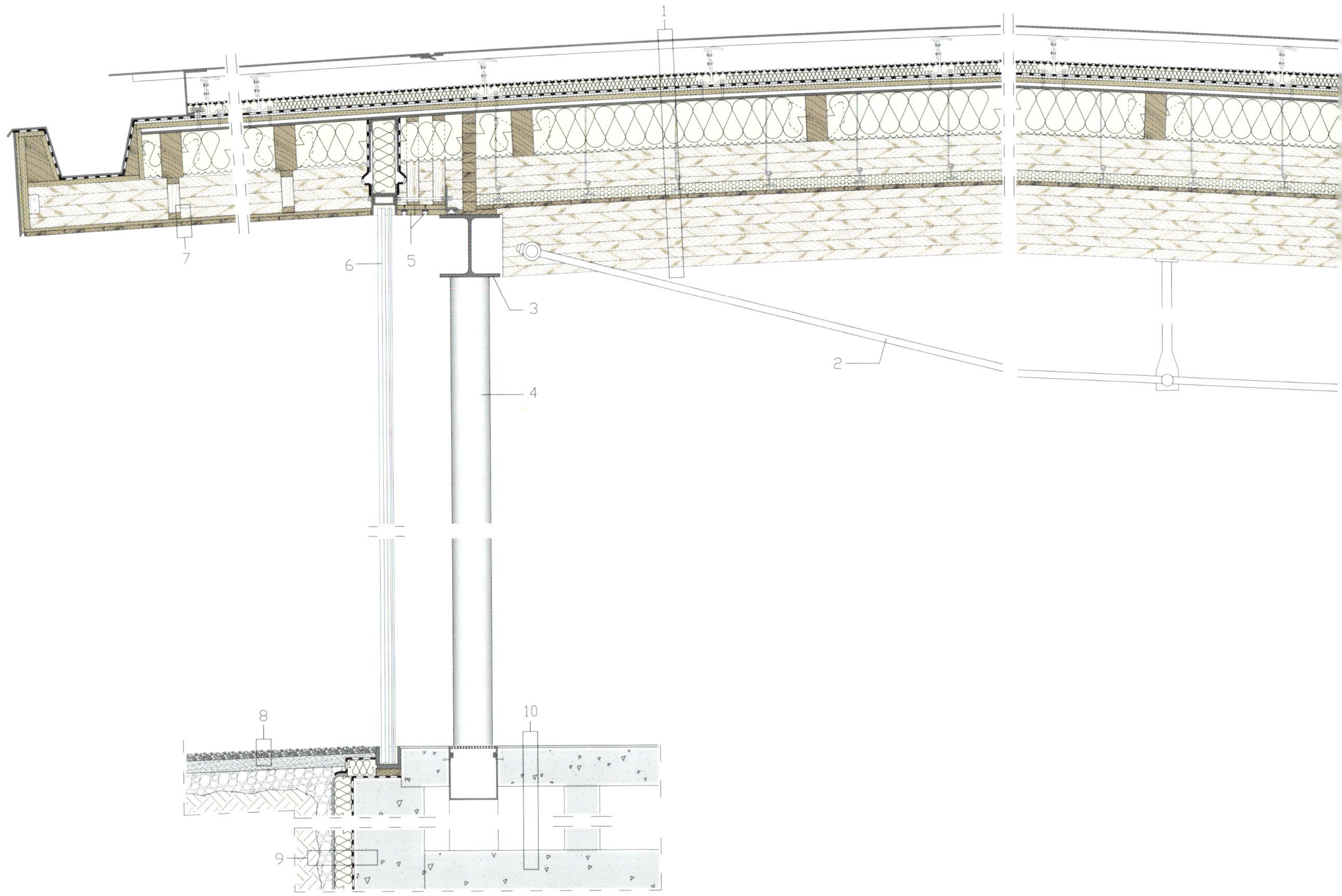

DETAIL A: CONSTRUCTION SYSTEM
VERTICAL SECTION - SCALE 1:25

1. Roof comprising curved aluminum sheeting on point fasteners, air space, sprayed waterproofing membrane, 1 5/8″ (40 mm) rigid insulation, waterproofing membrane, vapour permeable course, 3/4″ (20 mm) plywood panel, 1″ (25 mm) corrugated sheeting, frame of 7 1/4 x 3 1/2″ (185x90 mm) timber sandwiching insulation, 19 3/4″ (500 mm) glulam beam (parallel to plane of section), 1 3/4″ (45 mm) acoustic panel, false ceiling of Douglas fir slats on metal frame secured by tie rods
2. Steel tie-rod bracing
3. 9 3/8 x 9 3/8″ (250x250 mm) steel I-beam
4. Ø 6 1/2″ (165 mm) steel column
5. Plywood trim with curtain tracks
6. Floor-to-ceiling continuous glazed façade with aluminum frame and 5/8 + 5/8 - 1/2 - 1/8 + 1/8″ (17+15/12/7+7 mm) glazing units
7. False ceiling comprising Douglas fir slats, 5/8″ (15 mm) plywood panel, supporting frame of 2 x 1″ (50x25 mm) timber
8. Walkway comprising gravel, 2 3/8″ (60 mm) screed
9. Earth, gravel layer, drainage blanket, rigid insulation, waterproofing membrane, 11 7/8″ (300 mm) reinforced concrete structure
10. Polished concrete flooring, 5 7/8″ (150 mm) reinforced concrete slab, air space, reinforced concrete slab
11. Steel pipe profiles suspended by tie rods supporting lighting

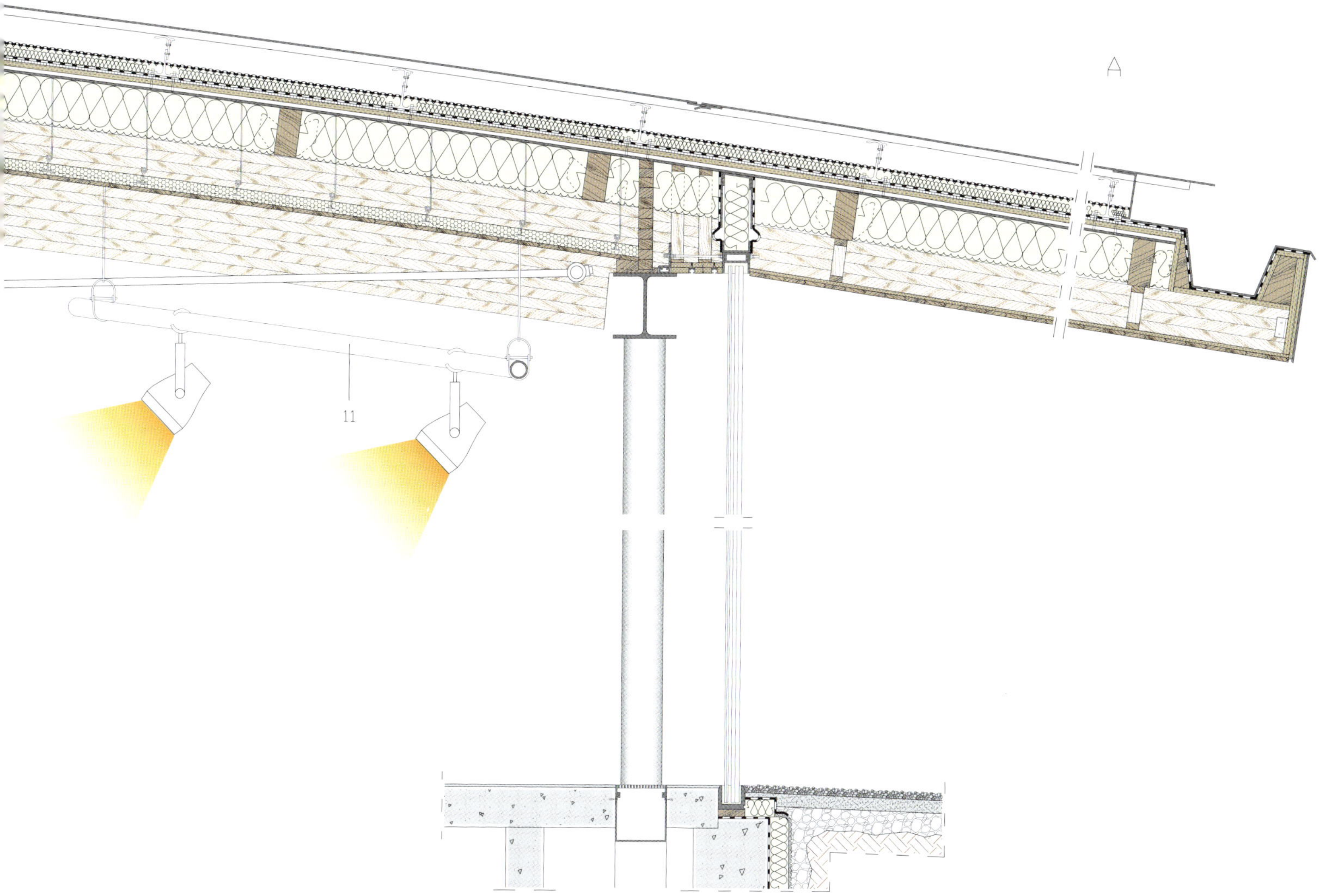
A
11

KIBERA HAMLETS SCHOOL

NAIROBI, KENYA

SELGASCANO AND HELLOEVERYTHING

It all started when architectural photographer, Iwan Baan, and architects SelgasCano visited the only "school" providing education for the children in Nairobi's Kibera Hamlets, one of Kenya's poorest slums.

The trip prompted SelgasCano to turn their brief for a summer pavilion for Copenhagen's Louisiana Museum of Modern Art into an opportunity to design and finance a structure that after its useful life at the exhibition could be easily dismantled, shipped and re-built in the Kenyan slum as a new school.

The project was made possible thanks to the collaboration of many: the Louisiana Museum, architecture studios SelgasCano of Madrid and Helloeverything based in New York, Kenyan architect Abdul Fatah Adam, photographer Iwan Baan, and the London creative workplace Second Home.

The whole process of ideation and realization of the pavilion highlights three key features dear to the Spanish architecture firm and all those who had a hand in the project: the innovative and sensible use of lightweight, economical materials, the belief that contemporary architecture must be adaptable, and that architectural projects are a way of transforming our world.

In Denmark, the project was significant as an experimental prototype challenging the structural rules and traditional assemblage practices of conventional building. In Kenya, the same building became a school - the Kibera Hamlets School - and the practical solution to the economic and logistical constraints of an educational establishment in that context.

Started as a football team, the community-based organization Kibera Hamlets then took on the schooling of more than 150 young children and adolescents in this poverty-stricken slum, becoming a school for kindergarten, primary and secondary school groups. Many of the children are orphans and the victims of violence; many are HIV-positive. As well as the school, the organization also has theater, sports and environmental activities, develops community practices to prevent violence, and provides healthcare.

The two-level building that formerly housed the school had wooden floors and makeshift corrugated iron walls. The classrooms were dark

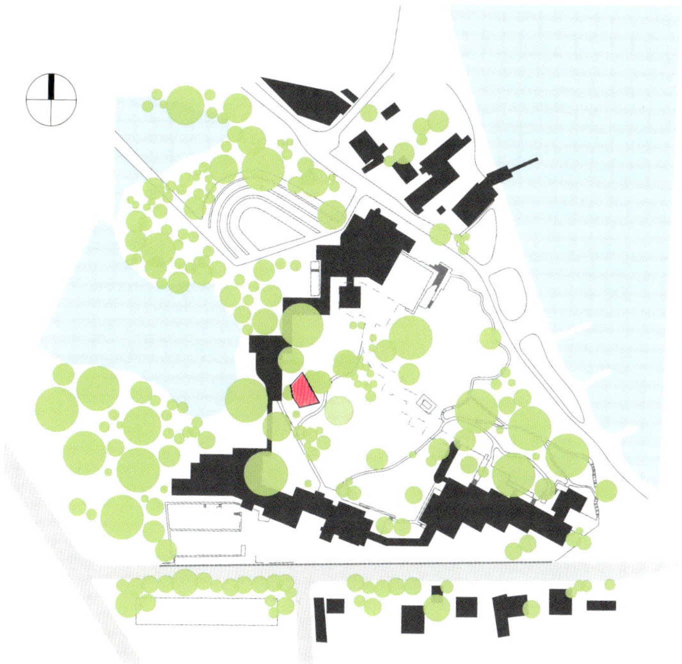

■ Temporary installation at the Louisiana Museum of Copenhagen
Floor plan - not to scale

■ Construction in Nairobi
Floor plan - not to scale

while the building itself was unstable and unsafe, not even providing adequate shelter from the elements. The new structure fits exactly into the existing plot. On the ground floor there are four classrooms, toilets and an open-air kitchen while on the upper level there are four more classrooms. A covered court and broad staircase serve as an auditorium and communal space as well as a distribution route.

The economic and functional constraints imposed by the particular social context and educational program, together with the need to design a lightweight structure that could be easily taken down and transported, acted as a stimulus rather than an obstacle in the designers' search for low-cost, ease-to-handle materials.

A frame of colored scaffolding pipes supports polycarbonate corrugated infills and roof. The ground and first level floors are made of concrete slabs and plywood panels while the parapets are wire netting. The choice of unconventional, lightweight, low-cost materials ticked two boxes: cost effectiveness and environmental sustainability. It also gave further impetus to new thinking about what can be built and with what when globally used technological solutions are slightly tweaked, and discarded material is recovered and re-used.

By using building materials and techniques familiar from Denmark to Kenya, the project was able to avail itself of local builder skills whose craftsmanship proved fundamental to the success and quality of the end result.

Color was used by SelgasCano to give the structure greater communicative force, helping to make it an approachable, user-friendly addition to the community. Ranging from yellow through to fuchsia, the colors symbolize fun and freedom in the midst of extreme poverty.

Small and low-cost, the SelgasCano project stands has an important means of transforming reality thanks to its ability to adapt to its specific economic and social environment. Not only does it improve the quality of life of Kibera Hamlets schoolchildren, it also benefits the whole slum, upgrading a public service offering by providing a space where color, transparency and simplicity express the hope for a better future.

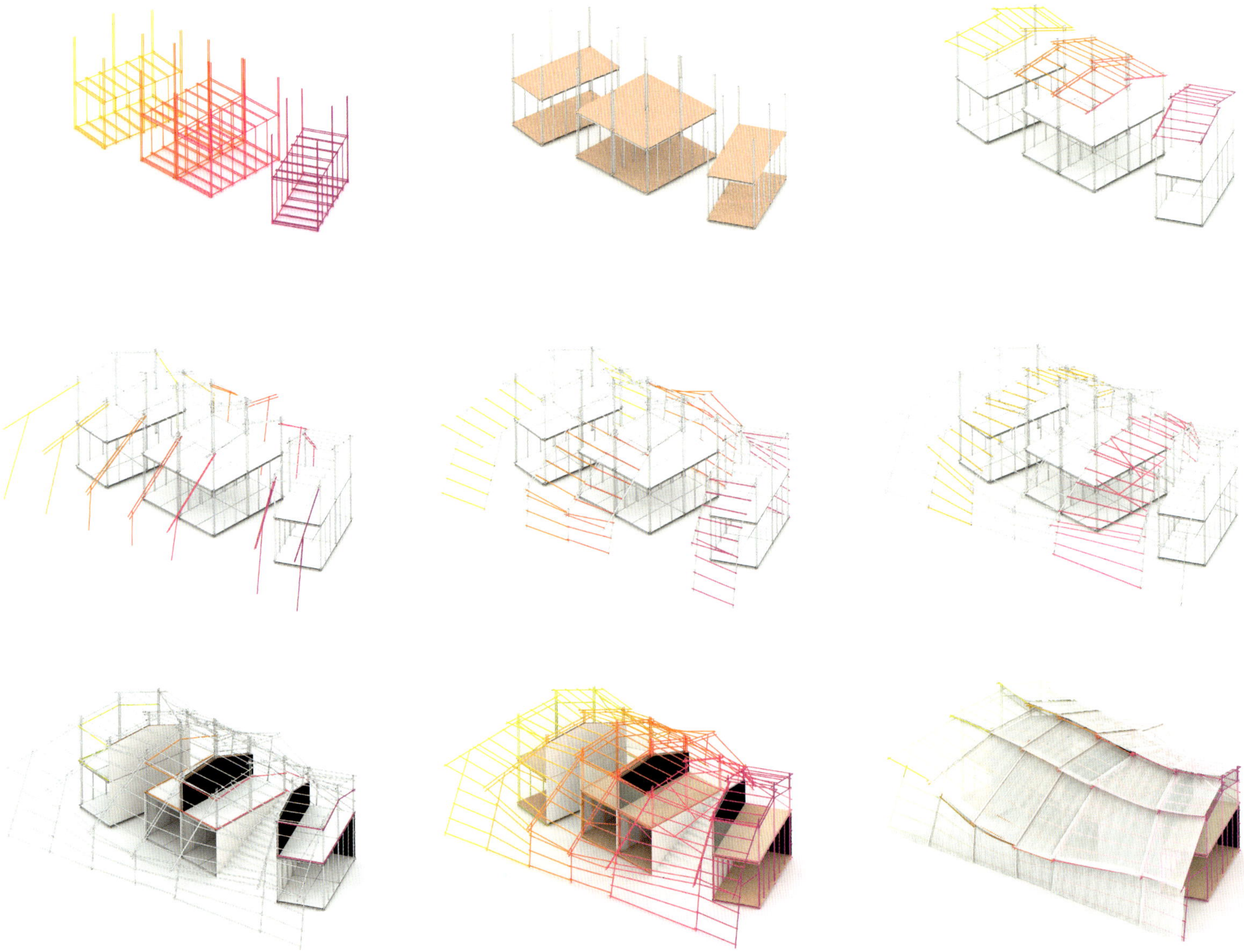

■ Design and building process

Frame in colored tubes and timber planks. Infills and roof in corrugated polycarbonate, parapets in metal mesh. The pavilion was designed to be flexible and adaptable to wherever it was placed.
The installation at the Louisiana Museum is a prototype aimed at verifying the feasibility of a lightweight, low-cost structure that could be easily knocked down and transported.

■ 1st level plan
Scale 1:200

■ 2nd level plan
Scale 1:200

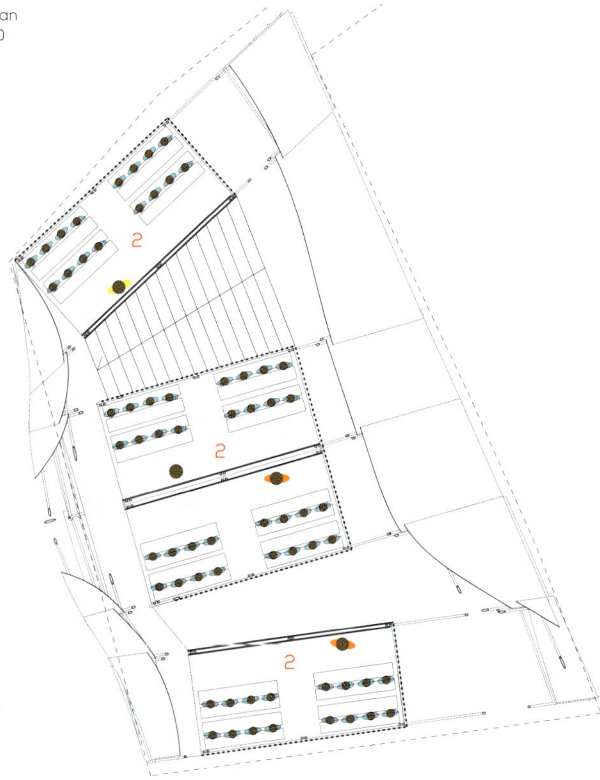

1. Open kitchen
2. Classroom
3. Storage

FREDERIKSBERG COURTHOUSE

COPENHAGEN, DENMARK

A city and its surrounding area are the product of the sedimentation and stratification of objects, materials, and architectures built down the ages. This is the thread that runs through the history of a place, the accumulation of specific colours, forms and materials that confer a consistency and coherence on heterogeneous elements from different eras, marking the continuity of human activity and community life and informing the distinctiveness of that particular urban fabric.

Designed by the firm 3XN, the extension of Copenhagen's Frederiksberg courthouse establishes a twofold relationship of continuity with its sister building from another era: a physical connection in the choice of materials and forms that re-interpret rather than contrast with the nearby neoclassical building; and a functional link in that the new extension is part of a single court of justice system.

The new volume sits comfortably alongside the complex designed by Hack Kampmann in 1921. Contemporary in style, it echoes the forms, colors and materials of the surrounding neighborhood. Its trapezoid shape conforms to the perimeter of the allocated plot. One of the long sides runs parallel to the existing building and court while one of the short sides faces the square in front of the courthouse complex and nearby church. The new volume yields to the shapes of the adjacent buildings, matching them in size and proportion. On the side overlooking a small walkway, the last two floors tilt back 45°, its cross section almost a mirror image of the building opposite. This ploy creates an airy corridor from the square to the road system beyond the complex. On the square side, it is the new building's ground floor that steps back 45° to allow the public space to penetrate inside the building.

Although contemporary in style, the materiality and texture of the new façade connect with the surrounding historical fabric. The contemporary feel is conferred by the original sequence of lights on the façade and the slightly different shade given to the traditional colour of the brick cladding. The overall appearance though is still one of continuity, not contrast.

The recent reform of security measures for courthouses is the basis for the internal distribution circuits, with separate circulation paths for employees, defendants and witnesses.

All office environments overlook a narrow central atrium that draws light deep into the building. Communal spaces are rigorously white, giving a sense of airiness and breadth while the working environments and internal corridors are in warmer, more welcoming colours. At night, coloured neon panels turn the central patio into a multicoloured lantern.

The architectural programme is informed by the intention to resonate with context. The brown hues and texture of the façades allow dialogue between old and new under the crisp clear northern light that penetrates and shapes the interiors, filtered by side-hung aluminum mesh sun shading.

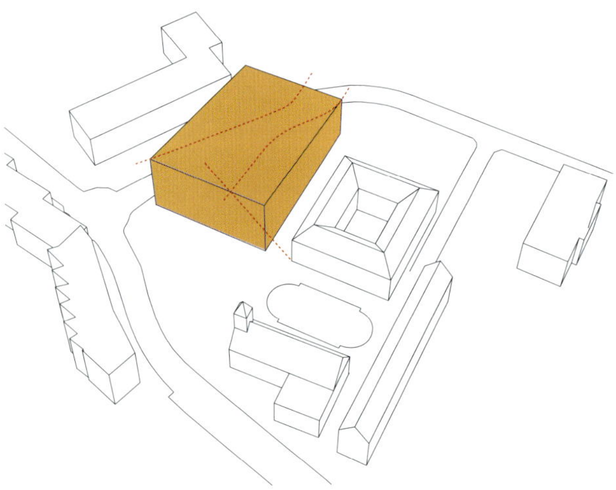

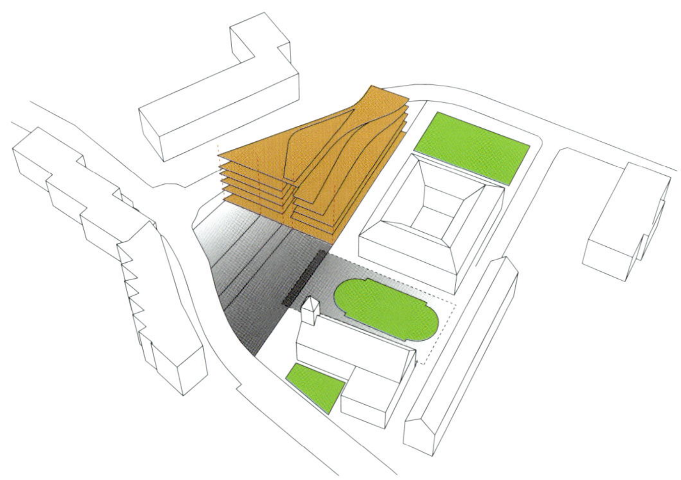

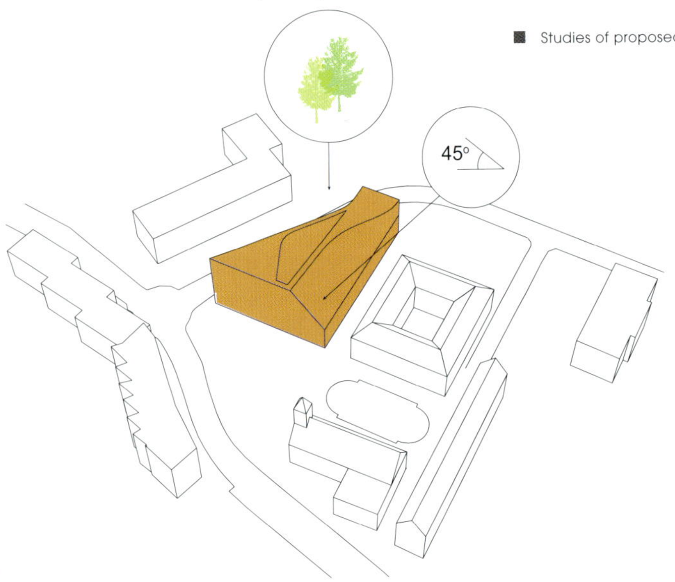

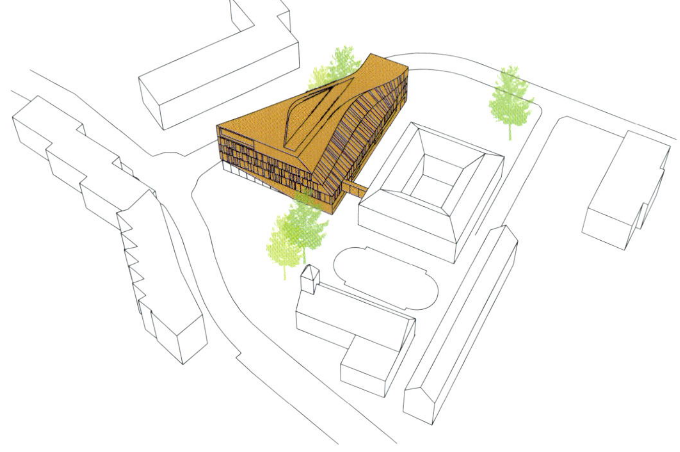

■ Studies of proposed volume distribution - not to scale

Planivolumetric scheme of program in its urban context - not to scale

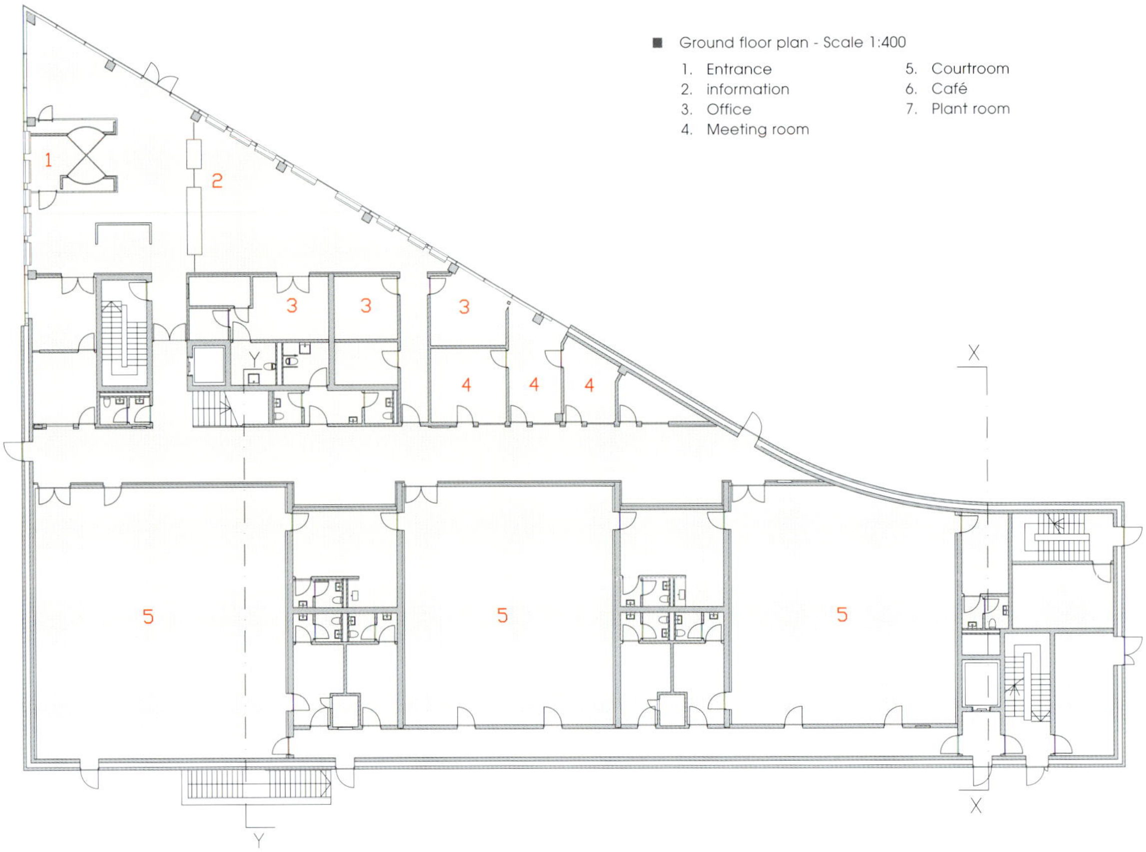

■ Ground floor plan - Scale 1:400

1. Entrance
2. information
3. Office
4. Meeting room
5. Courtroom
6. Café
7. Plant room

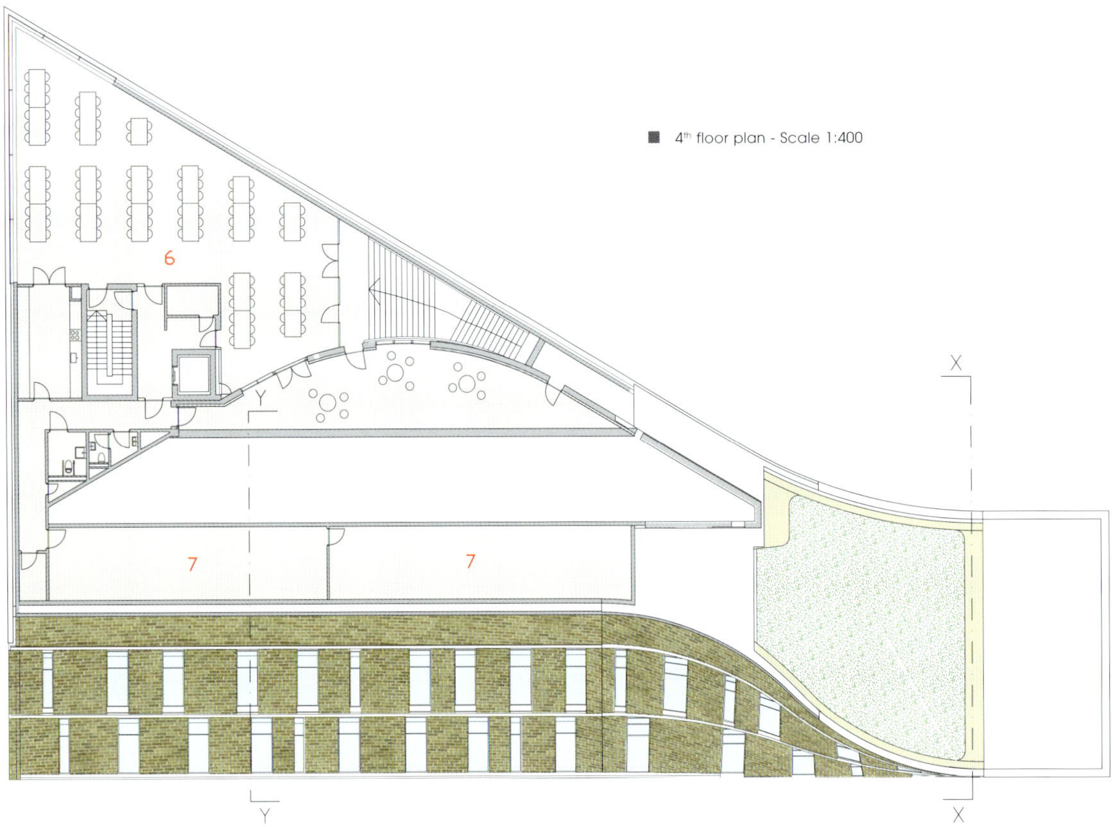

■ 4th floor plan - Scale 1:400

Competition model

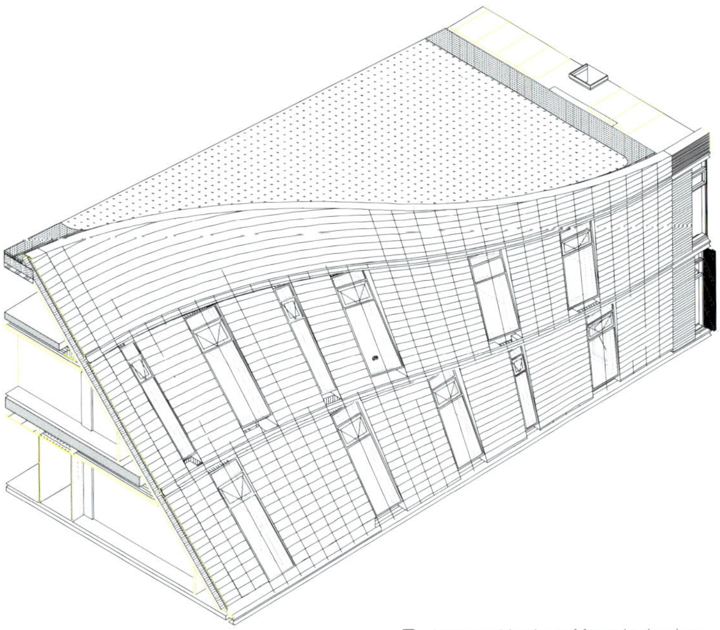

Axonometric view of façade structure - not to scale

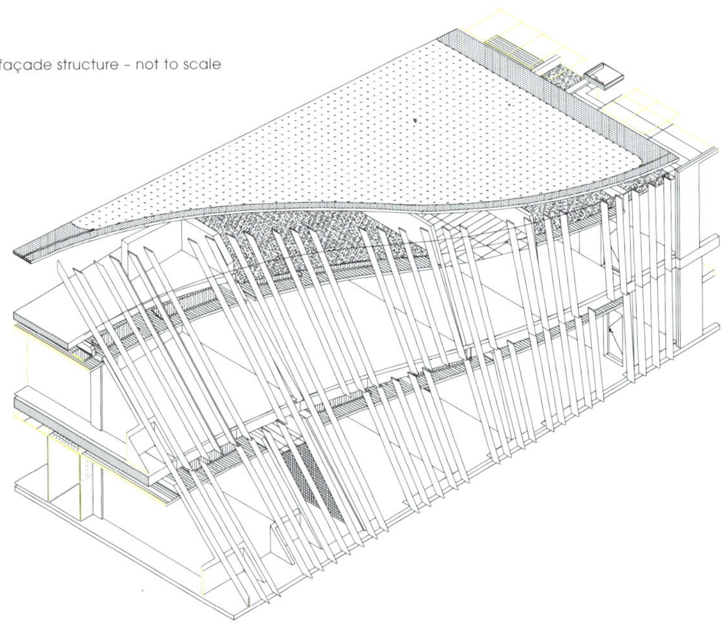

Competition model

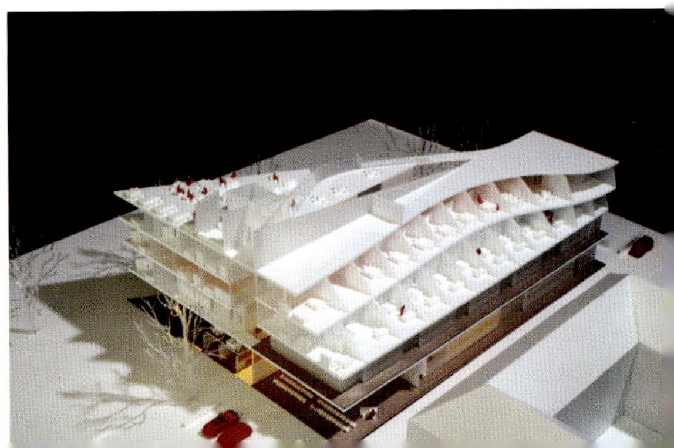

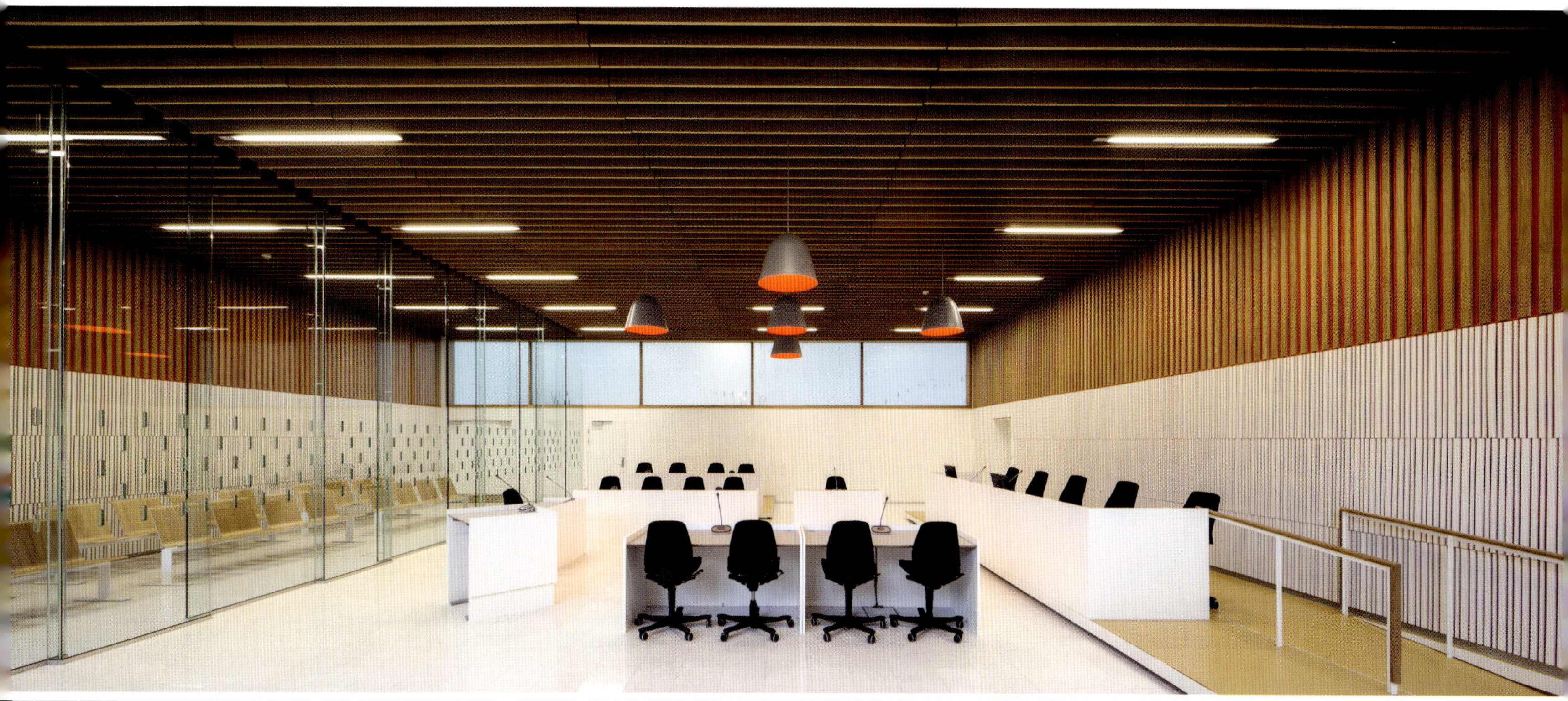

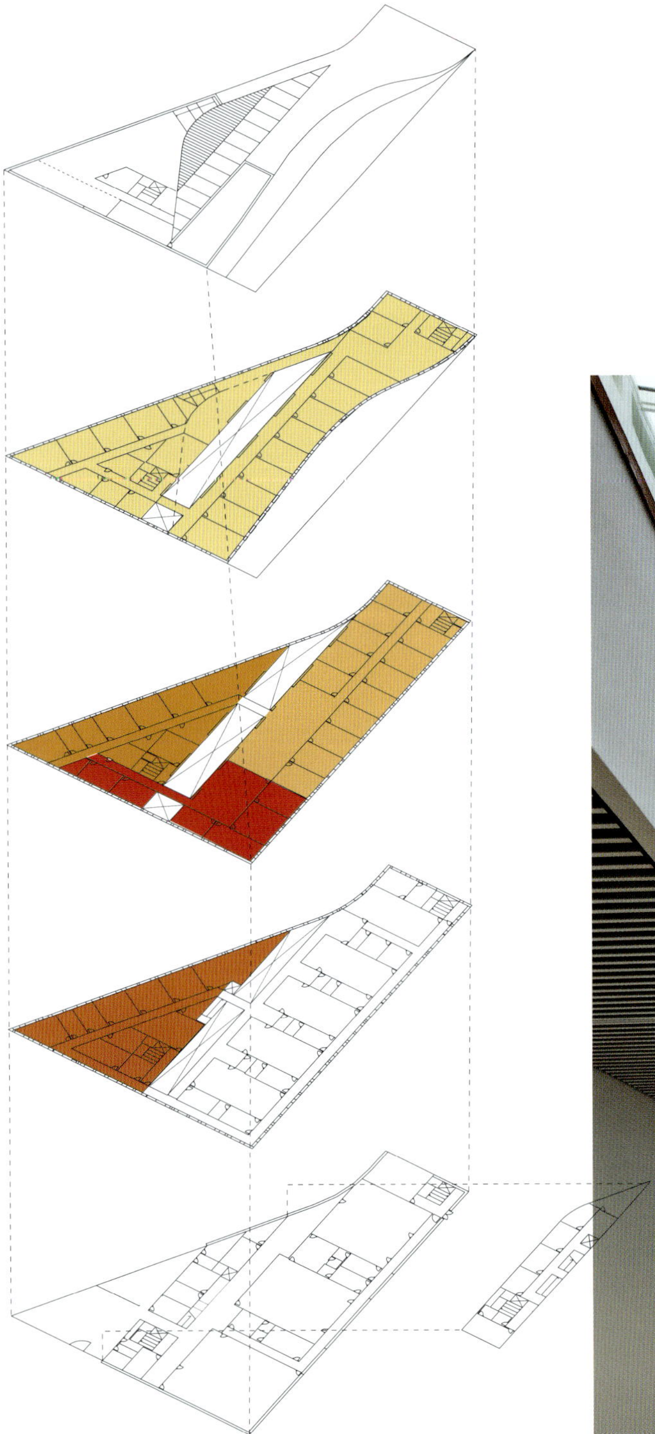

■ Spatial distribution scheme - competition - not to scale

- Central secretariat
- Judges
- Court clerk
- Administrative offices
- Department of Probate Court

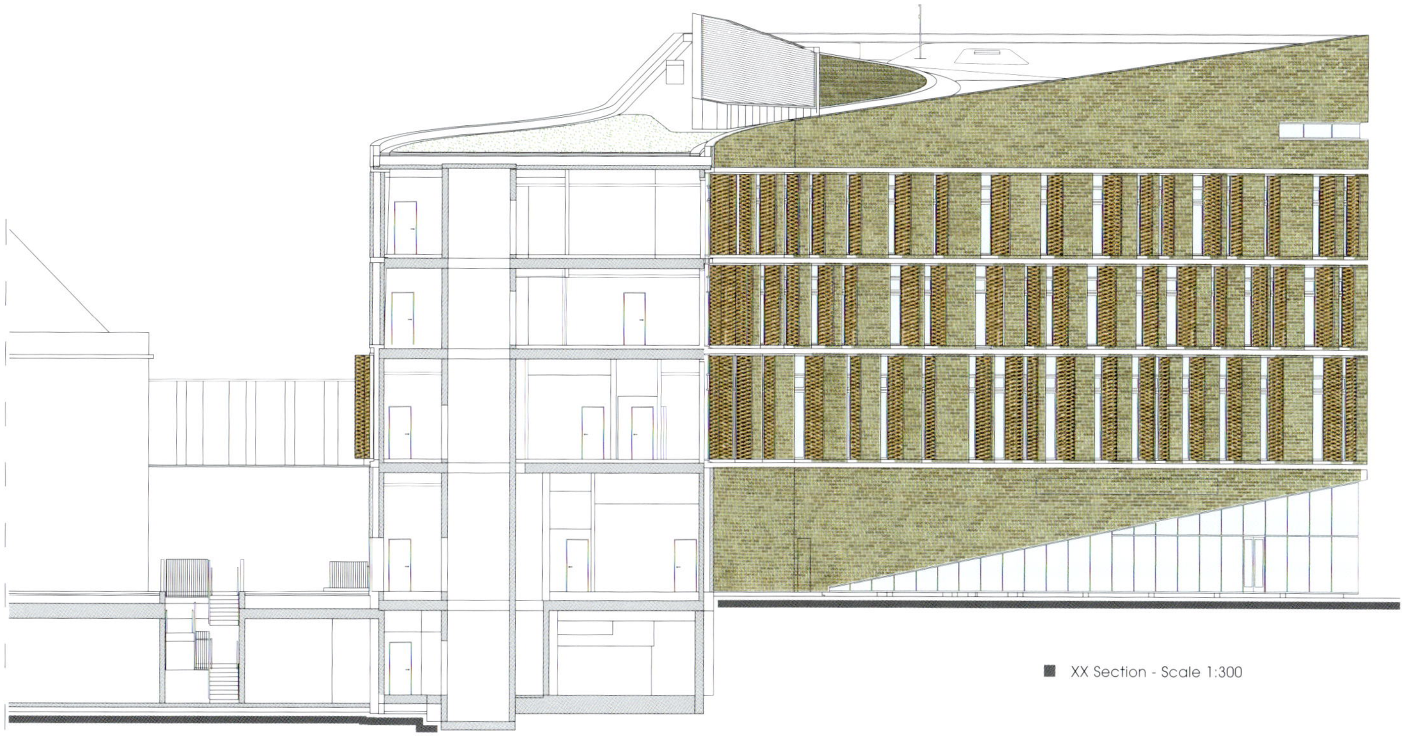

■ XX Section - Scale 1:300

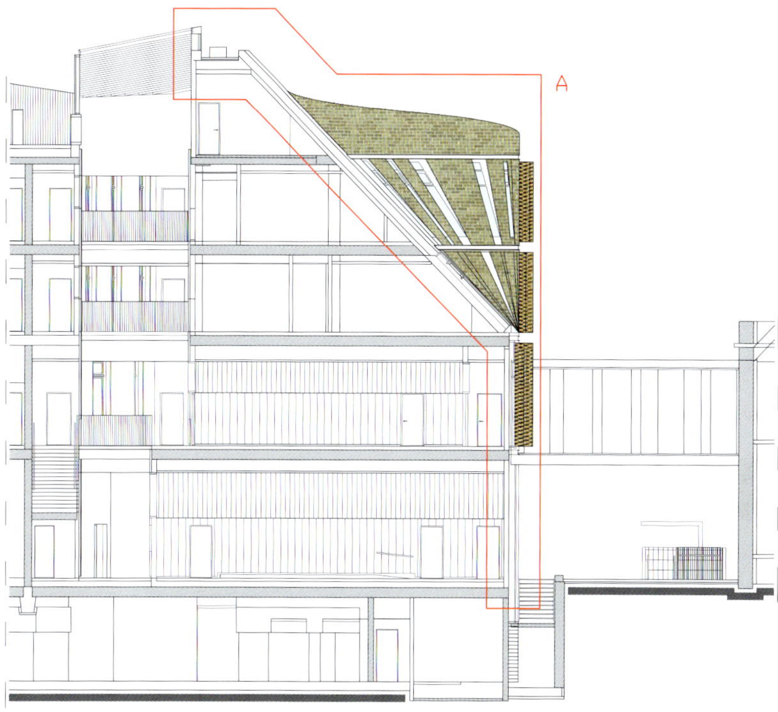

■ YY Section - Scale 1:300

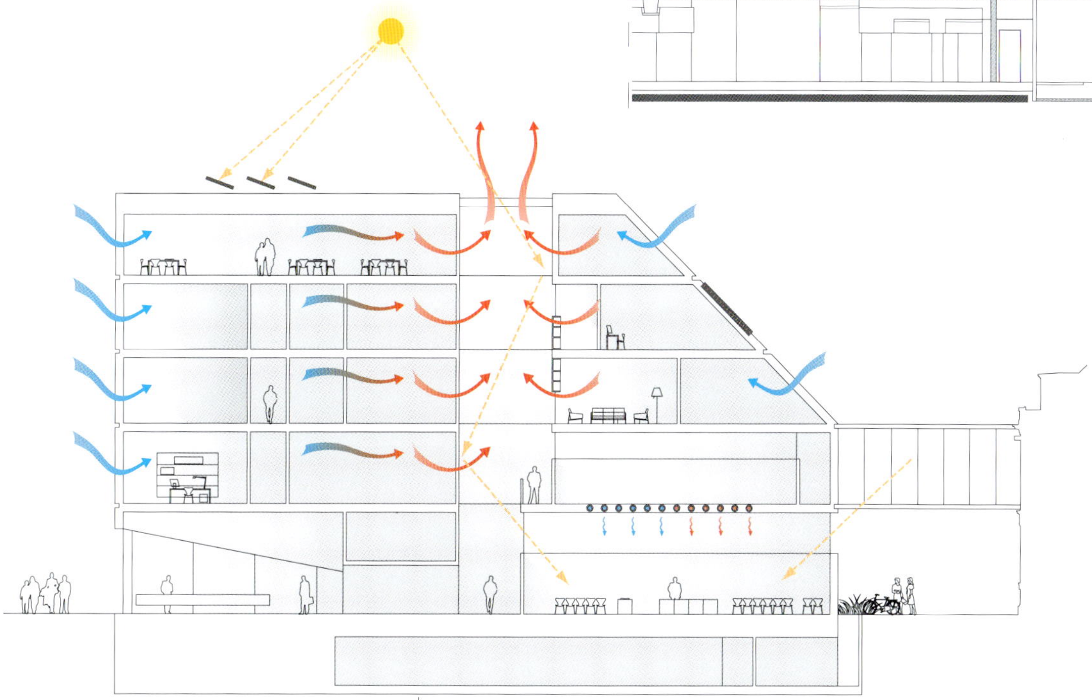

■ Cross-sectional view of natural ventilation and heating – not to scale

DETAIL A: CONSTRUCTION SYSTEM VERTICAL SECTION – SCALE 1:40

1. Skylight with aluminum frame and 5/16 - 1/2 - 5/16 - 1/2 - 5/16″ (8/14/8/14/8 mm) glazing
2. 2 3/4″ (70 mm) aluminum sandwich panel with insulation core (can be opened for ventilation)
3. Green roof with 2 3/4″ (70 mm) top soil, filtering layer, 1 5/8″ (40 mm) studded plastic mat, asphalt membrane root barrier, double layer 13 3/4″ (350 mm) insulation, 4 7/8″ (125 mm) corrugated sheeting, vapour barrier, 1/2″ (12.5 mm) gypsum board
4. 1 3/8″ (35 mm) flame-retardant panel
5. Wall with double 1/2″ (12.5 mm) gypsum board, supporting frame of 6 7/8″ (175 mm) steel C-profiles sandwiching insulation, double 1/2″ (12.5 mm) gypsum board sandwiching vapour barrier
6. Roof formed by clinker tiles, supporting frame of 1 3/4 x 1″ (45x25 mm) timber, asphalt membrane, secondary frame of 1 3/4″ (45 mm) timber, asphalt membrane, 3/4″ (20 mm) timber panel, 2″ (50 mm) ventilation space, double 13 3/4″ (350 mm) rigid insulation, vapour barrier, 1 3/4″ (45 mm) rigid insulation, double 1/2″ (12.5 mm) gypsum board
7. Recessed heating convector with 4″ (100 mm) aluminum grille on 1″ (25 mm) flame-retardant soundproofing panel
8. Linoleum flooring, screed, footfall matting, 3 1/2″ (90 mm) foamed concrete screed, 15 3/4″ (400 mm) reinforced concrete slab, false ceiling consisting of 4 x 1 1/4″ (100x30 mm) aluminum profiles with interior insulation on aluminum T-profile and tie rods suspended from slab
9. Aluminum window with 5/16 - 1/2 - 5/16 - 1/2 - 5/16″ (8/14/8/14/8 mm) glazing
10. Aluminum profile floor course sandwiching insulation
11. Floor-to-ceiling aluminium window with 5/16 - 1/2 - 5/16 - 1/2 - 5/16″ (8/14/8/14/8 mm) glazing
12. Side-hung aluminium mesh sun shading
13. 4 3/8″ (110 mm) clinker cladding, 4″ (100 mm) rigid insulation, frame of steel C-profiles with 7 1/8″ (180 mm) insulation, 15 x 15″ (380x380 mm) steel L-profile, 7 7/8″ (200 mm) reinforced concrete structure
14. Sheet aluminium window trim

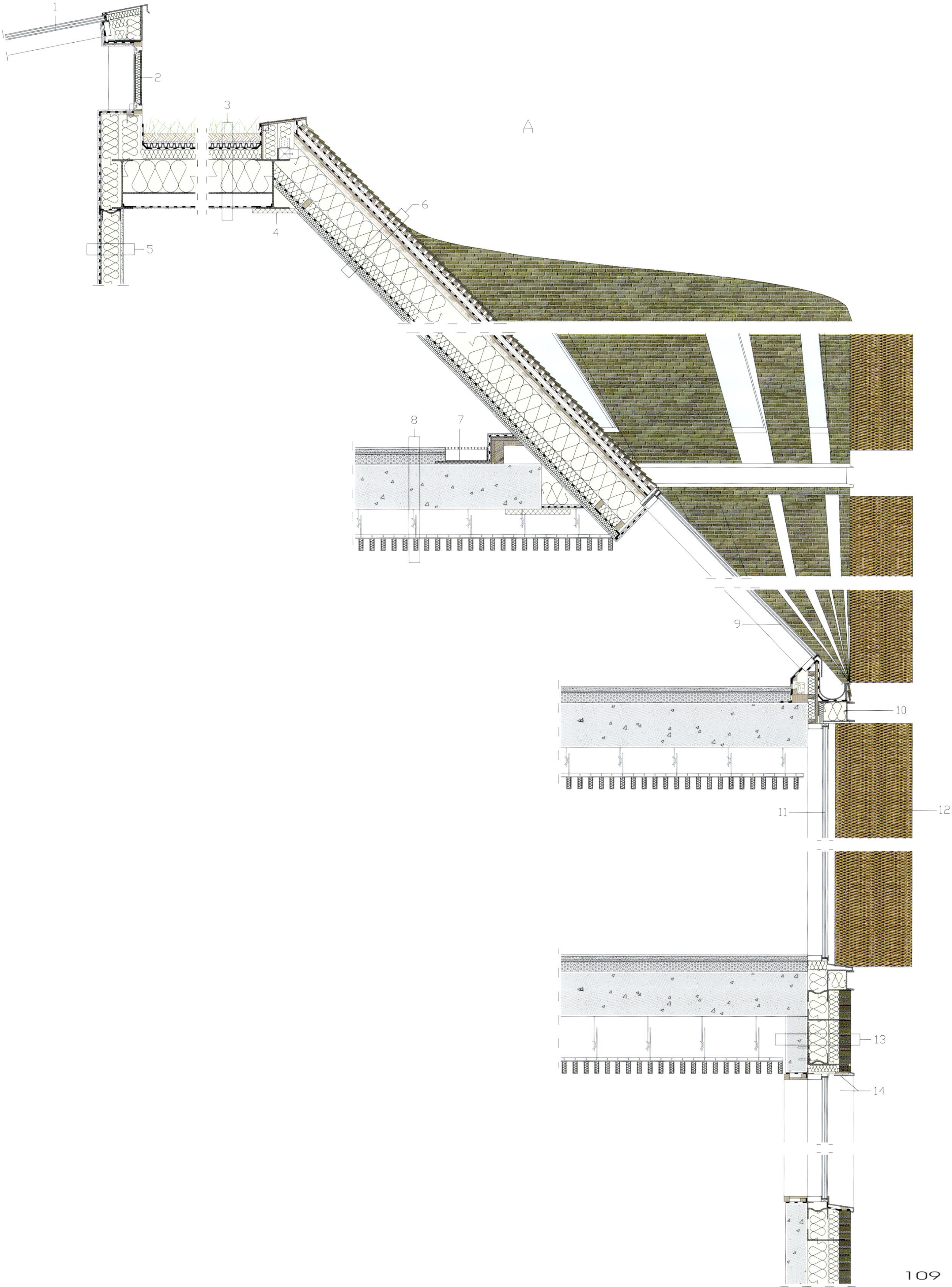
A
1
2
3
4
5
6
7
8
9
10
11
12
13
14

COPENHAGEN INTERNATIONAL SCHOOL NORDHAVN

COPENHAGEN, DENMARK

C.F. MØLLER

Take an architecture firm like C.F. Møller, founded in 1924, which over its long history of almost a century has made sustainability a signature feature; add an international school for pupils from 3 to 19, founded in 1963 and now the largest of its kind in Denmark. The result is one of the most innovative and interesting architectural projects of 2017.

In architecture, experimentation with composition and technology is always in its element when it comes to designing educational spaces because ideally, places of education should constantly change with the generations, not only adapting to technological advances but also to developments in educational practice, which in turn go hand in hand with changing social trends.

CIS Nordhavn is a school building for the Copenhagen International School in the new district of Nordhavn. Inaugurated on March 7th, 2017, the 26,000 sq m building is the largest school in the Danish capital with 1,200 pupils and 280 employees. Standing on an artificial promontory surrounded by water and green areas - to be completed with the arrival in the next few years of the subway - this large school facility has been designed to be part of its urban context, being on the route connecting the port to the nearby city neighborhood.

The main school building is subdivided into four smaller "towers" placed asymmetrically on a ground-floor base. Rising from 5 to 7 stories, the towers have been designed to meet the needs of children at different stages of development. For example, the classrooms for the youngest pupils are particularly large. A full range of functions is provided in and around the classrooms, each of which has designated green spaces and a series of ancillary facilities. These include three full-size basketball courts and a theater with a large auditorium for the public along with other adjoining rooms.

Dividing the school into four units also helps develop a sense of community and identity as well as facilitating the child's sense of spatial awareness. You get the sense that the Reggio Children idea of classrooms around a communal square has here been combined with the more ingenious distribution logic of Hogwarts of Harry Potter fame!

The ground floor base contains communal spaces, including a foyer, sports facilities, a canteen, a library and public activity areas. This spatial distribution allows the classroom units to be closed off outside normal school hours while the common areas can remain open for school and local community events.

The base includes a communal roof terrace, which functions as a school playground for the whole school, especially the younger pupils. This huge recreational area provides a secure environment, ensuring that pupils do not stray from the premises or get too close to the water.

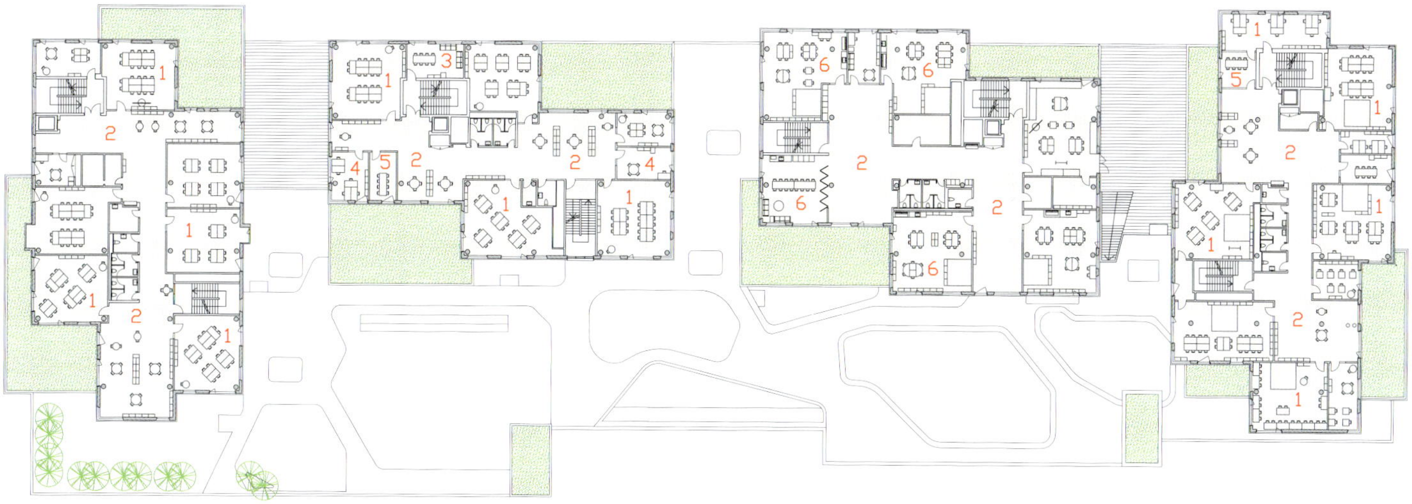

■ Ground floor plan - Scale 1:800

1. Classroom
2. Hall
3. Teachers lounge
4. Office
5. Meeting room
6. Workshop

■ Perspective cross-sectional view - not to scale

■ North elevation - Scale 1:800

The unusual shape of this school building gives rise to an interesting layout. Equally unique is the Copenhagen International School's outer skin made up of 12,000 solar panels, each individually angled to create a sequin-like effect. As well as recalling J.K. Rowling, the building design also has a little of Paco Rabanne! By no means an unmistakable school building, this intriguingly extrovert construction strikes the observer for its lively dialogue with the nearby water and the ever-changing light of northern skies. Beside its architectural impact, the complex is also a powerhouse of energy saving. The photovoltaic skin will supply more than half of the school's annual electricity consumption. The total solar cell stretch of 6,048 sq m makes it one of the largest building-integrated solar power plants in Denmark, with an estimated production of over 200 MWh per year.

Equally environmentally minded is the position of most of the schoolrooms at the corners of each tower so as to optimize natural daylighting and provide views onto the outside from a wide variety of positions. LED lighting is used throughout and teachers can vary the color and intensity of the artificial lighting. All the furniture is made out of natural materials while the toilet flushes use recycled water. Last but not least, as well as contributing to the school's green profile, the solar cells also form a permanent part of the school's curriculum, allowing students to monitor energy production and use the data they collect in physics and math classes.

In the words of C.F. Møller architect and partner, Mads Mandrup: "We have created an exemplary educational building in the heart of Nordhavn that can instill new vitality in the whole neighborhood; a building whose transparent and porous base and handsome yet functional façade creates an innovative landmark". Mission accomplished.

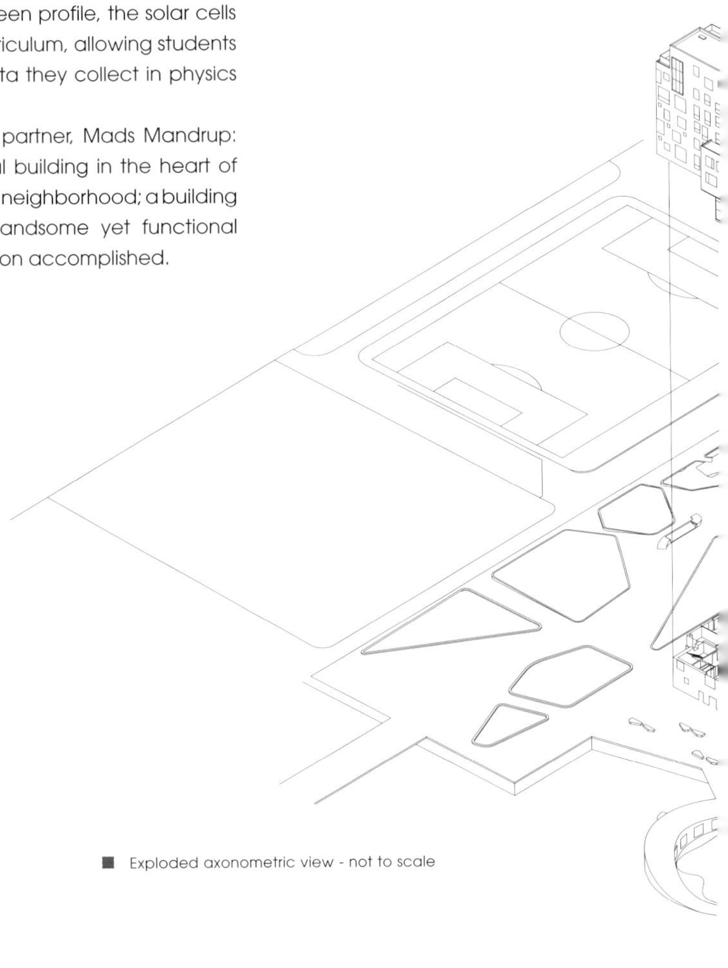

■ Exploded axonometric view - not to scale

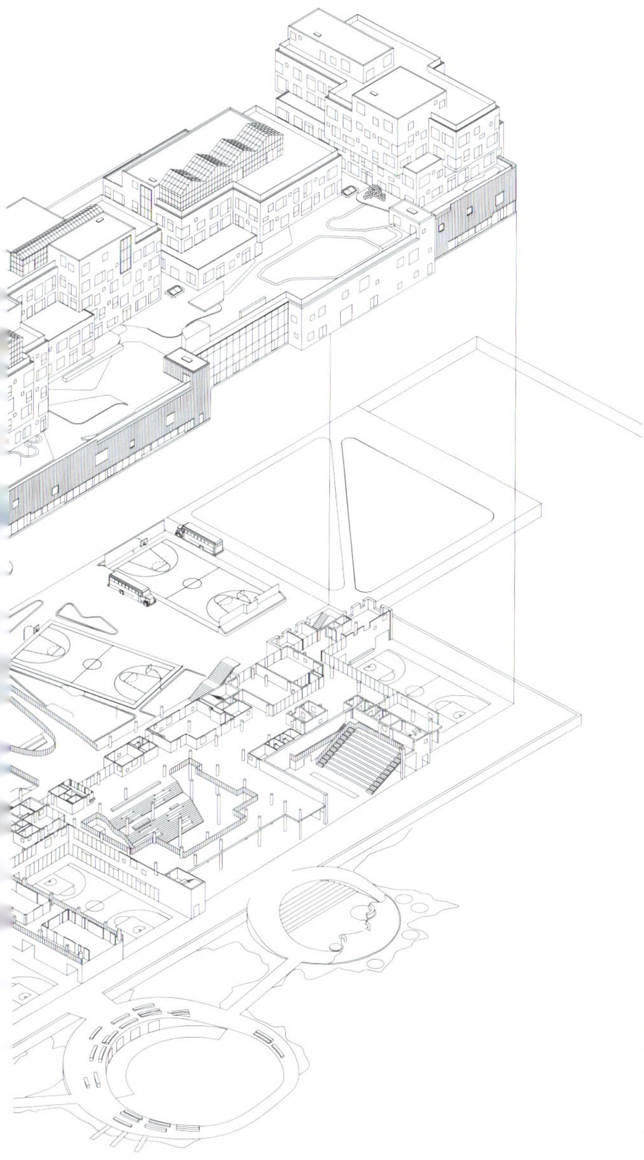

HYUNDAI
HYUNDAI
HYUNDAI
APL

■ Bioclimate cross-sectional view - not to scale

1. Green area and playground between the building and the city
2. Playground and garden roof for outdoor activities and storm water collection system
3. Positioning of classrooms at the corners to guarantee natural lighting and ventilation from two façades
4. Solar panels on the façade provide energy and can also be used for teaching purposes
5. Cooled ceiling
6. Area facing the port for outdoor activities
7. Broad views through the canteen and outdoors

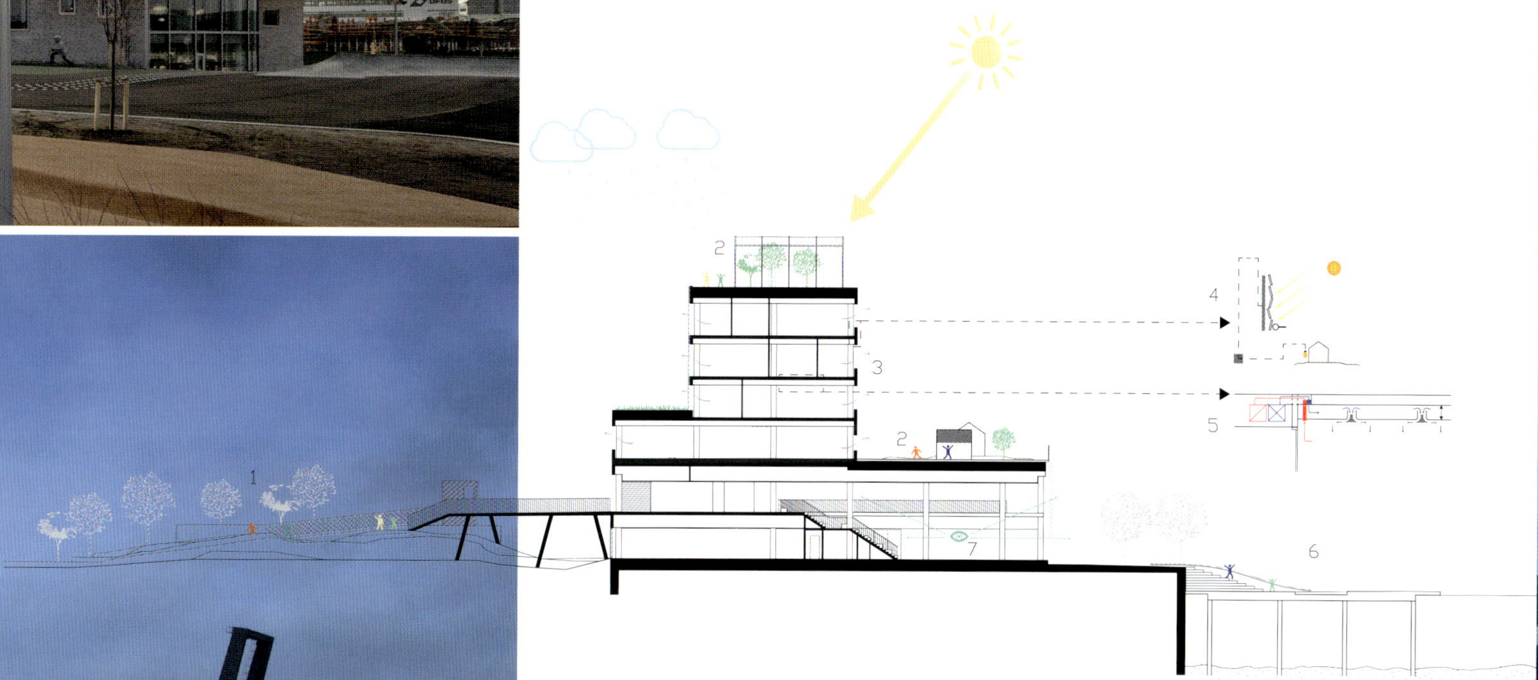

Picture Books

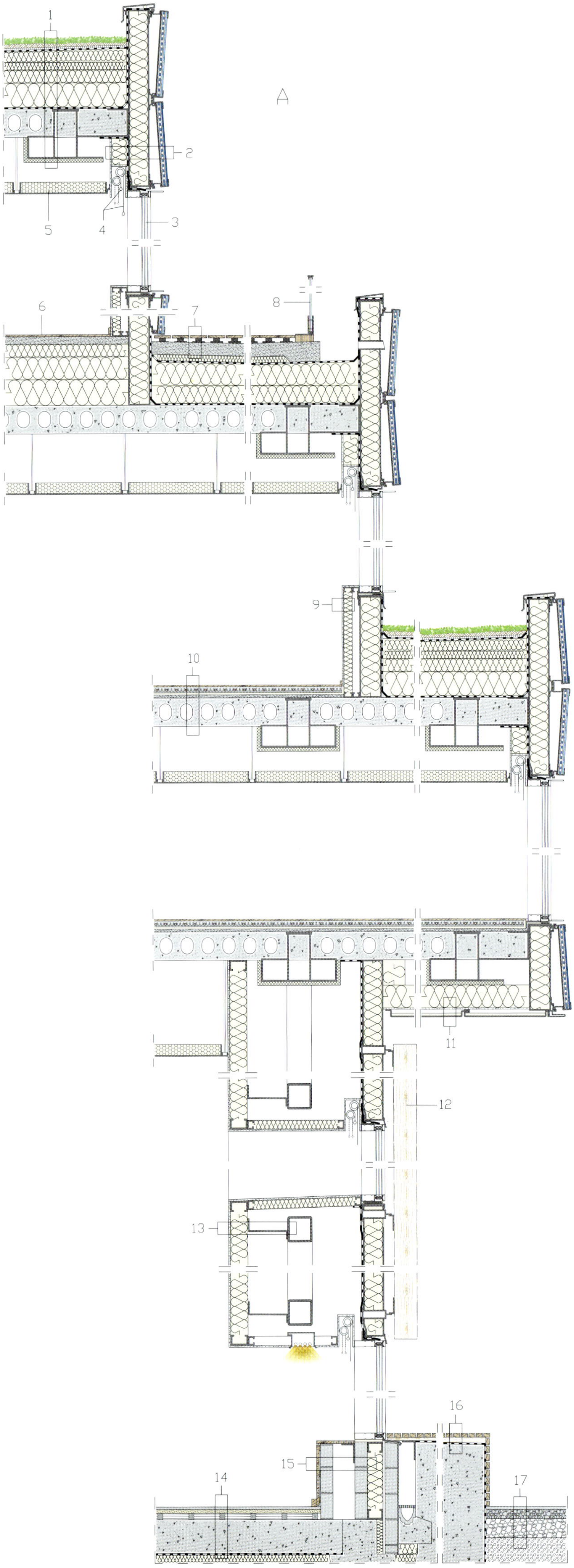

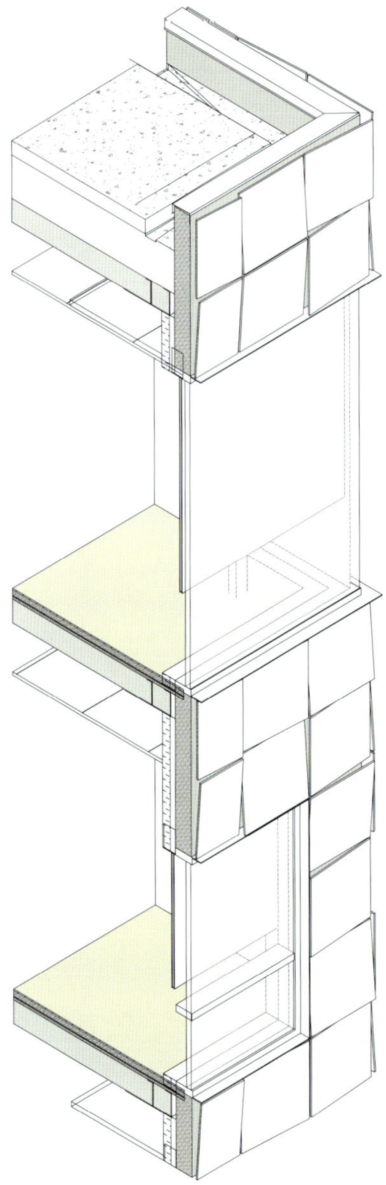

■ Exploded axonometric view of the façade's construction system

DETAIL A: FAÇADE CONSTRUCTION SYSTEM VERTICAL SECTION - SCALE 1:40

1. Green roof comprising soil, felt matting, waterproofing membrane, 4 3/4" (120 mm) max h insulation layer forming slope, 2 3/8 x 4 x 7 7/8" (60+100+200 mm) rigid insulation, waterproofing membrane, 8 5/8" (220 mm) cellular concrete slab, composite steel beam with flame-retardant treatment
2. Façade comprising 3/16" (4 mm) colored glass panels, protective film, photovoltaic cell, protective film and black film, point fasteners, 6 3/4" (170 mm) aluminum sandwich panel with insulation core, waterproofing membrane, insulation layer, 1/2" (12.5 mm) gypsum board bulkhead
3. Window with 1/4 - 5/8 - 1/4 - 5/8 - 1/4" (6/16/6/16/6 mm) aluminum glazing unit
4. Sun-shading blinds
5. Suspended ceiling comprising aluminum panels and acoustic insulation suspended by tie rods
6. Oak flooring
7. Timber decking on adjustable pedestals, screed forming slope, 2" (50 mm) rigid insulation
8. Railing consisting of double 3/8" (10 mm) glass in steel profiles
9. Interior wall covering comprising 1/2" (12.5 mm) gypsum board, frame of 2 3/4 x 1 5/8" (70x40 mm) aluminum C-profiles sandwiching insulation
10. 5/8" (15 mm) oak flooring, 2 3/8" (60 mm) screed with embedded radiant heating, acoustic matting, 1" (25 mm) screed, 8 5/8" (220 mm) cellular concrete slab
11. Suspended ceiling comprising sheet steel and insulation panels, 1/2" (12.5 mm) gypsum board, 6 7/8" (175 mm) rigid insulation
12. Ash fins fastened by 4 3/4 x 1 5/8" (120x40 mm) steel L-profiles to steel box profiles
13. Bulkhead formed by 1/2" (12.5 mm) gypsum board, supporting frame of 5 1/2 x 3 1/8" (140x80 mm) aluminum C-profiles sandwiching insulation, steel Z-profile anchor, frame of 7 7/8 x 7 7/8" (200x200 mm) steel box profiles
14. Gymnasium floor comprising linoleum, MDF panels, suspending frame, 10 1/4" (260 mm) reinforced concrete slab, waterproofing membrane, insulation layer
15. Finish comprising 7/8" (22 mm) oak panels on anchors, structure of 4" (100 mm) concrete blocks, air space, 5 7/8 x 4" (150x100 mm) steel L-profile, structure of 4" (100 mm) concrete blocks, insulation layer
16. Bench seat comprising 2 x 1 1/4" (50x30 mm) teak battens, timber supporting beam, waterproofing membrane, reinforced concrete structure
17. Polished concrete paving, drainage layer, compacted gravel, layer of gravel and sand

RENOVATION OF LES DOCKS

MARSEILLE, FRANCE

ALFONSO FEMIA
WITH 5+1AA

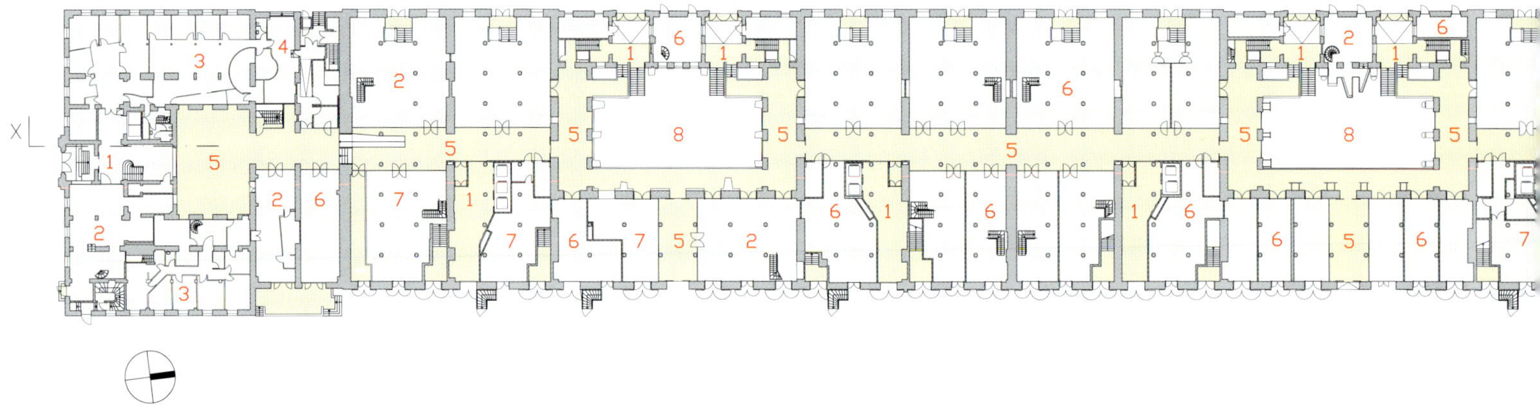

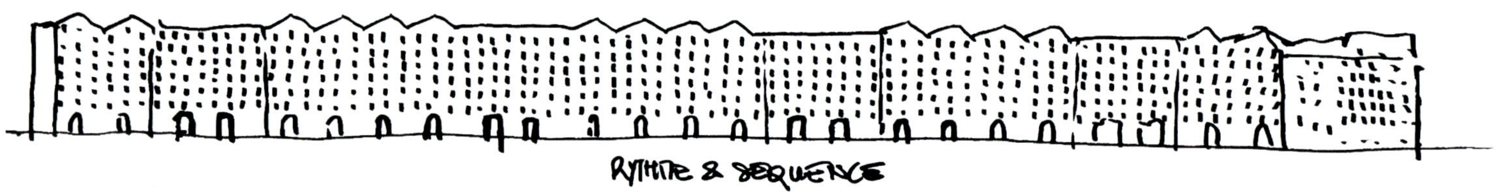

■ West elevation - Scale 1:1000

■ XX Section - Scale 1:1000

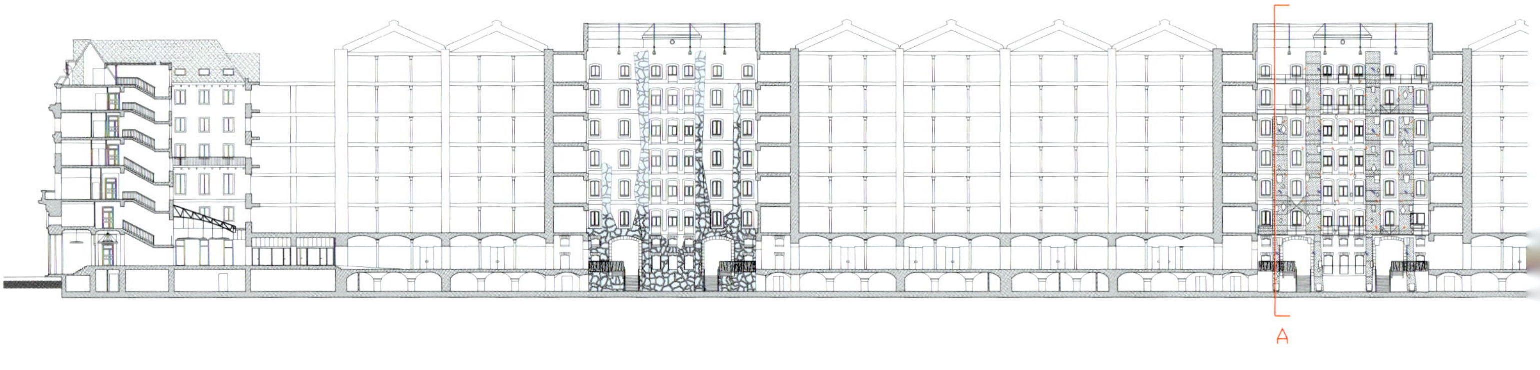

■ Ground floor plan - Scale 1:1000

1. Entrance
2. Restaurant and cafeteria
3. Office
4. Archive
5. Inner path
6. Retail
7. Technical room
8. Inner courtyard

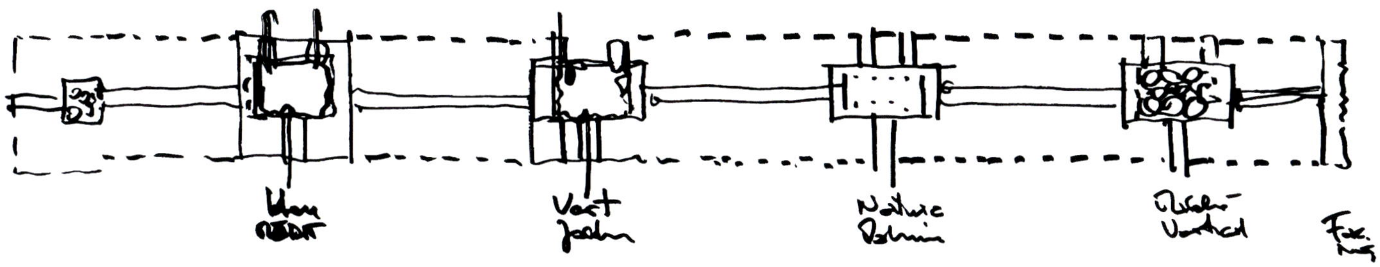

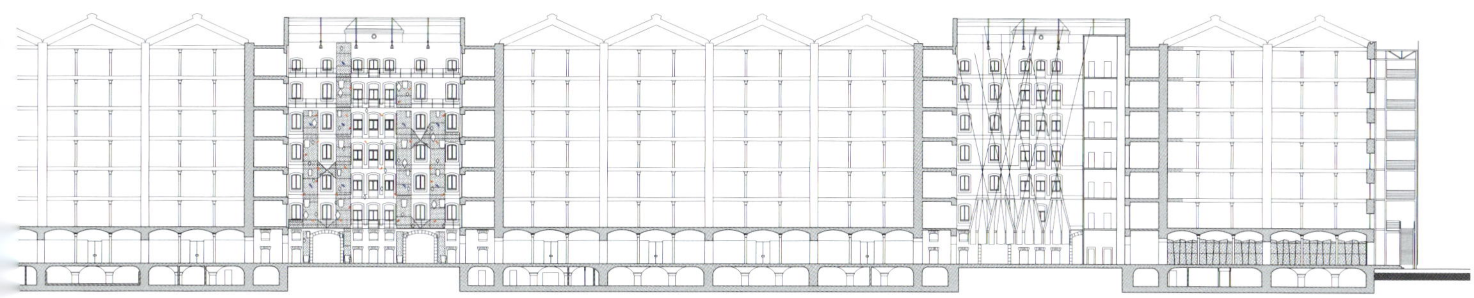

How to describe an intense, complicated project like the one just completed at Les Docks in Marseille, one of the largest buildings in France completely renovated for new use by the painstaking, knowledgeable intervention of the architects? Simple: with a letter.

Giorgio Tartaro rights to Alfonso Femia

_1

Dear Alfonso,

You asked me to assess, even harshly, an important piece of your personal and professional lives. I'll answer with impressions, the way I usually do when trying to formulate what I think; I let things flow - a flow of consciousness, understanding and acknowledgement.
The first thing that comes to mind. Others follow.
The archetypal letter.

Act One - Status quo ante

Went by car from the MuCEM, the harbor, Foster, other projects in the beehive of activity that is Marseille. Enter dark dusty worksite. Potential, what once was, plant and equipment being re-laid.

Couldn't bring myself to believe that all you were doing was a mere restoration job with some earth removal, everything based on those beautiful white tubes holding the plant and equipment. Had imagined a wider, more thoughtful intervention: a theme explained. You had talked once to me of a fantastic new life for these dark courtyards. But what I saw was a worksite, a dismal dark place. The size of the building and the way the project was to proceed would tell a very different story.

Intermezzo - The surroundings, horror and splendor

The opening towards the sea of this shopping mall by the harbor, the interminably long walk to get to the terraces and finally see the sea, and the massive harbor wall, all speak of the city's need to close itself off from the sea, the source of its wealth, but also an ever-present danger. It makes you understand the function of Les Docks as the city's strongbox, its coffer of riches; how the architecture, now as then, openly declares its function but also issues a warning. What jars today is the square in front of the hotel. Not so much on busy market days, but on ordinary days. Hope there's a renovation project for it or that the opening to the sea and the horizon you propose before Place de la Joliette will actually come about.

Inauguration - The scent of noises

Once again, I let myself be guided by your words, by details, scents and sounds that in the courtyards become background noise.

Designer luminaires, carefully chosen parquet flooring, transparent glass to replace walls, the succession of blue, green, grey metallic mesh... Arrive at the crenulated wall that conceals the fire escape staircase, long in the planning and now pierced with openings to exalt but at the same time lighten the great fortress that is Les Docks.

I look at the details to try and find signs of haste, mistakes, inappropriate features. Hard to find anything that jars. Apart from a few doorsteps, couplings or furnishings that don't quite fit (but we all know what happens afterwards when others have a say...). I look up to the panels supporting the ceramics and try to figure out how a damaged light will be reached; I look at the sequence of the vases set high on the walls and try to imagine what the courtyard will look like once the plants have grown. I stop. I think back on your past projects. Try and find links, and find them in the inclined, box-shaped staircase.
After that first visit, I expected a more mundane outcome, perhaps one that was starker and more essential. But it's become a *hortus mirabilis* of ideas now turning into concrete projects.

ANDRÉ SUARÈS
JOSEPH MÉRY
ERNEST HEMINGWAY

I am struck by something you once said that drives home the difference between what it could have been and how it is. Rain wets the ceramic and the grouting of the blue court. Your eyes light up, you stand up straight and say: "That's how I would have liked it, see?"; as if you had the Instagram options to create your own image, your photo, your creature. That's it. That's the difference. Between the drawing board, what's actually there, and the digital image; what is and how you would like it to be.

_2

Skin - Inner skin. Structures, courtyards and marvels

Here the inner skin is much more organic than in your previous work where contrasts either weave together or are sharply distinct.

Here, the skin is organic, made of plants. I watch people as they looked around, glass in hand, at the inauguration, observe them looking up to try and see where those "natural" skins you chose to clad pillars and stone structures actually finish.

An infinite gaze, in an attempt to find reiteration, alignments, connections, justifications and changes.

You must have had fun cutting those diagonals, subtracting points of visual focus, tiring rather than cheating the observer's eye.

Natural and artificial, a Möbius strip, they are among the most interesting and important themes of this project. Both in their affirmation and negation.

If the project is a metaphor - as 10 million motorists will understand each year as they encounter the "literary" wall going across the flyover - then Les Docks are its manifesto.

_3

Skin against skin

The north frontage had to be given thought. Don't get me wrong. I don't mean just how to cover that lovely but awkward pre-existing structure with a fire escape. The façade facing the square, in front of the buildings by Fuksas and the sloped square, had to be given character. People in cars on the flyover needed to be told something. The architecture needed to be explained, its story retold with signs, and invention, something that everybody would understand without understanding; make people pause without stopping.

What better than writing? The code *par excellence*, used by the Greeks and the Latins as explanation, warning, indication, charm.

"What to do?" that's what someone would have said.

Simple. Find a text in some way connected with Marseille, perhaps an "impression of Marseille". Make the lettering fit the building. Create those obligate words, the semantic orgasm "Les Docks", from a sort of literal entropy.

Engage visual studios and typographers, refer to Manutius and the Gutenberg press, make laser cuttings that skilful firms will correct to a 700 mm margin of error.

"Beautiful, cool." say the architects, developers and journalists. Someone stops to read it. Some recognize the names of poets and a few of the sayings.

Fact is, though, no one, apart from the authors, will ever read it all. Well, so what? Do you have any idea how many people quote Joyce and Ulysses without having even read Molly's monologue? Or how many people talk about Beethoven and can't tell the difference between the first notes of the *Fifth Symphony* and the *Ode to Joy*?

This it is an immanent wall, if you see it that way. You don't have to read it; you simply have to know it's there, that it exists, that for the first time writing - letters - are not there as a frieze under a tympanum or gate. For the first time, letters are architecture, transparent and immanent.

The sign finally comes into its own.

And serves a purpose. The word "text" means to weave... weave stories, views, moments, attention and distraction.

■ Study sketches of layout and cladding solution for the inner courts

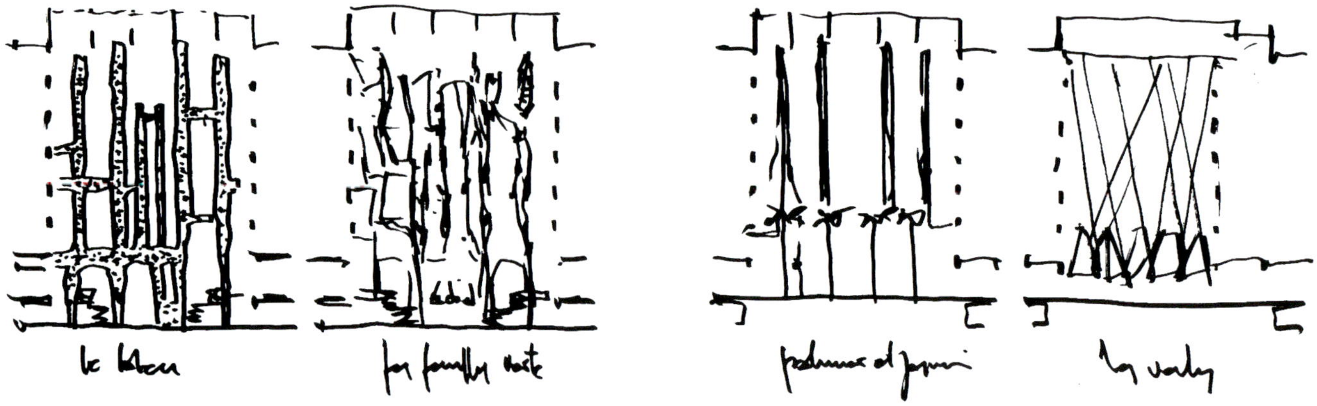

The new docks in Marseilles is a succession of colors, materials and images in which art and nature are interwoven with architecture and movement. Achieving such a merger of ideas necessitated the close cooperation of the architect, artists, artisans and industry. The "blue" courtyard required careful use of color. The cladding rises up from the floor onto the walls in a chromatic effect created through the mixing of 7 hues from deep blue to white. These colors were produced specifically for this project, working closely with the designers and creating a customized production process. The final crackle effect was done by mosaic artisans who placed the ceramic pieces on industrialized steel plates. The "green" courtyard truly started from the impression of the diamond-shaped leaf, created by the artist Danilo Trogu working with Alfonso Femia. The diamond-shaped leaves were created using 30/60x60 cm blocks and then attached directly to the galvanised steel structure that both supports and defines the pattern, with its solids and voids. The design leaves space for plants to grow, intertwining themselves with the frame to create and represent the symbiosis of nature, creation, material and art.

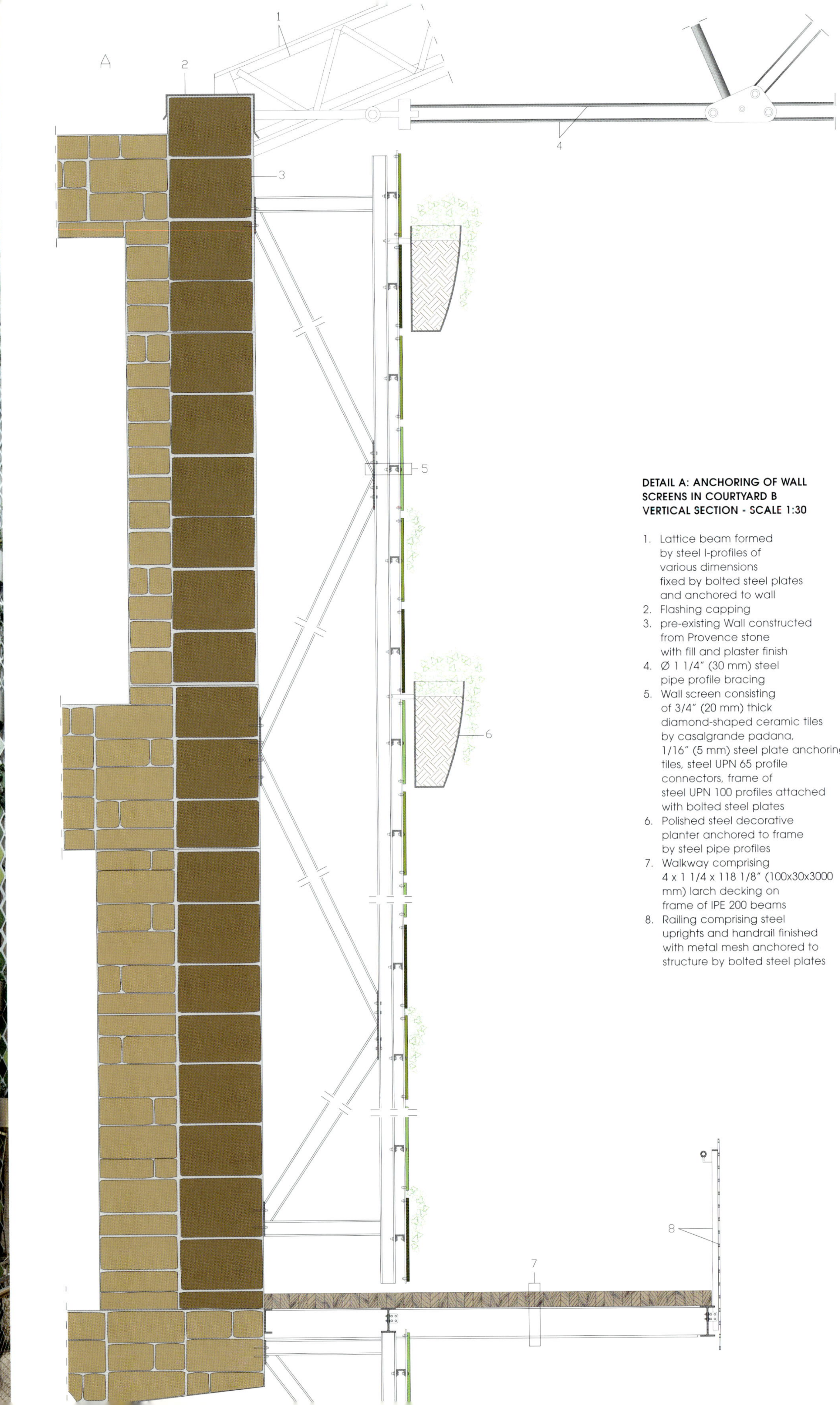

DETAIL A: ANCHORING OF WALL SCREENS IN COURTYARD B VERTICAL SECTION - SCALE 1:30

1. Lattice beam formed by steel I-profiles of various dimensions fixed by bolted steel plates and anchored to wall
2. Flashing capping
3. pre-existing Wall constructed from Provence stone with fill and plaster finish
4. Ø 1 1/4" (30 mm) steel pipe profile bracing
5. Wall screen consisting of 3/4" (20 mm) thick diamond-shaped ceramic tiles by casalgrande padana, 1/16" (5 mm) steel plate anchoring tiles, steel UPN 65 profile connectors, frame of steel UPN 100 profiles attached with bolted steel plates
6. Polished steel decorative planter anchored to frame by steel pipe profiles
7. Walkway comprising 4 x 1 1/4 x 118 1/8" (100x30x3000 mm) larch decking on frame of IPE 200 beams
8. Railing comprising steel uprights and handrail finished with metal mesh anchored to structure by bolted steel plates

PARISH COMPLEX
IN THE DIOCESE OF LODI

DRESANO, ITALY

A huge solitary white cylinder stands against the flat skyline in the open countryside that is Italy's northern Po valley plain around Lodi, near Milan. This is the first impression you get of the parish church at Dresano by Neapolitan architects Corvino and Multari, winners of the competition by invitation called by the Italian Episcopal Conference (CEI) in 2009. Yet the uncompromising stereometric form is part of a much-researched, complex program that had to resolve at least three problematic issues facing architects of places of worship. The result is an exemplary lesson in method and how potential problems can be transformed into opportunities to bring about one of the most mature, meaningful new constructions in a sector of such fundamental importance in Italy.

Problems

Top on the list is the very fact of designing a piece of religious architecture, a delicate problem-fraught brief for a number of reasons. First, there is the symbolic charge attached to any religious building. Then, there are the inevitable comparisons that will be made with the many Modernist masters who have successfully reinterpreted a tradition going back thousands of years that has given the world so many extraordinary achievements. Finally, there is the progressive secularization of contemporary society that has obliged religion to take on a different dimension and led the catholic church to rethink the way places of worship are used and hence articulated, with the need for new forms to combine an unchanged symbolic value and the new liturgical approach, continuing tradition but at the same time embracing current needs.

The second-order problem is the whole question of the place of modern buildings of worship in our modern world. Alongside its mission as a place of contemplation and introspection, a church is the focal point of its pastoral ministry but also the center of other activities involving the community. This is why here, the cloister is no longer an enclosed monastic space but part of the churchyard, scene of collective activities in a community fabric lacking places of civic socialization.

The third-order problem is the church building's relationship with context, here a considerable headache, given the particularly non-descript landscape and absence of any striking natural or architectural reference points. Which led the architects to carry out painstaking research into the area's past in order to find some.

As well as taking their cue from the ancient farmhouses that speak of an age-old peasant culture, the bedrock of this northern plain, the architects also refer to an interesting piece of the past they unearthed and took as a precedent for their building: the small 18th Century church of San Giorgio Martire, whose cube-shaped central plan includes an inner circular volume created by a series of radial pillars supporting the building's dome.

Themes

Redolent with symbolism, the circulum shape chosen recalls the cosmos and divine perfection, but also, for the Christian tradition, the power of prayer and the capacity of the scriptures to give "order" to the world, the circle being a metaphor for the chaos of earthly life turned into a harmonious whole. The reference is to a tradition rooted in Plato's Timaeus that led Alberti to view the circle as the ideal form for the central plan of the "Christian temple". However, the use of the circle here does not just make reference to ancient cosmogony. Corvino and Multari's brief made explicit that the church should reflect the new idea of the Church given by the Second Vatican Council concluded

in the mid 1960s, whereby the celebration of the mass has become a community experience of the Word and the Sacrament, in a return to the original meaning of the Greek *ekklesía*, which in the ancient *polis* meant a gathering of the whole community. The circle shape is therefore a concise, highly effective image of an assembly of equals in prayer, a gathering of brethren enjoying the same relationship with God, each at an "equidistant point from the center".

Another highly sensitive theme is the dialectic between a circle plan and the axial layout required for the entrance (here to the south) to be diametrically opposite the altar, towards which all the pews face. The dilemma is solved by placing all the sacramental furniture - the monstrance, or ostentorium, the baptismal font and confessional, but also the bracket for the wooden statue of the Madonna delle Grazie, the organ and the side chapel - outside this axis so as to avoid the risk of the longitudinal plan overshadowing the central role of the circular hall. The result is the clear perception of the centrifugal tension being countered by the re-direction towards a single point of a series of objects and activities, which, although single points in space, are held together in a unified whole by the enveloping circle.

This circle is contained within another circle. Which brings us to the third theme. Like the ancient church of San Giorgio Martire, here too the structural elements stand apart from the perimeter wall, creating an open ring and leaving the "real" walled circle of the ambulatory to encircle the body of the church and rise well beyond the lenticular profile of the roof. This adds a further theme to those of the circulum and the contrasting central and axial layout: architecture within architecture.

This leads to yet another theme: the double shell envelope. Corvino and Multari make the ambulatory look as if it has been "dug out" from the perimeter wall, the resultant space a walkway but also letting in the light. For it is especially this higher encircling volume, its profile converging towards the center of the body of the church, that captures the light and filters it down through a strip of X-shaped reinforced concrete elements serving as both diaphragm between interior and exterior and an expressive textured connection between church and cloister. The same structural elements are found on the rectangular base supporting the cylindrical volume. The protective iron oxide coating gives them the brick-brown color of the old farmhouses dotting the countryside, a reference to the time-honored history of the place.

Et Verbum caro factum est. Et habitavit in nobis (And the Word was made flesh and dwelt amongst us)

The architecture needs nothing else. It is an extraordinary space. The stereometric relationships and use of light in the assembly hall prove yet again that when put to masterful use, the simple geometries of archetypical forms can delivery semantic excellence and symbolic force. Devoid of any superfluous decorative add-ons, the clean elegant lines of both architecture and furnishings make it a place of prayer and contemplation. Above the entrance, a large burnished bronze plaque by one of Italy's most famous artists, Nino Longobardi, is engraved with a gigantic cross. Resembling both cave drawing and metropolitan tag, it proclaims the very essence of what this architecture is all about. Christ is not there. Longobardi has removed the simulacra of Christ's body on the cross - an ineffably lightweight cast aluminum figure - to the innocent purity of the church itself. He is no longer on the cross, crucified; He has descended from the cross to rest within the church of mankind, His place of preference.

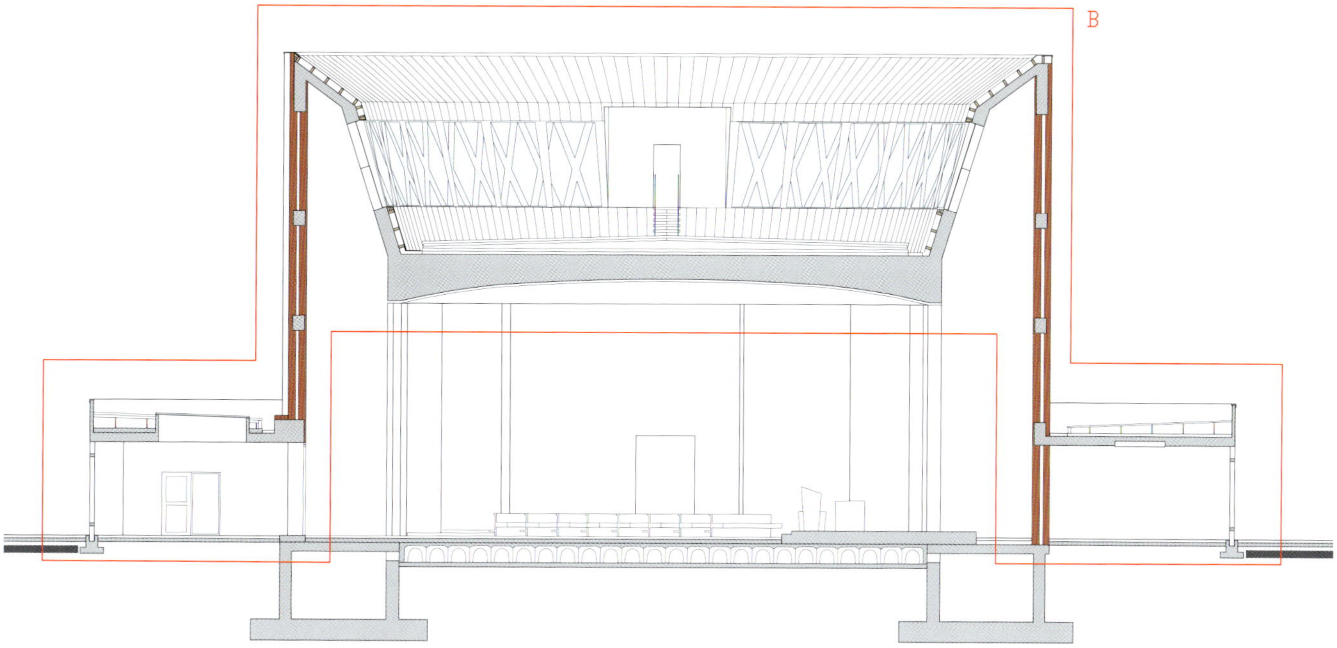

■ XX Section - Scale 1:250

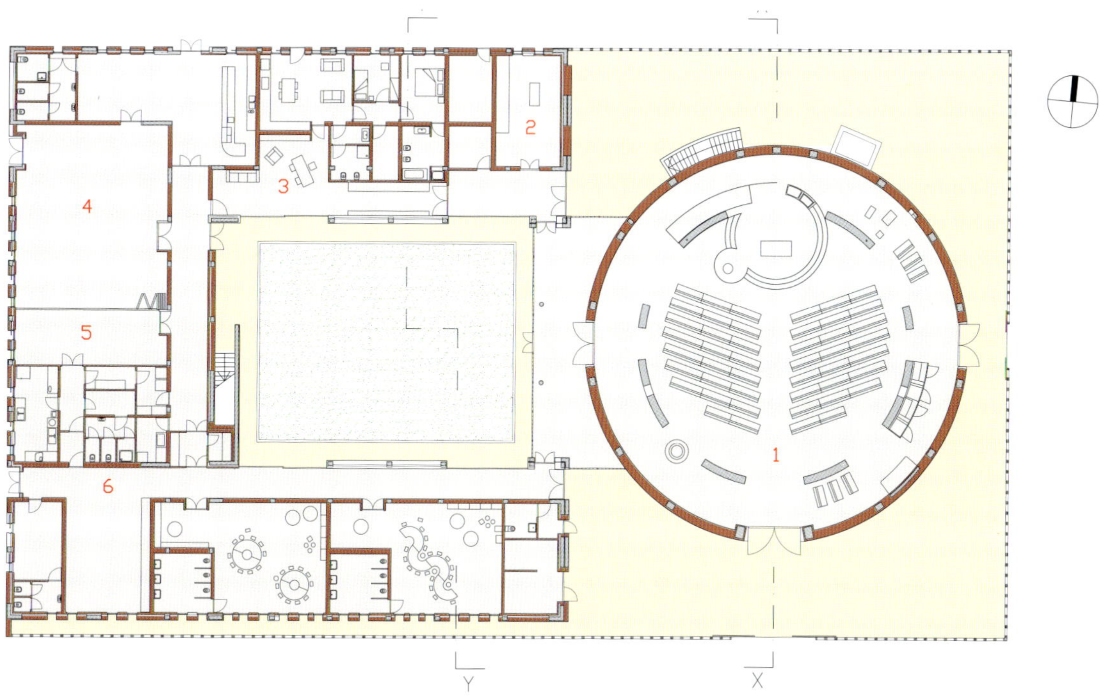

■ Ground floor plan
Scale 1:500

1. Main body of the church
2. Sacristy
3. Rectory
4. Parish hall
5. Canteen
6. Parish teaching and other activities

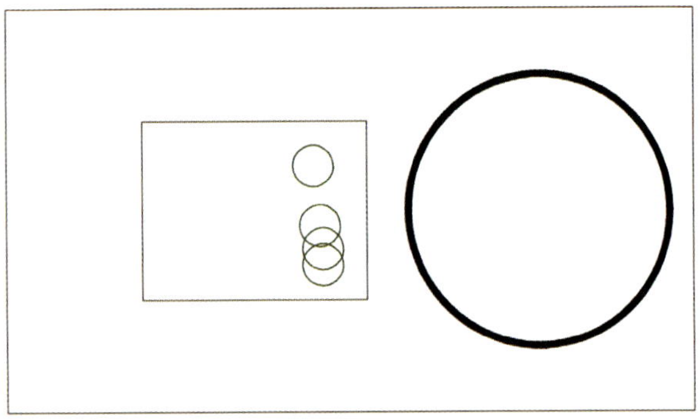

1

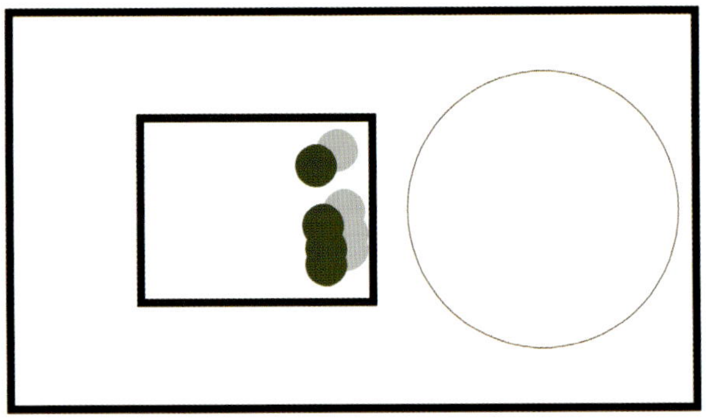

2

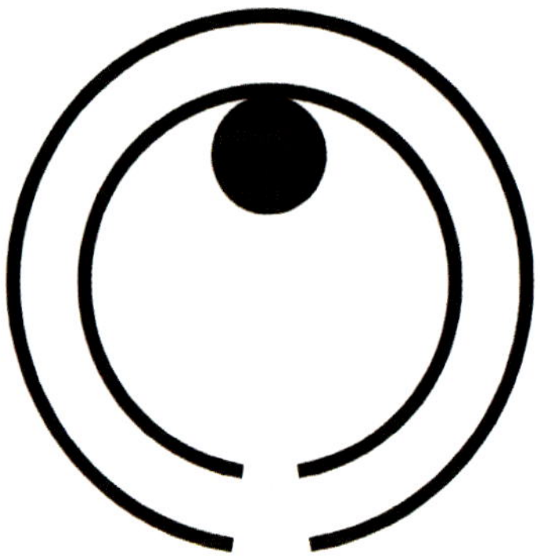

3

4

■ Conceptual sketch
indicating distribution circuits

1. The main body of the church in the circular plan
2. Parish activities and teaching environments grouped around a courtyard where existing trees have been preserved
3. Church plan consists of two concentric circles, symbolizing the embrace of the community by the Madonna delle Grazie
4. The assembled faithful become a symbolic image of pierced side of Christ

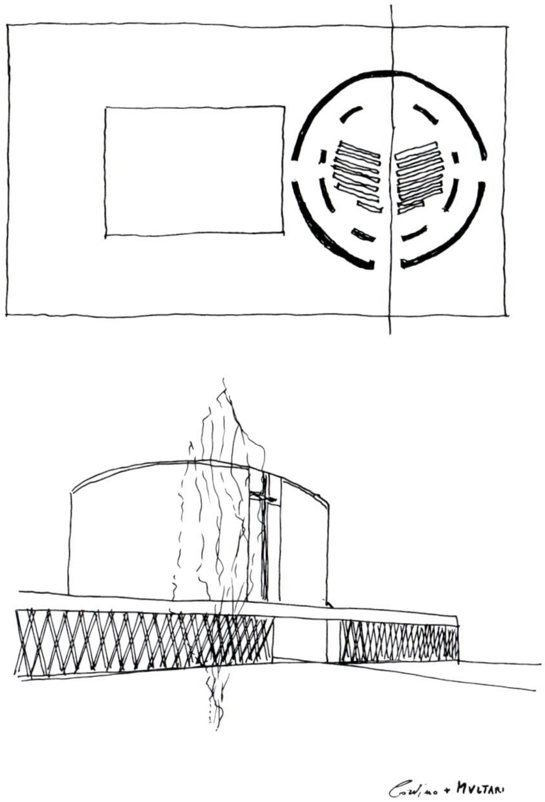

Perspective floor plan sketches

Concept sketch showing the idea of embrace as underlying concept of the project

DETAIL A:
CLOISTER CONSTRUCTION
VERTICAL SECTION
SCALE 1:30

1. Skylight with 3/16 - 1/2 - 3/16 + 3/16" (4/12/4+4 mm) aluminum glazing unit
2. Wall with double waterproofing membrane, 1/2" (12 mm) timber panel, 2" (50 mm) insulation layer, 3/8" (10 mm) gypsum board
3. Roof with seamed aluminum sheeting with drainage joints, supporting frame of 3 1/8 x 2" (80x50 mm) fir, adjustable pedestals, waterproofing membrane, 4" (100 mm) rigid polyurethane insulation, 5 1/2" (140 mm) screed, vapor barrier, 15 3/4" (400 mm) lightweight reinforced concrete slab, 4" (100 mm) rigid insulation, false ceiling comprising 1/2" (12.5 mm) gypsum board on metal droppers
4. Aluminum door with integrated horizontal blinds and 1/4 - 3/4 - 5/16" (7/20/8 mm) glazing unit with AGC security glass
5. Wall with plaster finish, 4" (100 mm) brick, 2" (50 mm) cavity
6. Floor comprising 1/2" (14 mm) porcelain stone tiles, 3 1/8" (80 mm) sand and cement screed with embedded heating system, 2 3/8" (60 mm) expanded clay and cement screed, 2 3/8" (60 mm) rigid polyurethane insulation, waterproofing membrane, reinforced concrete slab with plastic void formers
7. 5 7/8" (150 mm) masonry block wall with plaster finish
8. Wall with 3/4" (20 mm) plaster finish, 9 7/8" (250 mm) brick leaf, 4" (100 mm) rigid insulation, 2" (50 mm) cavity, 3 1/8" (80 mm) brick leaf, 3/4" (20 mm) plaster

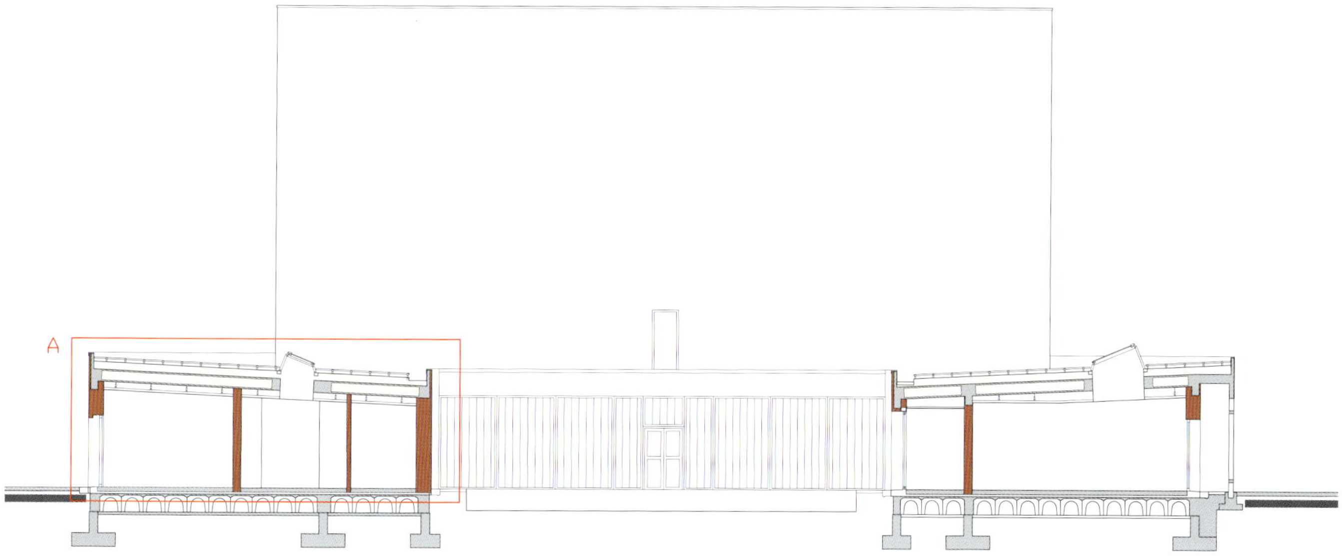

■ YY Section - Scale 1:250

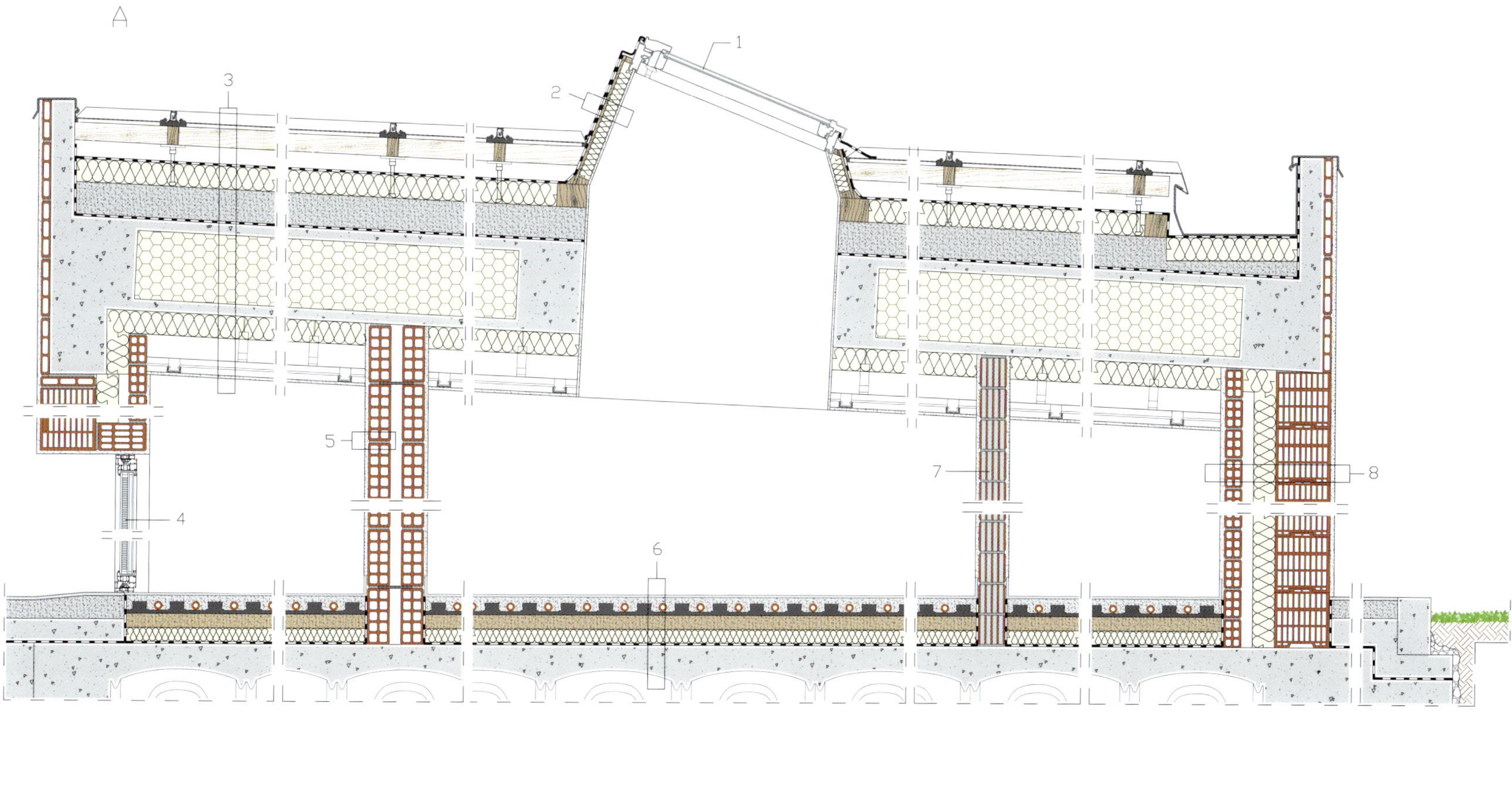

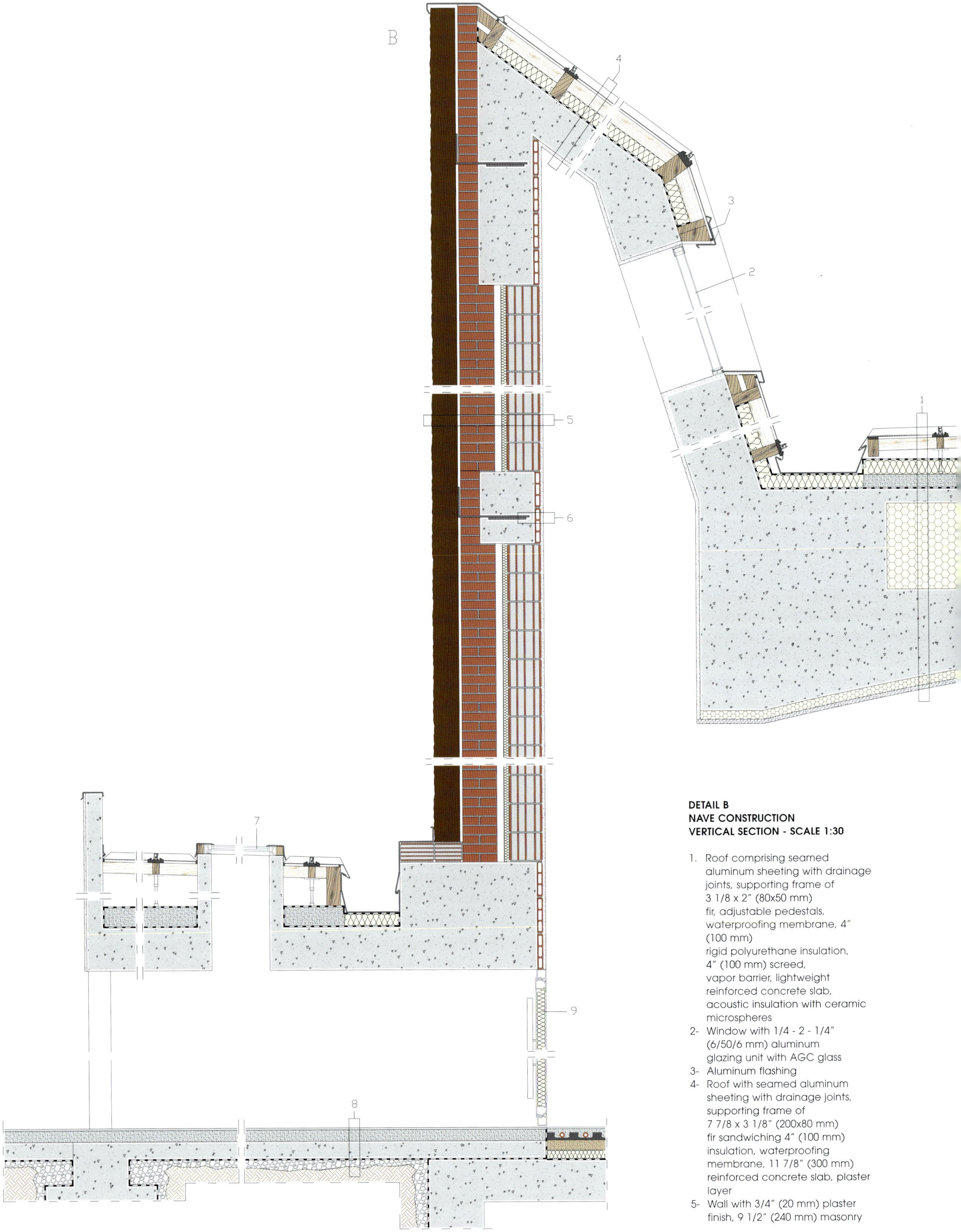

DETAIL B
NAVE CONSTRUCTION
VERTICAL SECTION - SCALE 1:30

1. Roof comprising seamed aluminum sheeting with drainage joints, supporting frame of 3 1/8 x 2" (80x50 mm) fir, adjustable pedestals, waterproofing membrane, 4" (100 mm) rigid polyurethane insulation, 4" (100 mm) screed, vapor barrier, lightweight reinforced concrete slab, acoustic insulation with ceramic microspheres
2- Window with 1/4 - 2 - 1/4" (6/50/6 mm) aluminum glazing unit with AGC glass
3- Aluminum flashing
4- Roof with seamed aluminum sheeting with drainage joints, supporting frame of 7 7/8 x 3 1/8" (200x80 mm) fir sandwiching 4" (100 mm) insulation, waterproofing membrane, 11 7/8" (300 mm) reinforced concrete slab, plaster layer
5- Wall with 3/4" (20 mm) plaster finish, 9 1/2" (240 mm) masonry

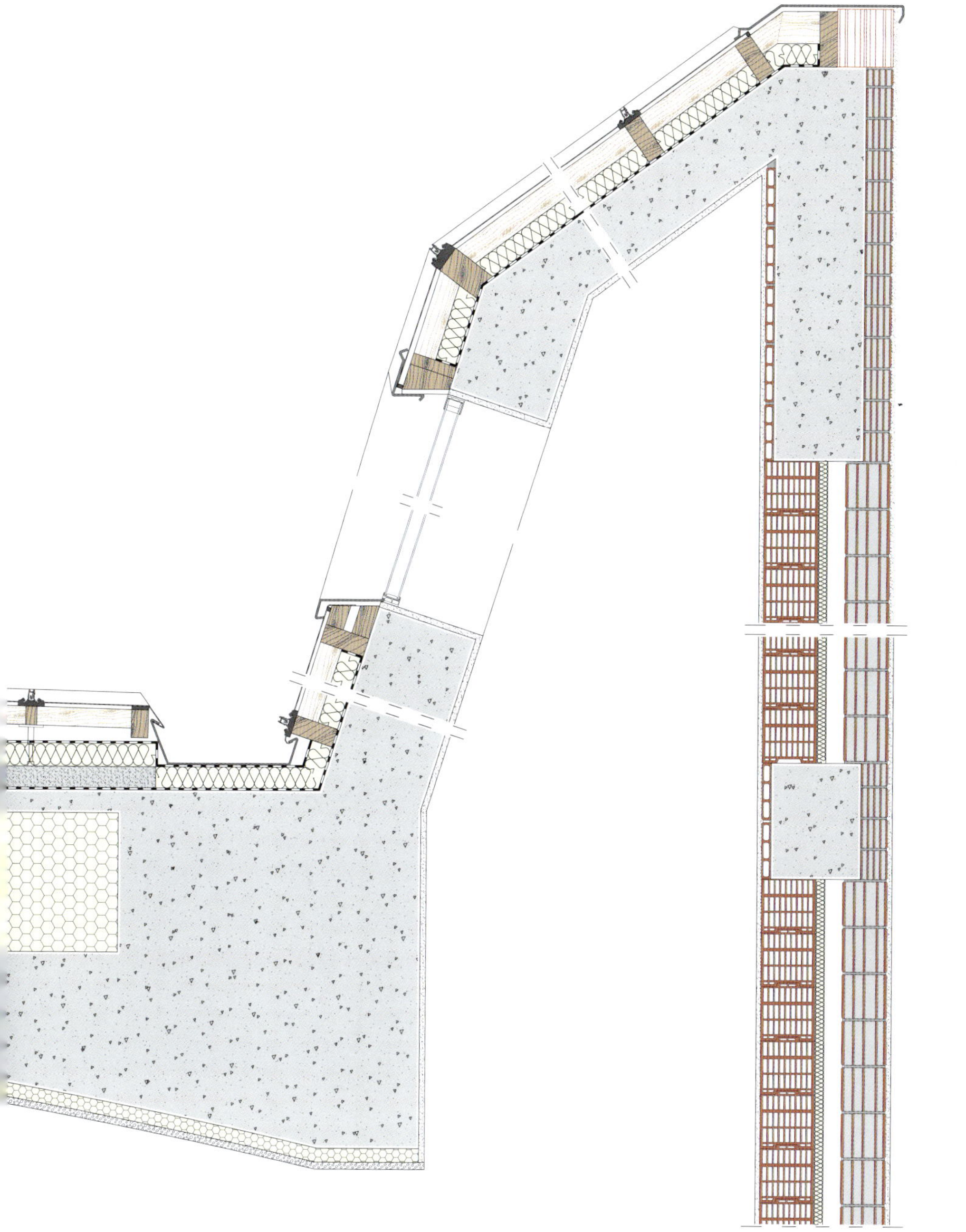

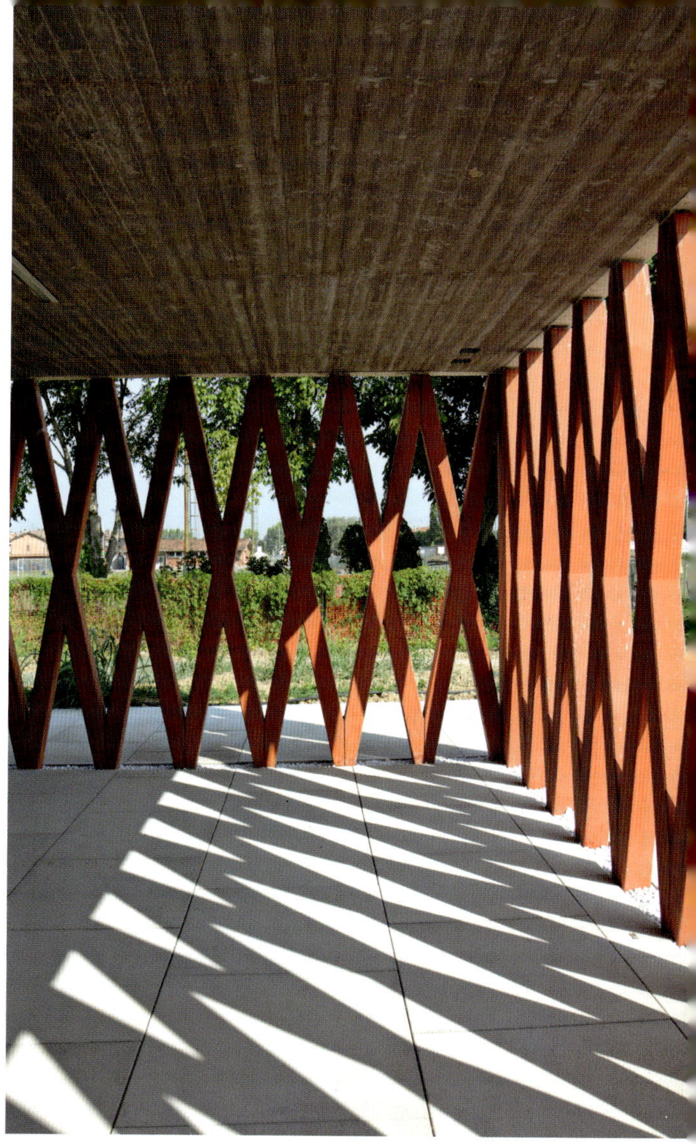

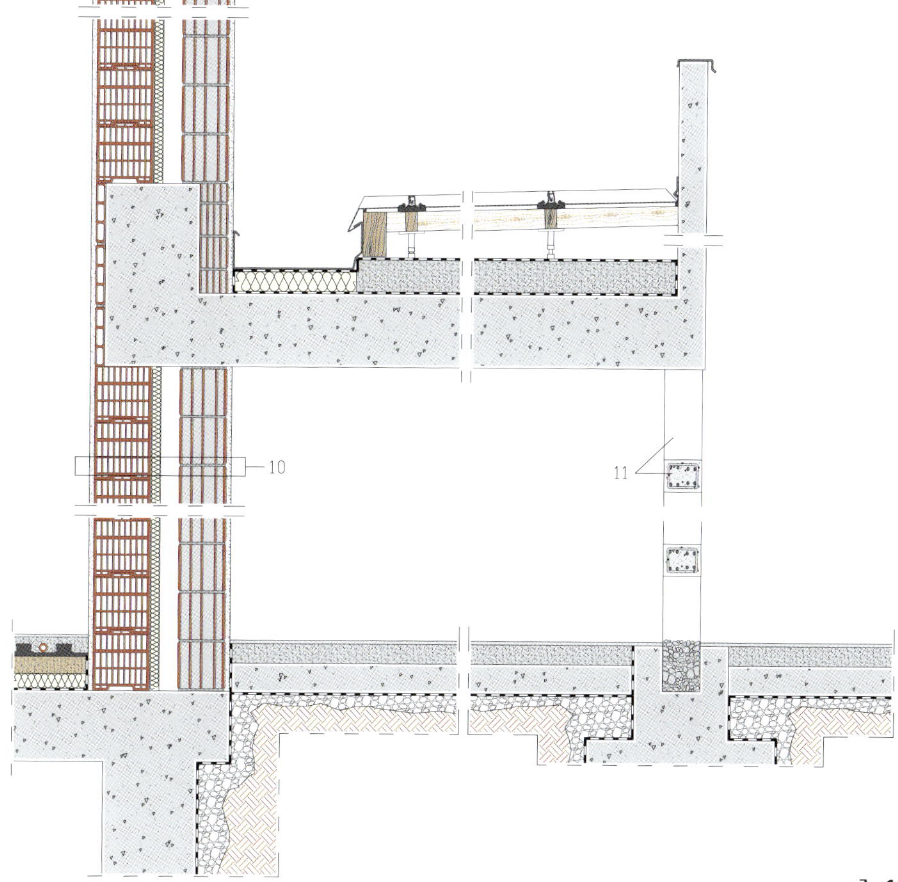

blocks, 2" (50 mm) cavity, 1 5/8" (40 mm) rigid insulation, 9 7/8" (250 mm) brick leaf, lost-wax bronze statue with lead-colored bicomponent resin treatment

6- 3/4" (20 mm) plaster layer, brick fill, 15 3/4" (400 mm) reinforced concrete beam, steel plate with profile securing sculpture

7- Skylight with 3/8 - 1/2 - 3/8" (10/14/10 mm) aluminum glazing unit

8- 1/2" (14 mm) bush-hammered porcelain stone pavers, 3 1/8" (80 mm) lightweight concrete screed, 4 3/4" (120 mm) reinforced concrete slab, waterproofing membrane, gravel, earth

9- Secco Sistemi sheet steel door with insulation core

10- Wall with 3/4" (20 mm) plaster finish, 7 7/8" (200 mm) masonry blocks, 3 1/8" (80 mm) cavity, 1 5/8" (40 mm) rigid insulation, 9 1/2" (240 mm) masonry blocks, 3/4" (20 mm) plaster layer

11- Perimeter sun shading comprising overlapping pre-cast 12 5/8 x 6 1/4" (320x160 mm) reinforced concrete beams

LA SEINE MUSICALE

PARIS, FRANCE

SHIGERU BAN ARCHITECTS EUROPE
WITH JEAN DE GASTINES ARCHITECTES

Shigeru Ban is best-known for his experimental houses and lightweight structures, but after building Pompidou 2, he enlarged his practice and opened a second office in Paris. His latest achievement is La Seine Musicale, a complex that occupies one end of the Île Seguin, a narrow sliver of land in the river that is part of Boulogne-Billancourt, on the western boundary of the capital. Renault made cars there until 1992, when they closed their factory - the largest of its kind in France. The land was cleared and the tycoon François Pinault commissioned Tadao Ando to build a museum for his collection of contemporary art. Discouraged by local opposition to his plans, he abandoned the scheme and moved it to Venice, where Ando converted the Palazzo Grassi, and then the Dogana.

To resolve a tangle of competing proposals, Jean Nouvel masterplanned the island as a linear axis of arts, commerce, and parkland. Ban won the competition to design a cultural resource that should appeal to a broad audience and provide a gathering place for Parisians and neighboring communities, much like the City of Music on the opposite side of the capital. Constrained by space and budget, he created an austere wedge of spaces that step down to the narrow tip of the island where the concrete block sprouts a bubble of glass enclosing a 1,150-seat concert hall.

The broad frontage, accessed by a narrow bridge from the north bank, is dominated by a giant LED screen for live transmission of events, outdoor movies, or - inevitably - advertising. A broad flight of steps leads up to a green roof. During the day, industrial doors to the right of the screen fold up to admit the public to a concourse that links the two performance spaces, as well as retail, administrative offices, rehearsal rooms and a music school. It's a bold attempt at achieving openness in an impassive block, but the first impression is intimidating. Lacking the crowds that may assemble for a popular performance in the arena, which can hold up to 6,000 fans, the plaza and façade feel hard and overscaled - a victim of the *folie de grandeur* that afflicts so many Parisian projects. The space cries out for a tree-shaded lawn where people could sit and picnic as they watched the screen. The fault lies less with the architect than with the client's overly ambitious program, which tries to crowd too many functions onto a confined and elongated site.

Everything pales beside the concert hall, which may be judged one of the most perfect of its kind in an age of exemplary performance spaces. The flattened glass sphere is supported by a diagonal grid of laminated beams that articulate the exterior and cast a pattern of shadows within. A triangular sail of photovoltaic panels follows the course of the sun, shading the glass and generating power, while slowly shifting its profile. Still to come is a sculpture terrace at the tip of the island, which may distract from the obtrusive post-modern buildings on the south bank of the river.

Steps lead up from the end of the internal concourse to a gallery that encircles the hall and is lined with an iridescent tile mosaic that shifts color as the light changes. The concert hall is designed to bring audience and players together in a magic circle of red plush seats and walls of milled oak strips that resemble a woven basket. The density of the weave is varied to modulate the sound in different degrees. Shallow balconies surround a steeply-raked wedge of seating. Ban has made inventive use of cardboard tubes, a signature element he adopted as a frugal but resilient structural support in large-scale buildings and emergency shelters. Here he employs tubes for the seats, upholstering the front and veneering the backs. In profile they resemble a convention of Michelin Men. Tubes of varied diameters are cut in thin sections to clad the undulating ceiling - to diffuse the sound and create a richly varied geometry that evokes Islamic decoration.

In color and pattern, Ban's creation makes a nod to the great 19th-century concert halls, without lapsing into historicism. The sight lines are exemplary and the acoustics are thrillingly good. At the conclusion of its recent European tour, the Cincinnati Symphony Orchestra performed John Adams's *Short Ride in a Fast Machine*, a newly revised edition of George Gershwin's *An American in Paris*, and Dvořák's lyrical *Eighth Symphony*. As an encore, the French conductor, Louis Langrée, offered Leonard Bernstein's *Candide overture* as a homage to Voltaire. Every piece sounded fresh-minted, every note resonated. A full house responded vociferously. The chief credit must go to acoustical wizard Yasuhisa Toyota, but it was Ban who turned his technical demands into a room of that calms and inspires, and which demonstrates the enduring appeal of serious music in an era of noisy, ephemeral fads.

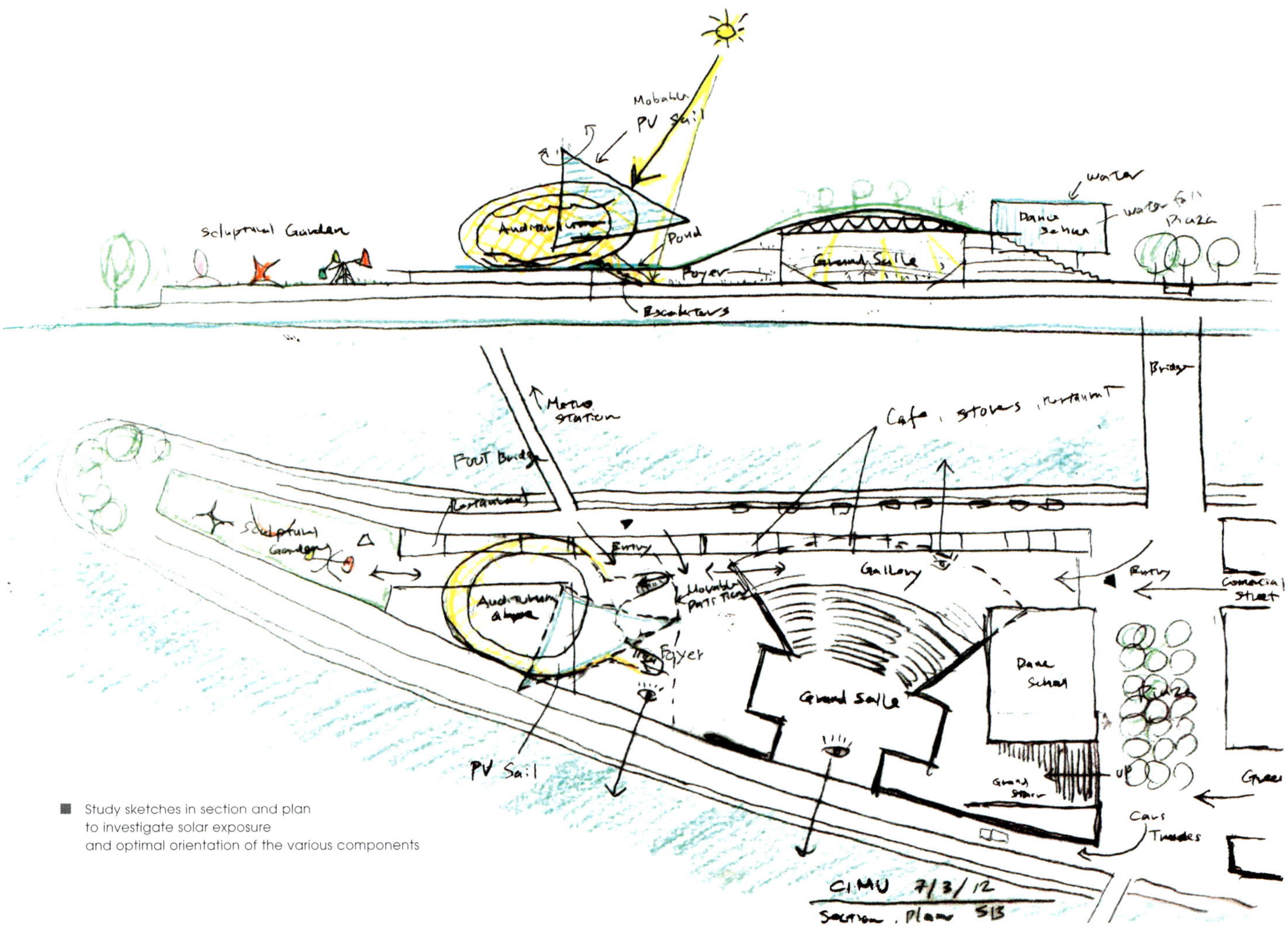

Study sketches in section and plan to investigate solar exposure and optimal orientation of the various components

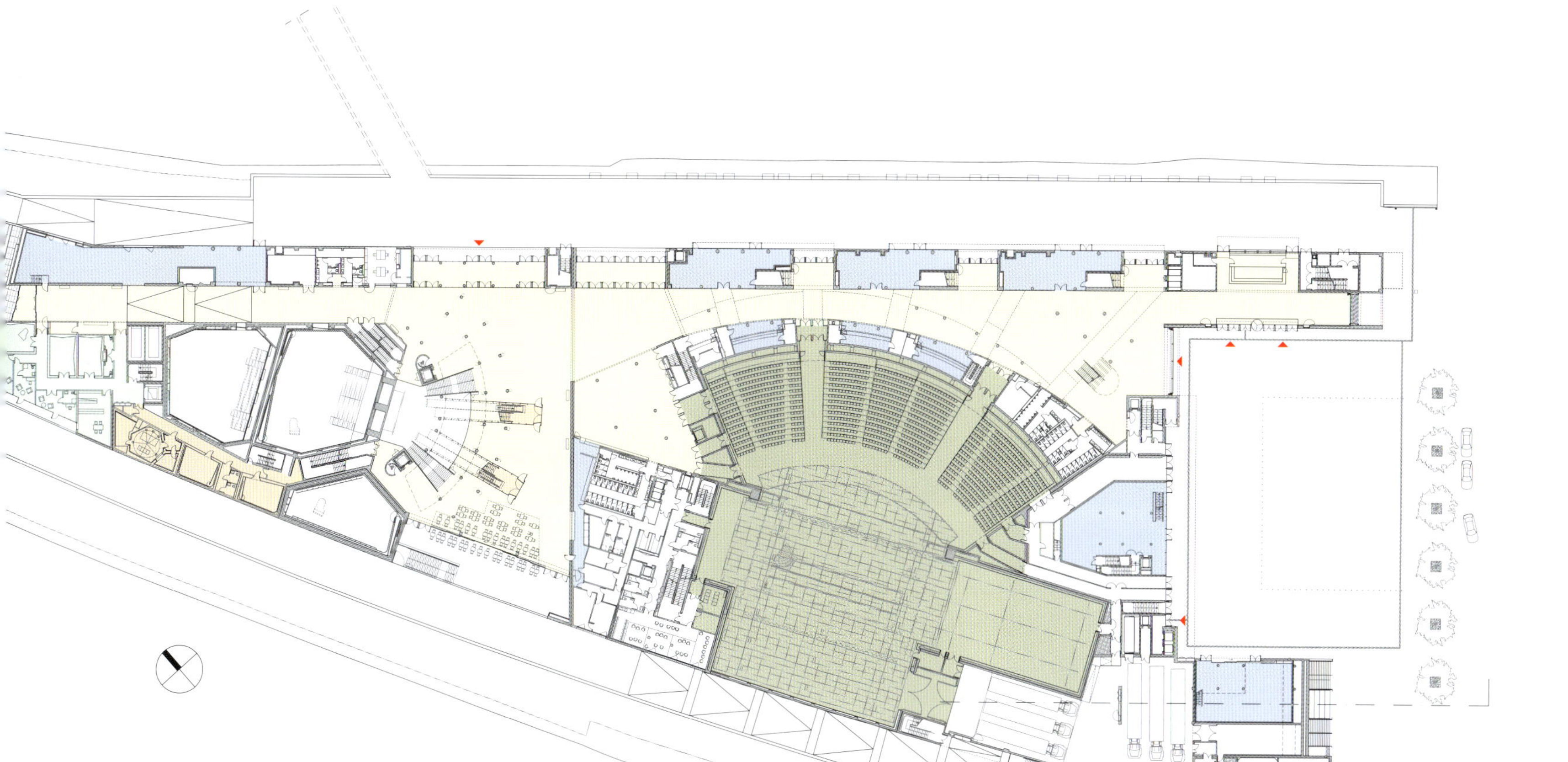

■ Ground floor plan - Scale 1:1200

- Foyer
- "Auditorium" classical music concert hall
- "Grande Seine" multi-purpose concert hall
- "Maîtrise des Hauts-de-Seine" choir school
- Resident orchestra area
- Rehearsal and recording rooms
- Event space
- Restaurants and retail

Views of the "Auditorium" study model showing the outer shell, the photovoltaic "sail", and internal spatial organization

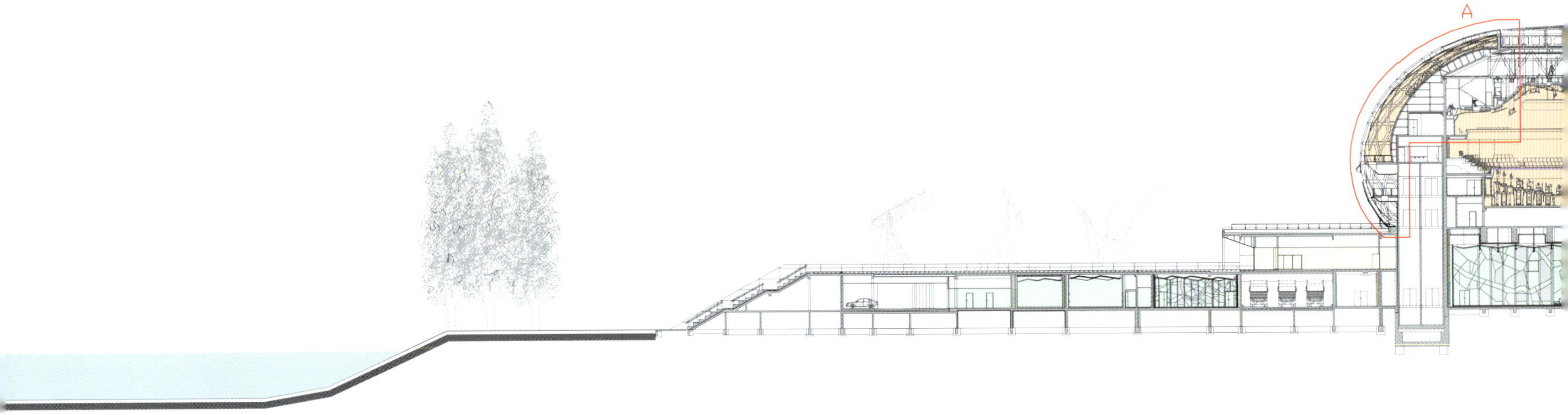

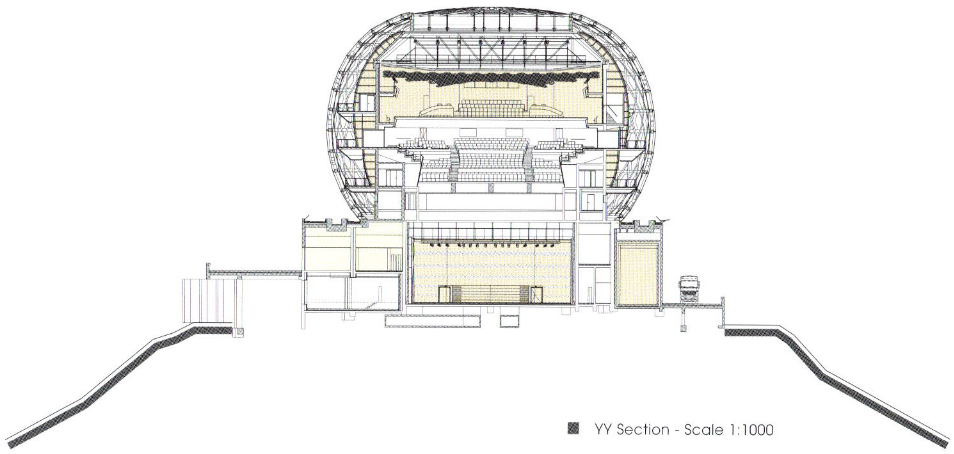

■ YY Section - Scale 1:1000

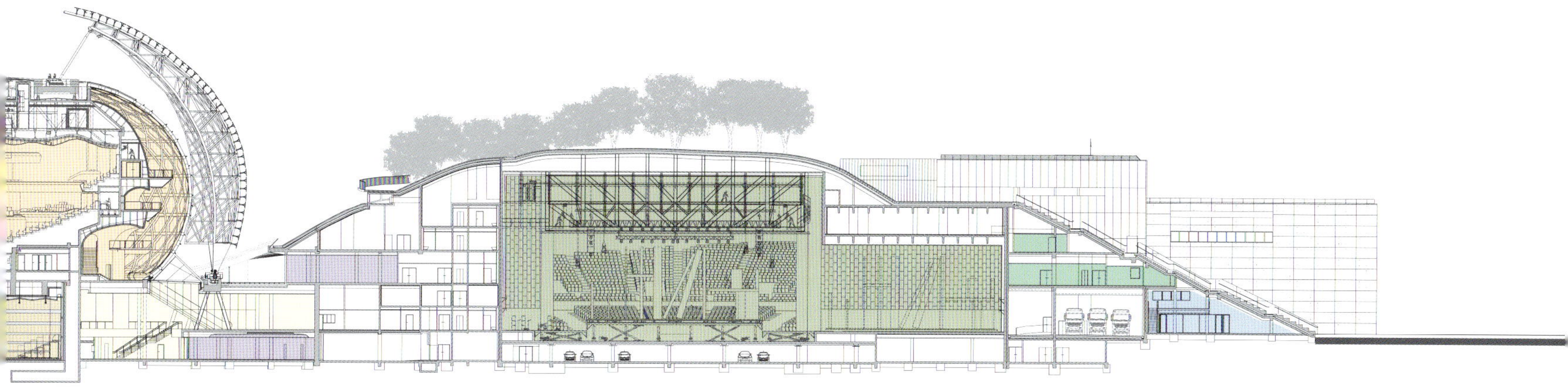

■ XX Section - Scale 1:1000

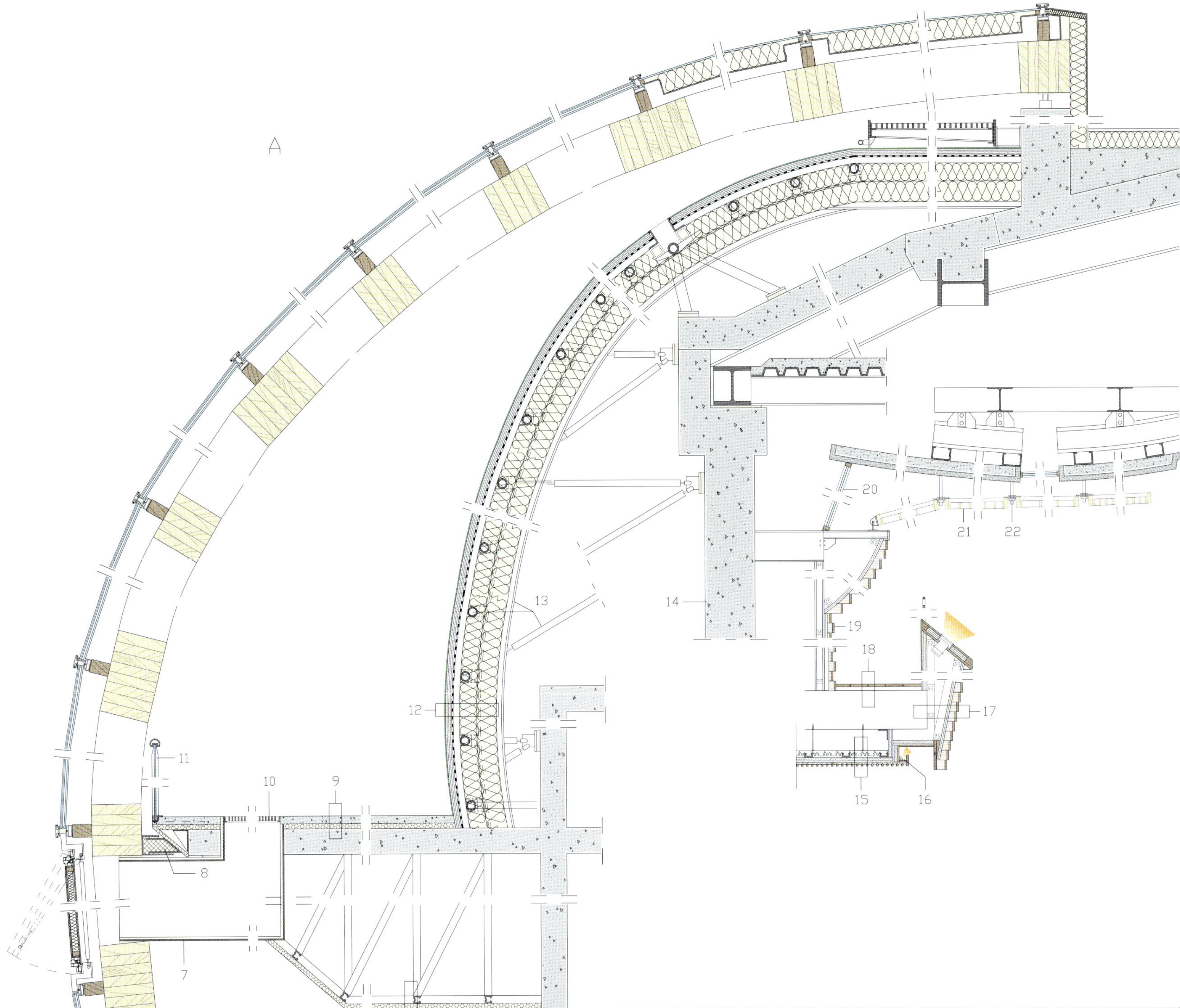
A
1
2
3
4
5
6
7
8
9
10
11
12
13
14
15
16
17
18
19
20
21
22

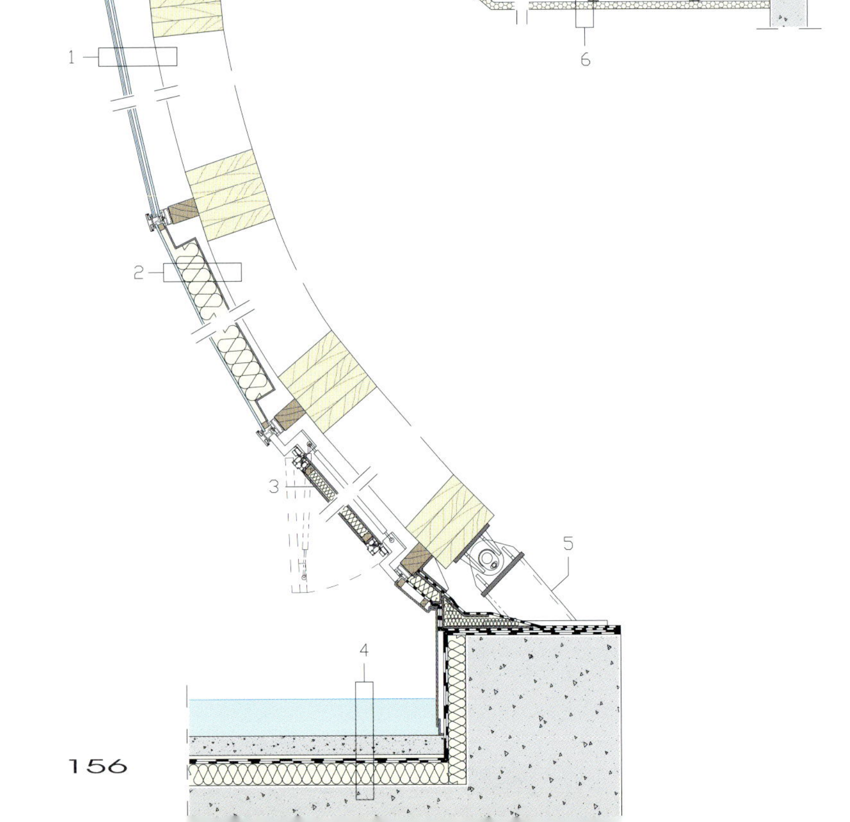

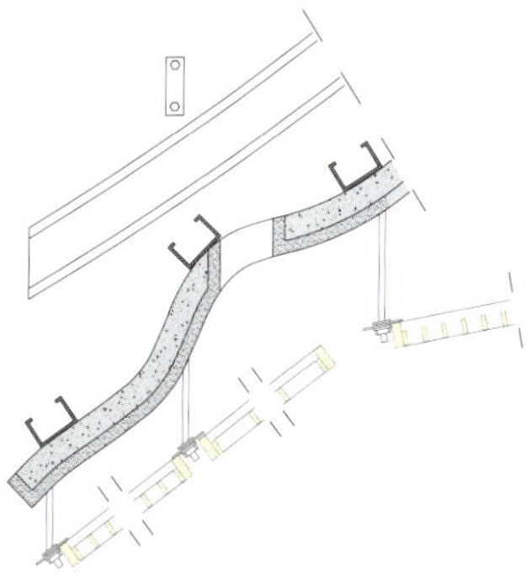

DETAIL A: AUDITORIUM
VERTICAL SECTION - SCALE 1:40
DETAIL B: ACOUSTIC CEILING
HORIZONTAL SECTION - SCALE 1:20

1. Building envelope comprising glazed curtain wall with 1/2 - 3/4 - 5/16 + 5/16″ (13/18/8+8 mm) aluminum glazing units fitted with Guardian Glass "SunGuard SuperNeutral" glass, structural framing of glulam beams in decreasing size from 157 1/2x126″ (400x320 cm) at base to 126x126″ (320x320 cm) at roof level
2. 1/2″ (12 mm) opaque enameled glass, wood framing with insulation fill of variable thickness, aluminum sheet trim
3. Panel for natural ventilation and expelling exhaust air with steel frame, automatic opening system, aluminum framing, 2 3/8″ (60 mm) steel panel with super mirror polish finish and rockwool insulation core
4. Pool lining comprising 4″ (100 mm) concrete, 3/4″ (20 mm) waterproofing layer, 1 1/8″ (30 mm) double waterproofing membrane, 4 3/4″ (120 mm) rigid insulation, 9 7/8″ (250 mm) reinforced concrete slab
5. System anchoring glulam beam structure to slab consisting of steel brackets and plates
6. Acoustically absorbent 1 5/8″ (40 mm) suspended ceiling painted white, lattice structure of 2 3/8 x 2 3/8″ (60x60 mm) aluminum C-profiles
7. Plaster boards natural ventilation and smoke exhaust duct
8. Perimeter fascia comprising double folded aluminum sheets with rockwool fill fixed to building envelope and acting as vertical fire barrier
9. Foyer floor comprising polished 2″ (50 mm) concrete slab with (10 mm) polished small grain Palladian flooring, 1 5/8″ (40 mm) acoustic insulation, 7 7/8″ (200 mm) reinforced concrete slab
10. Circular 1 3/4″ (45 mm) thick steel ventilation grill
11. Railing comprising 1/2 + 1/2″ (12+12 mm) laminated glass with polished steel handrail
12. Auditorium envelope comprising 3/4 x 3/4 x 3/16″ (20x20x4 mm) glass mosaic, quadruple 2 3/8″ (60 mm) acoustically insulating drywall, 1 1/8 x 2″ (30x50 mm) aluminum C-profile framing, 5 1/2 + 6 1/4″ (140+160 mm) mineral wool acoustic and thermal insulation panels
13. Structure of curved vertical IPE 200 beams and horizontal Ø 3 1/8″ (80 mm) steel pipe profiles, connecting structure to auditorium envelope comprising steel plates and Ø 2″ (50 mm) steel pipe profiles, 1 1/8″ (30 mm) neoprene joint for acoustic insulation
14. 15 3/4″ (400 mm) reinforced concrete auditorium shell
15. Suspended ceiling comprising corrugated oak battens, triple 1 1/2″ (37.5 mm) drywall, framing of 1 3/8 x 2 3/4″ (35x70 mm) aluminum C-profiles and shaped steel plates, steel tie rods suspended from slab
16. Linear LED lights recessed in suspended ceiling
17. Balcony rail comprising corrugated and perforated oak and acoustical insulating fabric panels with MDF backing, 1/2 + 1/2″ (12.5+12.5 mm) drywall, 1 5/8 x 2 3/8″ (40x60 mm) steel C-profile framing, recessed lighting
18. Balcony flooring comprising 3/4″ (20 mm) oak floorboards, 1 1/8″ (30 mm) wood fiber panel, 11 3/4″ (300 mm) reinforced concrete slab
19. Partition wall comprising transparent corrugated oak panels, 1/2 + 1/2″ (12.5+12.5 mm) drywall, acoustical insulating panel with frame of 1 3/8 x 2″ (35x50 mm) steel C-profiles
20. High acoustically insulating glass closing off control rooms
21. Concert hall suspended ceiling constructed from solid ayous hexagons of identical size. Cardboard pipes of different sizes inside this structure act to improve acoustics by scattering sound waves
22. Structure supporting suspended ceiling comprising steel tie rods, threaded bars, washers, and bolts connecting hexagons

Wolfgang Amadeus Mozart

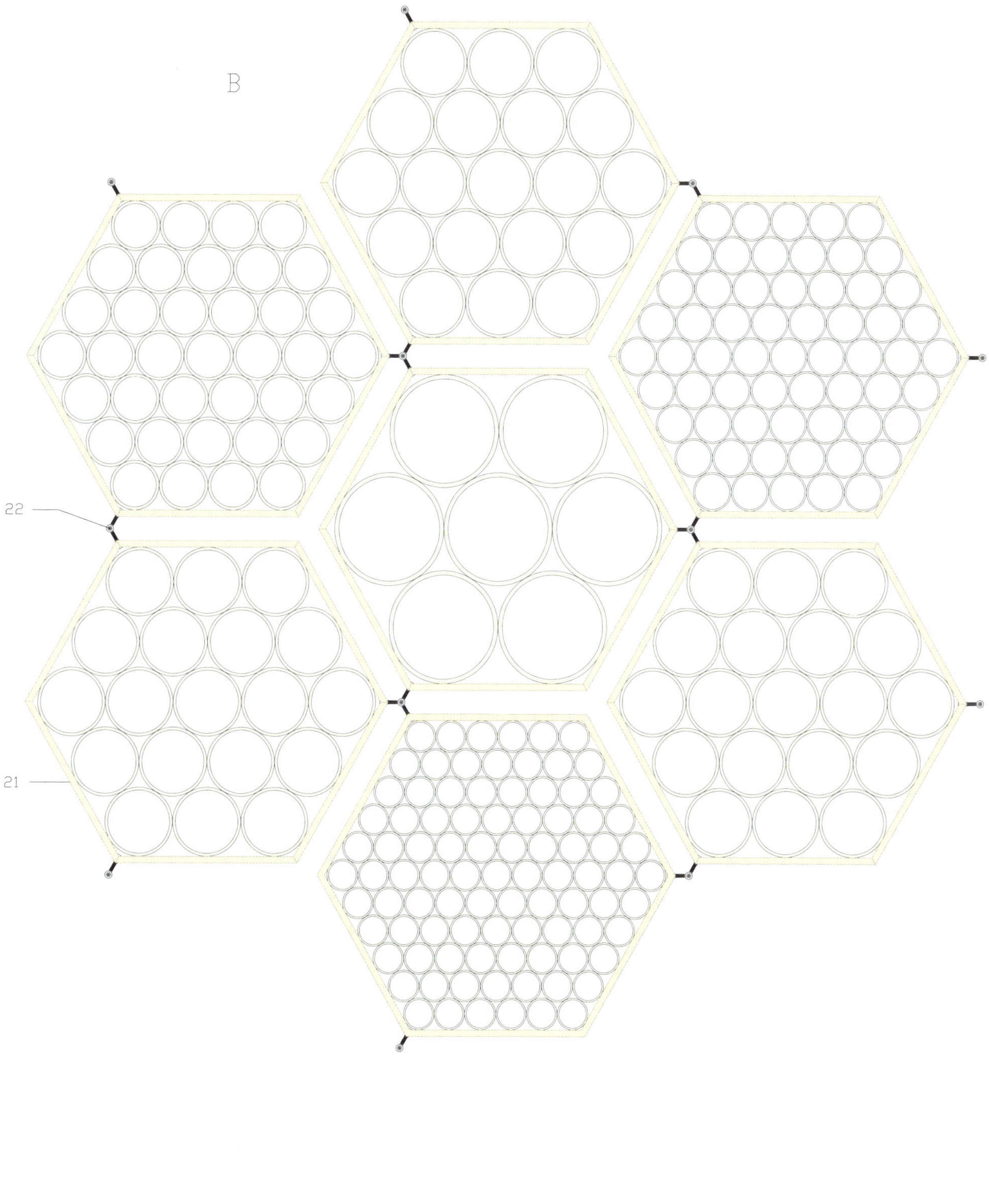
B
22
21

LIYUAN LIBRARY

JIAOJIEHE, BEIJING, CHINA

LI XIAODONG
ATELIER

Over recent decades China has undergone frenetic far-reaching changes. The inflow of investments into the cities has been especially massive, leading to successive waves of demolition and new urban expansion. The little library at LiYuan designed by the Li Xiaodong Atelier has all the appearance of taking a brave stand against this apparently unstoppable headlong dash. Everything about the project, from its programme and position to the materials and distribution circuit, is geared to creating a place of contemplative tranquillity in deliberate defiance of the hectic pace of modern-day China.

The little library is located on the edge of the village of Jiaojiehe, within walking distance for its inhabitants and a couple of hours' drive from the bustle of Beijing.

From the choice of site onwards, it has been conceived not just as providing a book-lending community service but as offering quiet, highly personal space and moments: after a short walk outside the village, the library visitor can enjoy a period of communing with self and nature.

Everything - materials, color palette, and construction techniques - are all designed to blend this little construction into its natural surrounds, allowing it to dematerialize to the point of dissolving the point of demarcation between exterior and interior.

The utter simplicity of the parallelepiped structure, mimicking ancient Chinese rural houses built with the few materials nature offered, only apparently foregoes any semblance of architectural design. The irregular wooden sticks creating a filter between inside and out were harvested from nearby woodland. Recalling the firewood collected by the locals and stacked against their houses, they are here held together on a burnished steel frame. The entrance to the reading room is below the natural ground level and reached by a terrace over water that runs right up to the rock on which the whole building stands.

Inside, a series of different levels mark out the different functional areas on a seamless groundplan. Light-colored wooden slats clad the floors and wooden lattice structures line walls and ceiling. On the walls, these transom and mullion frames serve as bookshelves and windows giving views onto the natural landscape. Defused light filters inside through the irregularly textured façade shielding the glazing.

The little library of LiYuan represents a major break with what's going on in contemporary China. The simple program in the midst of nature turns its back on relentless urban life; its very *raison d'être* - reading and thinking - demands a slower, more humane pace where human life and respect for place are once again essential values.

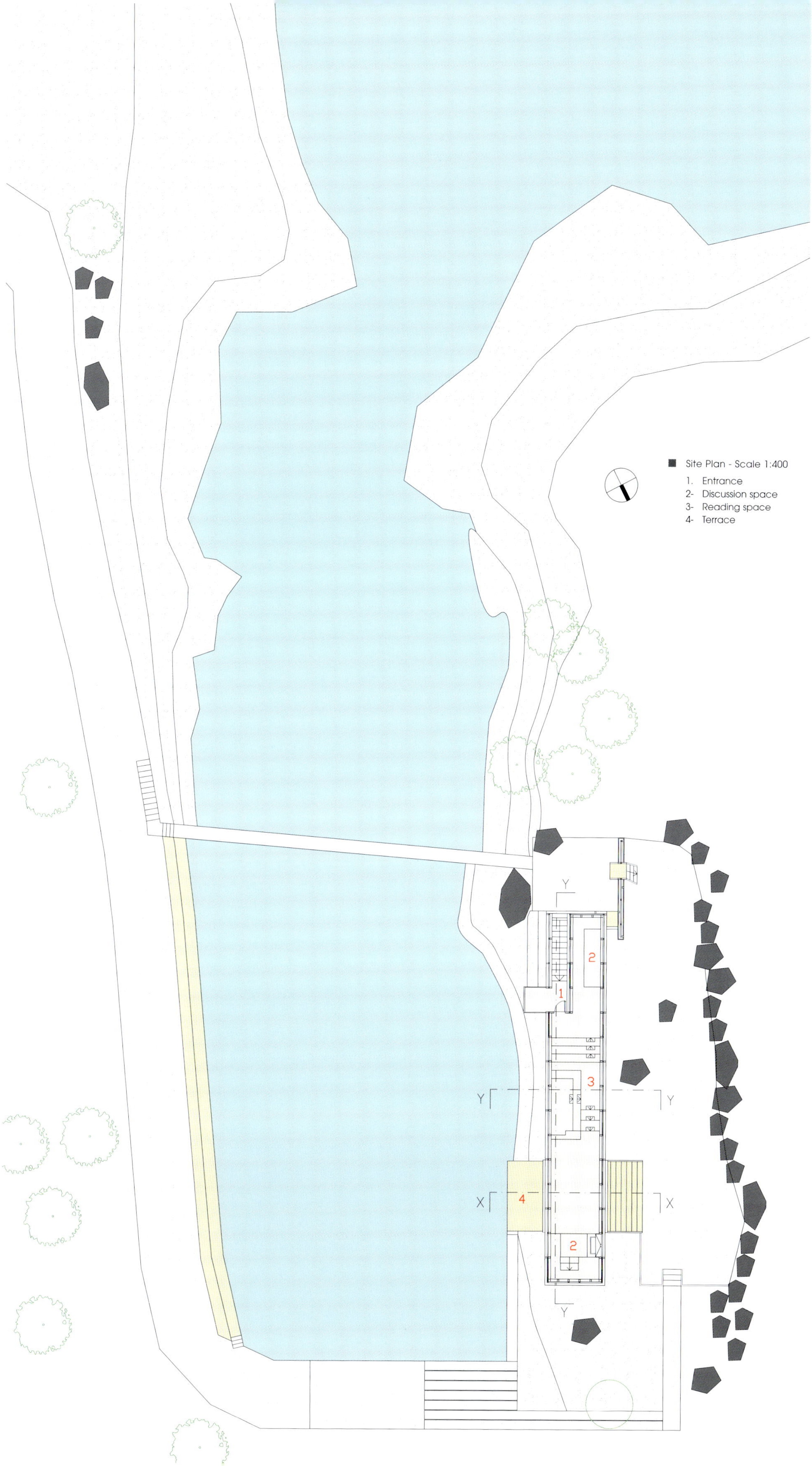

Site Plan - Scale 1:400

1. Entrance
2- Discussion space
3- Reading space
4- Terrace

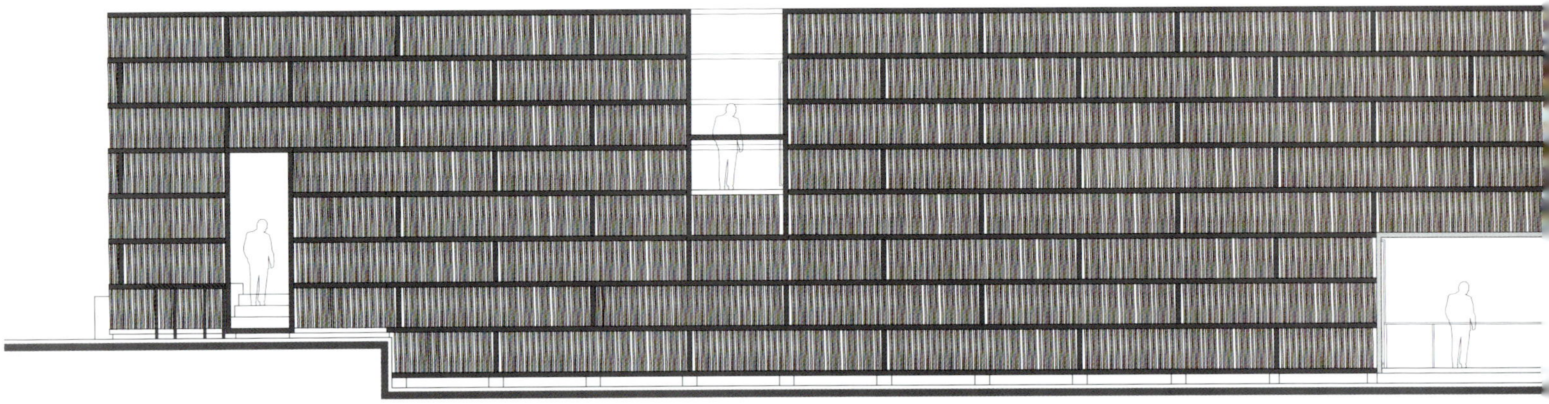

West elevation - Scale 1:150

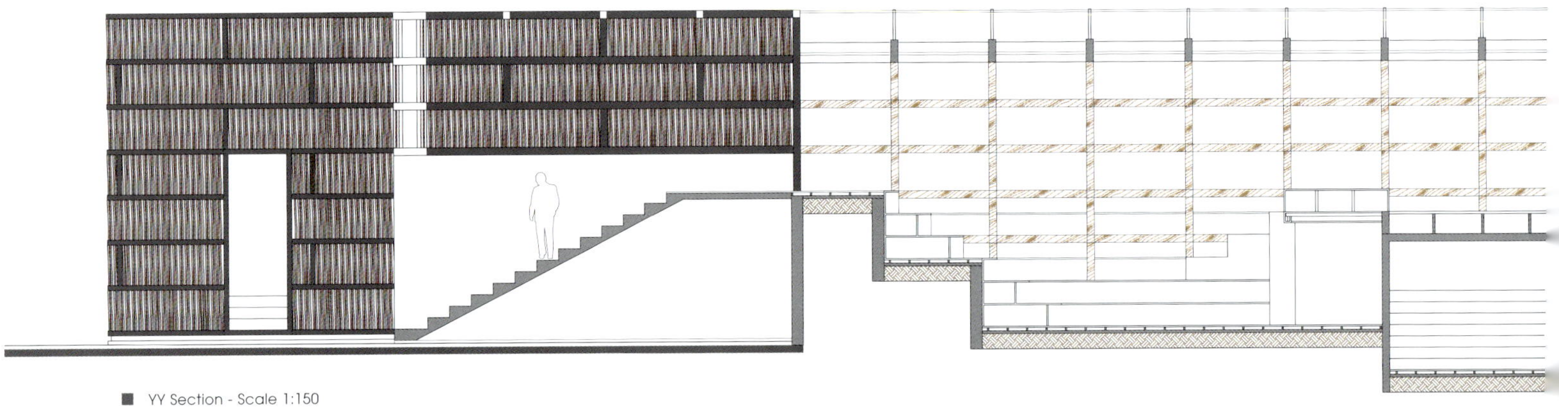

YY Section - Scale 1:150

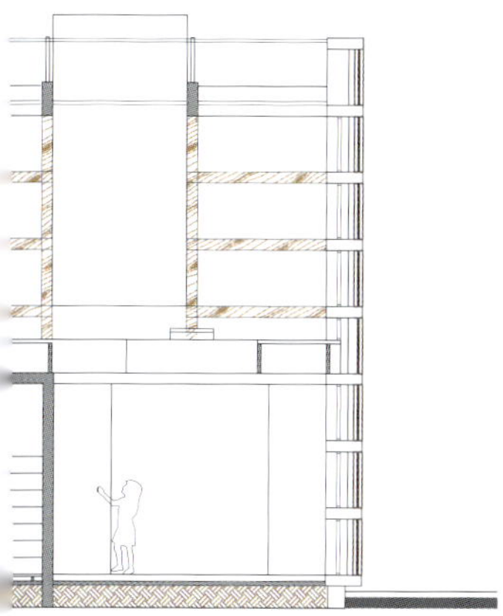

■ South elevation - Scale 1:150

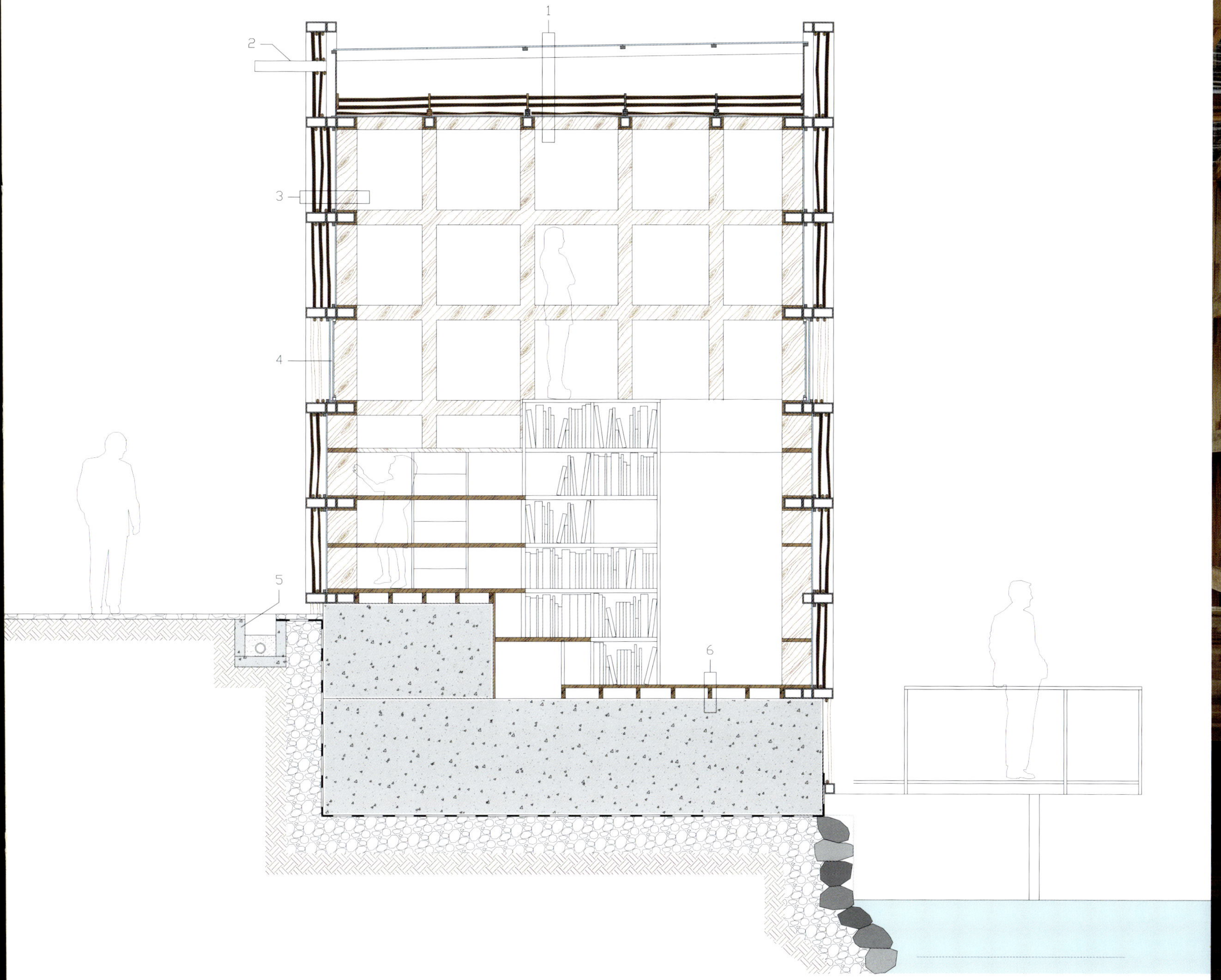

CONSTRUCTION SYSTEM
XX SECTION - SCALE 1:50

1. Double-skin roof consisting of glass panels, air space, sun-shading layer formed by sticks from local trees secured to timber beams, glass roof supported by structure of 4 x 4" (100x100 mm) steel box profiles finished with 3/4" (20 mm) thick timber panels - To accommodate changing weather conditions, the external panels can be opened during summer for cooling, while in winter they take advantage of sunlight to create a heat chamber
2. Eaves consisting of 4 x 4" (100x100 mm) steel box profiles (parallel to plane of section)
3. Façade with sun-shading made of woven sticks from local trees, frame of 4 x 7 7/8" (100x200 mm) and 4 x 4" (100x100 mm) steel box profiles, glass panel, internal frame of 7 1/8 x 4" (180x100 mm) steel box profiles finished in 3/4" (20 mm) thick timber panels
4. Operable window with 1/2 - 7/8 - 1/2" (12/22/12 mm) steel double glazing unit
5. Gutter formed by pre-cast concrete sections
6. 1 1/4" (30 mm) floorboards on 1 5/8 x 4" (40x100 mm) timber joists

THE ROY AND DIANA VAGELOS EDUCATION CENTER NEW YORK, USA

DILLER SCOFIDIO + RENFRO

Our lives are increasingly fragmented and filtered through digital media, even as the public realm of our cities is being privatized and sold off to the highest bidders. A few enlightened architects are pushing back, fostering social intercourse and creating stages that all can share. The New York firm of Diller Scofidio + Renfro (DS+R) has led the way, turning an abandoned freight track into the High Line, Manhattan's most popular promenade, and breaking down social barriers at Lincoln Center for the Performing Arts. Over the past year, they have infused learning hubs for the arts and medicine with that same exuberance, and are creating a cultural center for Rio de Janeiro that may rival the Pompidou as a people space. Connectivity is the thread that links these four diverse structures, drawing on early experiments and the desire to create a more democratic environment for life, work and play.

Elizabeth Diller and Ricardo Scofidio established their studio in 1979, and were joined by Charles Renfro in 1997. "We were both trained as architects, but neither of us intended to do client-oriented buildings," says Diller. "When we began to engage in public work, it was from the vantage of art, rethinking the conventions of space in the public realm." That goal found expression in the Blur, a virtual pavilion of water vapor on Lake Neuchâtel that was the biggest draw of the 2002 Swiss Expo. Soon after, they completed an apartment building in Japan and the boldly cantilevered Institute of Contemporary Art on the Boston waterfront. Their architectural practice began to surge and they now have a bulging portfolio.

"I love working on complex buildings, achieving a consensus on space and program, but we still make time to do books and independent projects," says Diller. "Three of the projects in the money-losing division of our studio are an opera for the High Line, an installation on blushing for the Istanbul Biennale, and an exhibition on Pierre Chareau."

Columbia University has had to expand into the low-income, tight-packed community that surrounds its original Beaux Arts campus in Upper Manhattan. The newly completed Roy and Diana Vagelos Education Center is a model of urbanity and a bridge between town and gown.

It is a state-of-art hub of education for the university's renowned medical center, in which 14 stories of classrooms, labs and clinical facilities on the north side open onto a boldly articulated cascade of social and study areas of varied height and plan to the south.

This division challenged structural engineer Dan Cecil of LERA to fuse structure and architecture, using innovative techniques and materials. Post-tensioned floor slabs are composed of self-consolidating concrete that had to weave its way through a massive steel skeleton. To reduce the weight of the slabs, the builders used a void-forming technology, eliminating the need for peripheral columns. Staircases double as supporting elements and the exposed concrete turns the south façade into a self-shaded sculptural composition. Clear glazing reveals the bustle within. It opens onto a publicly accessible garden - a rare spot of green in this neighborhood - and it is flanked by exterior stairs leading up to the second-floor terrace that opens out of a 275-seat auditorium. In fine weather, these stairways serve as bleachers.

To achieve a LEED Gold rating, the glazing has a low-e coating to reduce solar heat gain, and a ceramic frit on the outer surface that reduces reflectivity. Solar-activated shades complement the intelligent skin. As project leader Chris Hillyard explains, advances in medical practice and education are accelerating, and the program was enhanced during the six years of design development and construction. The repetitive 3-meter-high spaces to the north are easy to reconfigure for new equipment and teaching methods. The cascade is unlikely to change, for it offers a hierarchy of spaces for private study and socializing, woven together in three-story sections. Informal lounge areas look out to the city and in to areas above and below in a dynamic manipulation of interior volumes. Acoustic plaster in the ceilings and soft furnishings mute noise, making the spaces lively but not cacophonous.

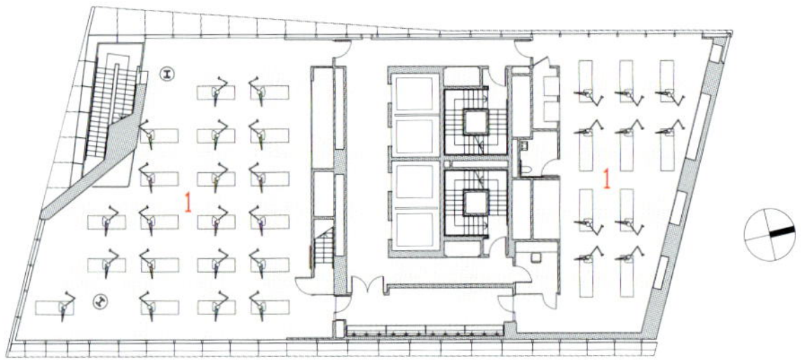

■ 5th floor plan - Scale 1:600

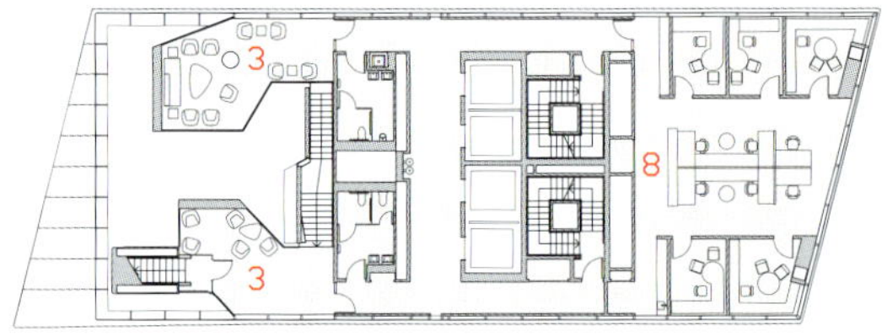

■ 11th floor plan - Scale 1:600

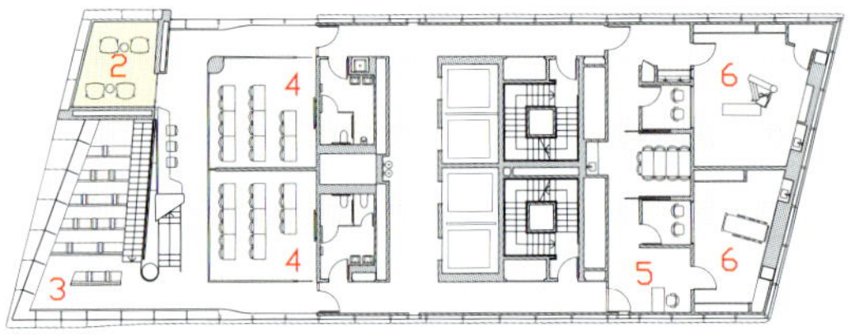

■ 8th floor plan - Scale 1:600

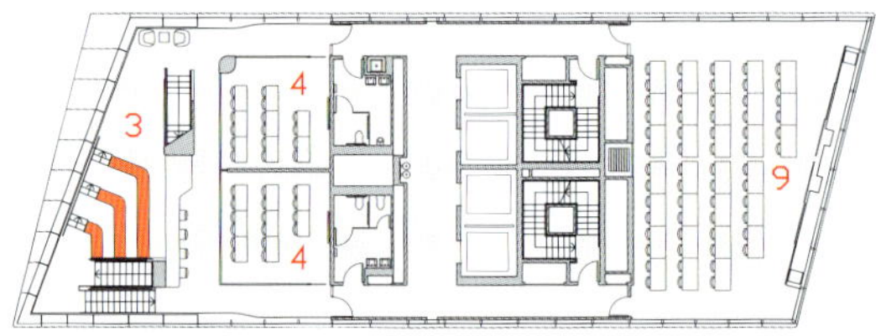

■ 12th floor plan - Scale 1:600

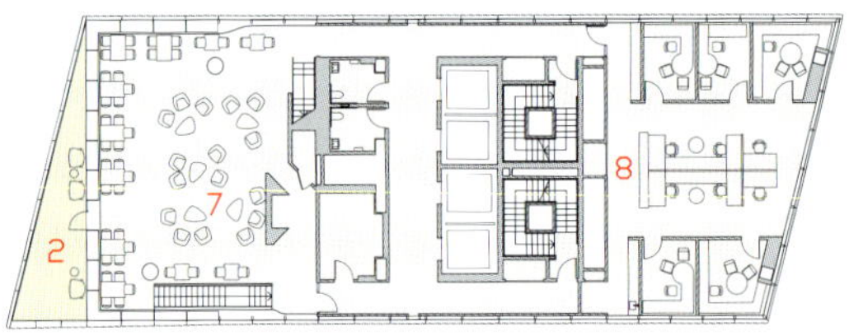

■ 10th floor plan - Scale 1:600

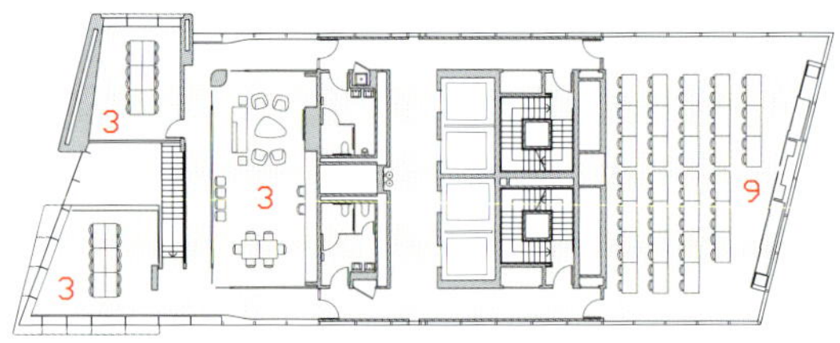

■ 14th floor plan - Scale 1:600

1. Anatomy laboratory
2. Terrace
3. Study area
4. Meeting room
5. Reception
6. Multipurpose room
7. Café
8. Administration
9. Classroom

■ Ground floor plan - Scale 1:400

1. Entrance
2. Lobby
3. Café
4. Meeting room
5. Office
6. Administration
7. Waiting room
8. Waste and Recycle
9. Loading area

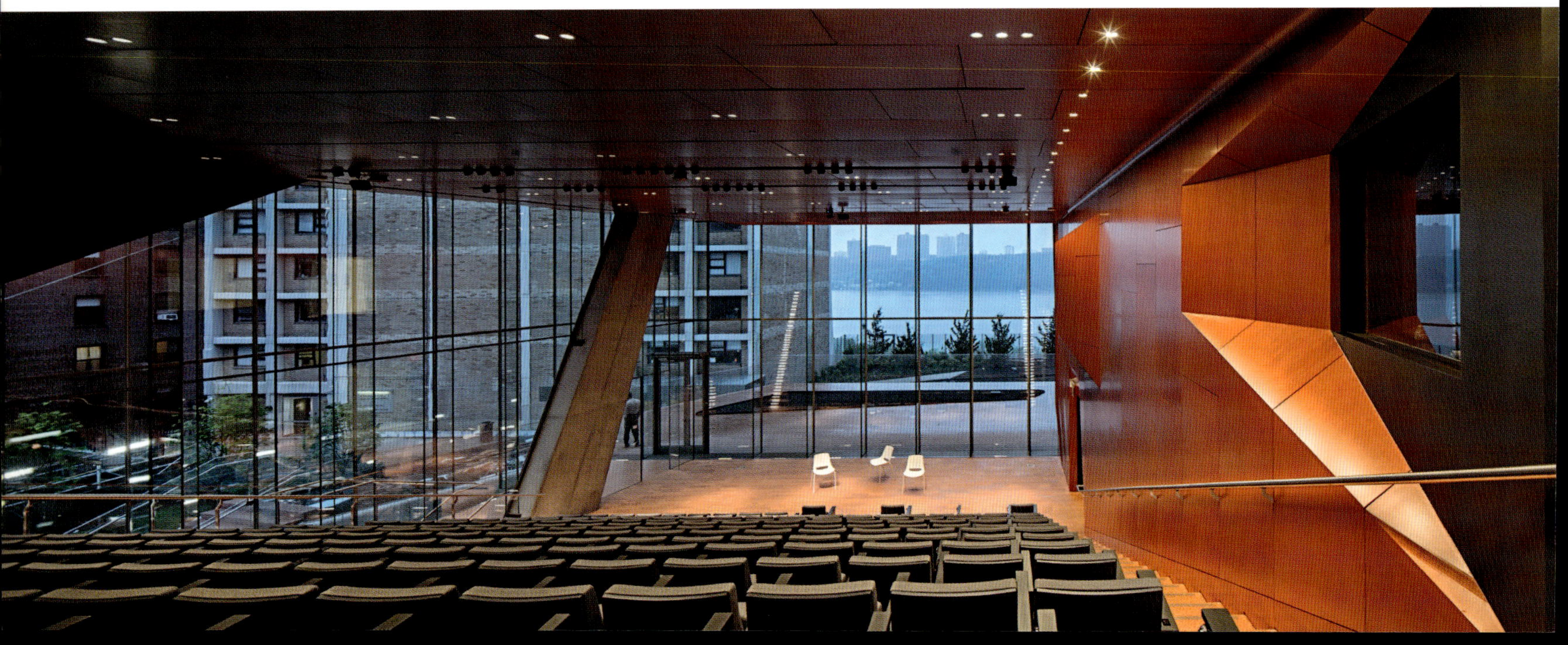

■ Vertical circulation and communal spaces distribution at the different levels

■ Perspective view of the artificially lit building highlighting the contrast between the transparent glazed and concrete segments, rendering

A

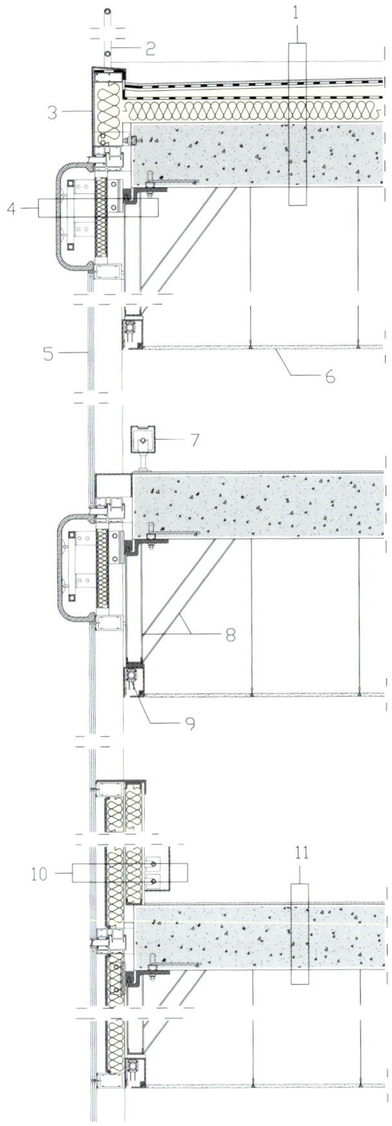

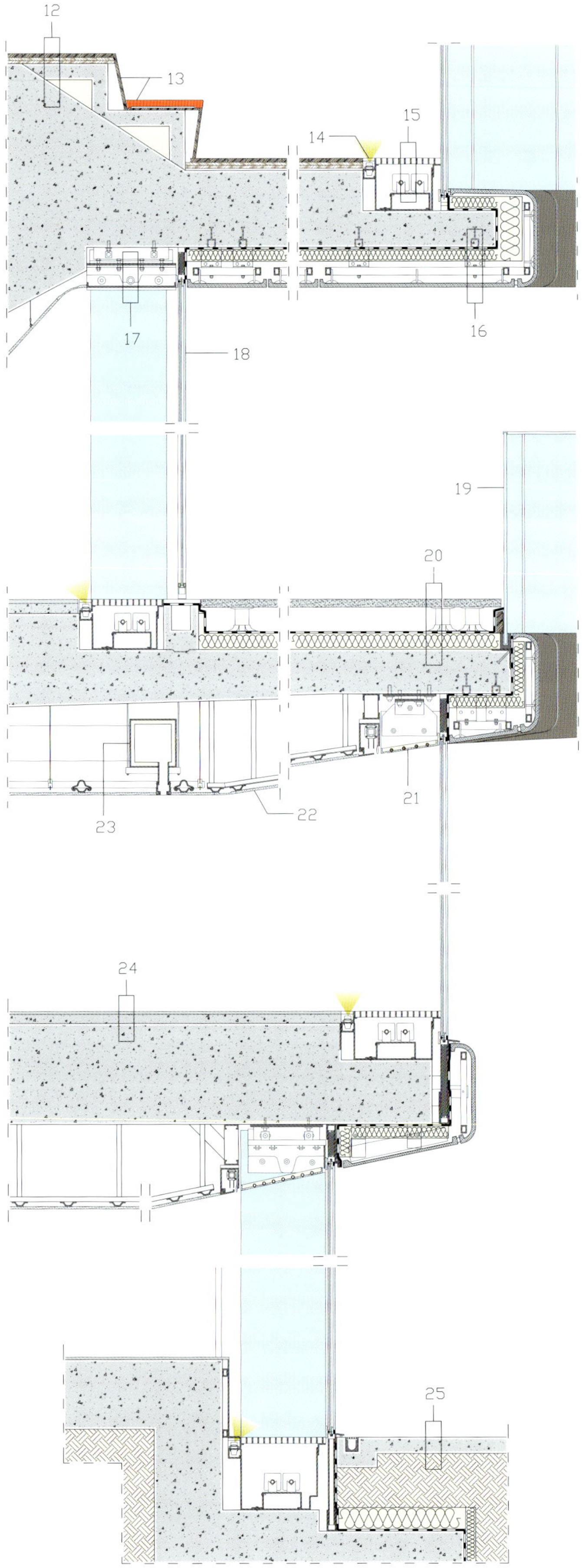

DETAIL A: CONSTRUCTION SYSTEM VERTICAL SECTION - SCALE 1:40

1. Roof comprising 1/2″ (13 mm) polished concrete paving, waterproofing membrane, protective bitumen layer, rigid insulation forming slope, 5 1/8″ (130 mm) rigid insulation, vapour barrier, 13 3/4″ (350 mm) pre-stressed reinforced concrete slab
2. Railing with Ø20 mm steel pipe profile frame
3. Steel flashing trim
4. Floor course comprising 1″ (25 mm) fiberglass-reinforced concrete panels, supporting structure of steel brackets, steel box- and L-profiles, 2 3/4″ (70 mm) sheet metal sandwich panel with insulation core, steel plates and profiles anchored to slab supporting structure
5. Floor-to-ceiling glazed curtain wall with 3/8 - 3/8 - 3/8″ (10/10/10 mm) aluminum double glazing units
6. False ceiling comprising sound-deadening gypsum board anchored to slab by metal droppers
7. Floor radiators
8. Structure supporting sun-shading system comprising vertical and diagonal 3 3/4″ (95 mm) steel C-profiles and horizontal 3 3/4 x 1 3/8″ (95x35 mm) steel C-profiles
9. Motorized sun-shading system anchored to structure by steel plates
10. Glazed curtain wall with 3/8 - 3/8 - 3/8″ (10/10/10 mm) aluminum double glazing units, air space, sheet metal panel, rigid insulation, frame of 3 3/4 x 1 3/8″ (95x35 mm) steel C-profiles sandwiching insulation, 5/8″ (15 mm) gypsum board, wall-mounted radiators
11. 1/2″ (12 mm) polished concrete floor, 14″ (355 mm) pre-stressed reinforced concrete slab
12. 1″ (25 mm) floorboards, double 3/4″ (20 mm) plywood subfloor, cast concrete stairs, foamed concrete forming steps, pre-stressed reinforced concrete slab
13. Bench seat with foamed polyurethane cushion and timber backrest
14. Floor recessed lighting
15. Protective steel grille, floor radiators
16. 1″ (25 mm) fiberglass-reinforced concrete panels, supporting brackets, steel box- and L-profiles, 3″ (75 mm) rigid insulation, vapor barrier, pre-stressed reinforced concrete slab of varying thickness
17. Metal housing and trim, system securing glazed wall (parallel to plane of section) comprising steel L-profiles and plates anchored to slab by steel plates and bolts
18. Continuous glazed façade with 1/2 - 5/8 - 5/16 - 5/64 - 5/16″ (12/16/8/2/8 mm) aluminum glazing units
19. Laminated glass wall mounted in aluminum U-profiles
20. Terrace decking comprising pre-cast concrete panels on adjustable pedestals, waterproofing membrane, 4″ (100 mm) rigid insulation, 11″ (280 mm) pre-stressed reinforced concrete slab
21. Ceiling-mounted radiant panel heating
22. False ceiling comprising 5/8″ (15 mm) fiberglass-reinforced gypsum board on frame of Ω-profiles suspended from slab
23. Sheet steel ventilation shaft with insulation suspended from slab by steel brackets and tie rods
24. Epoxy resin flooring, 2 3/8″ (60 mm) screed, 17 3/4″ (450 mm) reinforced concrete slab, earth
25. 4″ (100 mm) pre-stressed reinforced concrete slab with exposed aggregate finish, earth

■ XX Section - scale 1:400

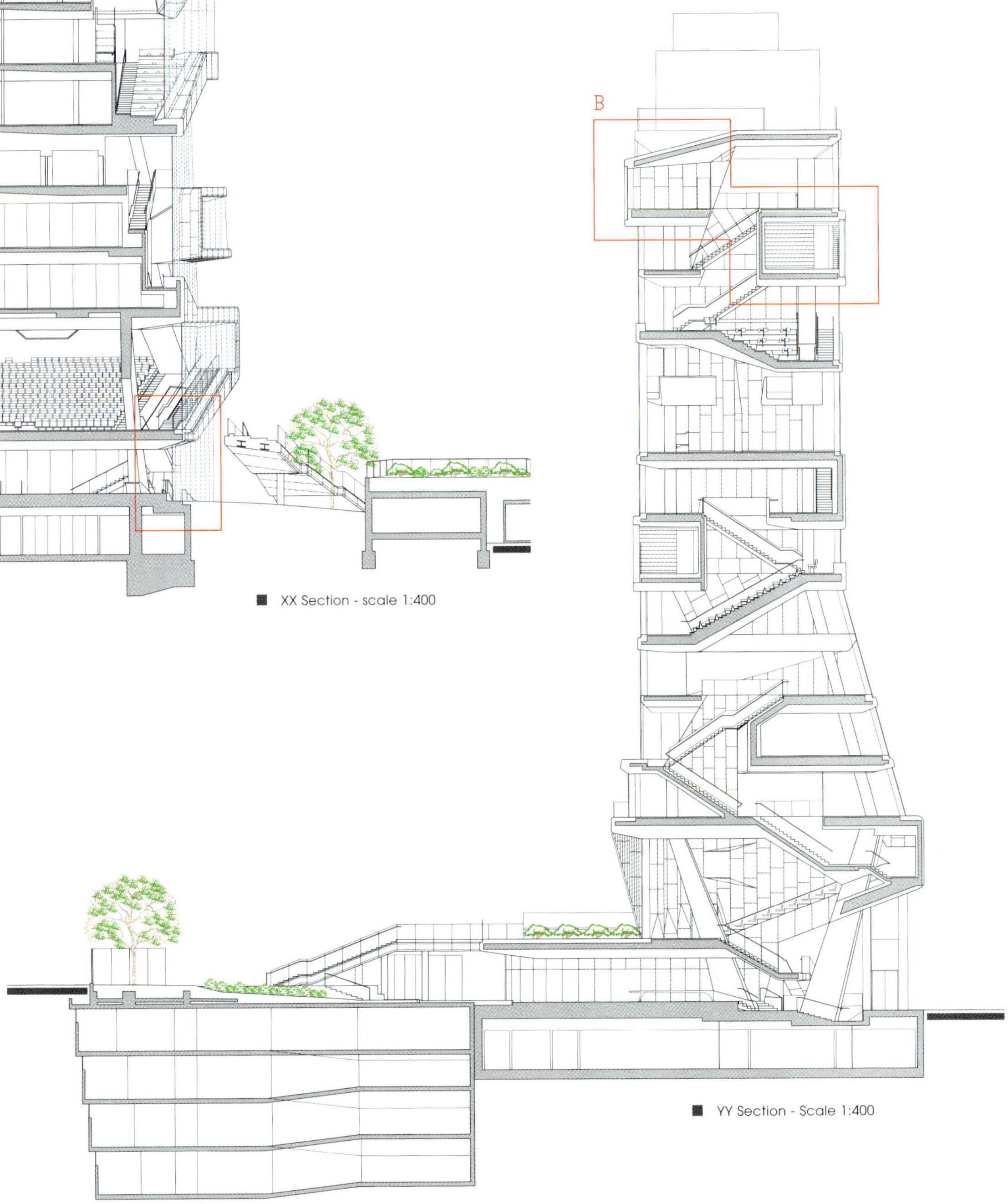

■ YY Section - Scale 1:400

MAQUET
MAQUET

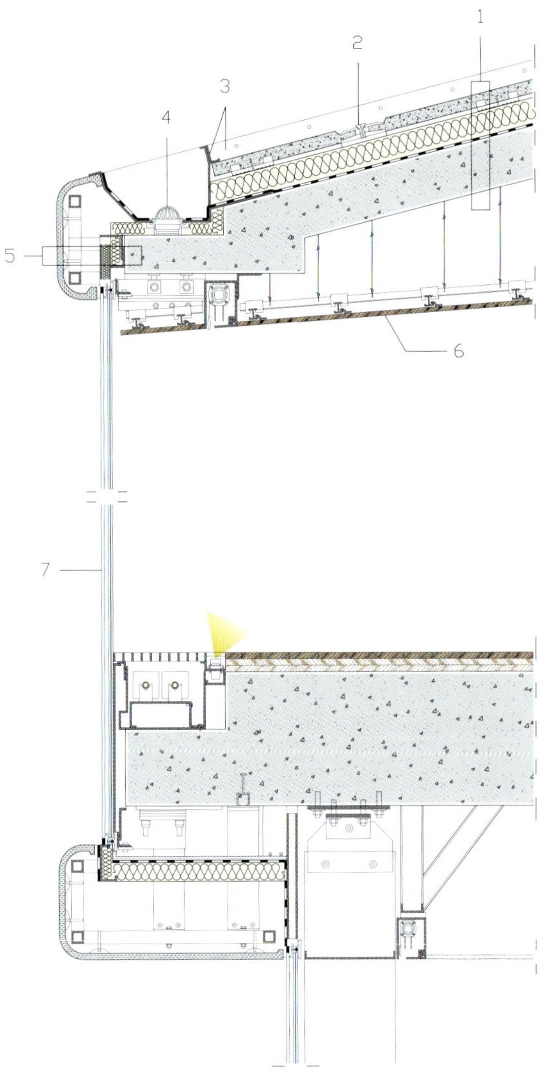

B

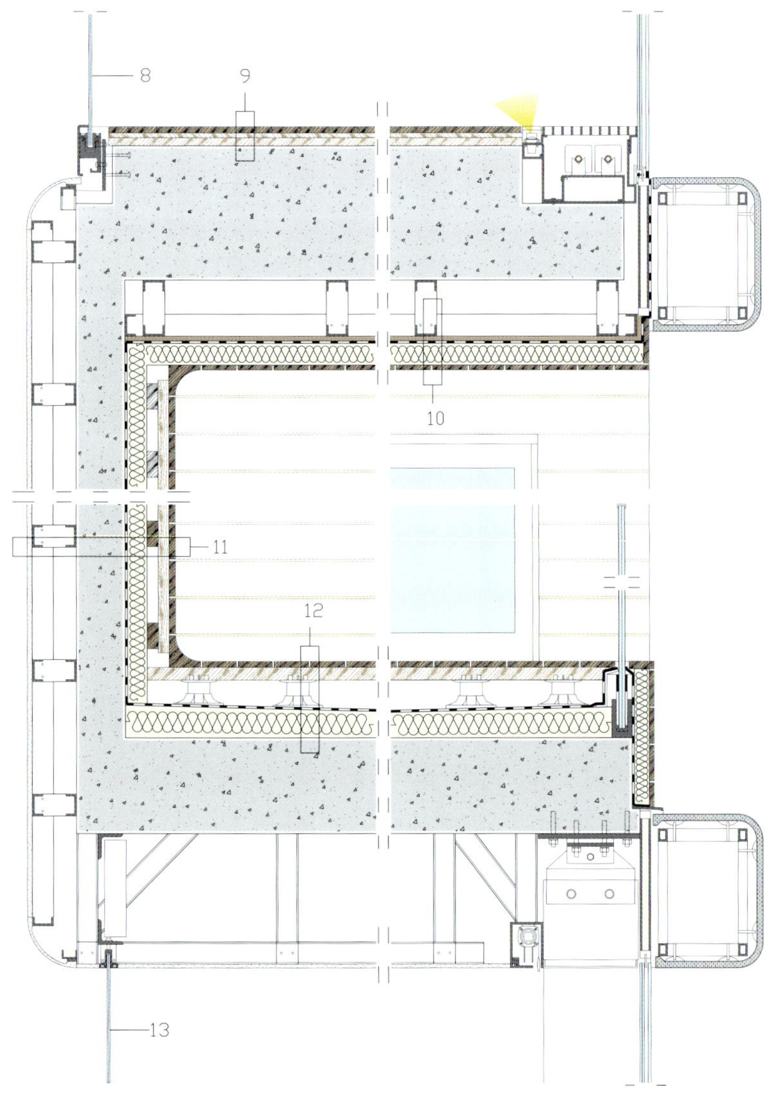

DETAIL B: CONSTRUCTION SYSTEM
VERTICAL SECTION - SCALE 1:30

1. Roof comprising pre-cast concrete panels, 4″ (100 mm) rigid insulation, waterproofing membrane, 7 7/8″ (200 mm) pre-stressed reinforced concrete slab
2. Fall arrest roof anchor
3. Sheet metal trim
4. Gutter and drain filter
5. 1″ (25 mm) fiberglass-reinforced concrete panels, structure of 2 x 2″ (50x50 mm) galvanized steel box profiles fastening panels anchored to slab by plates and bolts
6. False ceiling comprising timber panels fastened to metal frame suspended from slab
7. Floor-to-ceiling curtain wall with 1/2 - 5/8 - 5/16 - 5/64 - 5/16″ (12/16/8/2/8 mm) aluminum glazing units
8. Railing comprising 1/2″ (12 mm) laminated glass mounted in steel profiles and plates anchored to slab
9. 1″ (25 mm) floorboards, 3/4 + 1 1/4″ (20+30 mm) double plywood subfloor, 20 1/2″ (520 mm) pre-stressed reinforced concrete slab
10. Exterior false ceiling comprising 3/4″ (20 mm) timber battens, 3″ (75 mm) rigid insulation, waterproofing membrane, 3/4″ (20 mm) plywood panel, supporting frame of 3 1/2 x 1 3/4″ (90x45 mm) steel C-profiles
11. 3/4″ (20 mm) timber batten cladding, structure supporting cladding comprising 4 x 1 3/4″ (100x45 mm) timber, 3 1/8″ (80 mm) rigid insulation, waterproofing membrane, 7 7/8″ (200 mm) pre-stressed reinforced concrete slab, frame of 3 1/2 x 1 3/4″ (90x45 mm) steel C-profiles, interior gypsum board walls with 3/4″ (20 mm) plaster finish
12. 1″ (25 mm) terrace decking, timber joists, adjustable steel pedestals, waterproofing membrane, 5 1/8″ (130 mm) max h rigid insulation forming slope, 15″ (380 mm) pre-stressed reinforced concrete slab
13. 1/2″ (12 mm) tempered smoke protection barrier in steel profiles anchored to slab by L-profiles

ROZET CULTURAL CENTER

ARNHEM, THE NETHERLANDS

NEUTELINGS RIEDIJK ARCHITECTS

A Rotterdam partnership, of Willem Jan Neutelings and Michiel Riedijk, has created a succession of memorable public buildings. In Hilversum, the Institute of Sound and Vision expresses its role as an audio-visual archive and showcase with a vibrant glass façade that pulls multi-colored light into a lofty atrium, which steps down to the storage vaults. The architects took advantage of solid ground; in much of the Netherlands, the water level is so high that multi-level basements are prohibitively costly.

In Antwerp, the firm designed MAS: a civic museum in which the galleries are stacked and rotated, clad in red sandstone, and separated by a spiraling band of wavy glass that lights the ascent. At every level you have a treasure chest that contains some aspect of the city's history and a view from each side in turn over the townscape of today. That concept of a public route extending through a cultural building to link it to the life of the community is exemplified in the giant inner stair that bisects a library complex realized in Amersfoort in 2013.

A similar spinal stair carries the residents of Arnhem through the newly completed Neutelings Riedijk project called Rozet. The trapezoidal site is part of the central route that links the station to the central Kerkplein. Its multiple role as library, heritage center, art education complex, and community college makes Rozet a vital public amenity; it even offers free literacy courses and is part of a national network of libraries. "There's a tendency to exclude undesirables from privatized spaces such as malls," observes Neutelings. "Libraries have a far broader role than reading and borrowing books; they are one of the last civic spaces in Western society, a place where everyone is welcome. In all our libraries, we emphasize that spirit of inclusivity, creating a hierarchy of open spaces for gathering and small pockets for study."

Rozet is a bridge between the historic center and the post-war city,

and its staircase is an interior street with entries to the varied activities at each of the five above-ground levels. These complementary roles are boldly expressed in the façades, which are composed of precast concrete elements with a sandy tone that suggests stone. The edges are angled to catch the light, as do the embossed rosettes. These form an infinitely varied pattern and thus symbolize the gathering and sharing of knowledge within the building. Face-on, the building reveals its inner life and structure; obliquely it becomes a ribbed mass of masonry. The vertical windows with their deep reveals soften the light, while offering tightly framed glimpses of the city.

The architects employed varied tools to make Rozet a model of sustainability. The interior street is naturally ventilated and requires no heating since it is considered an extension of the outdoors.

The roof is green and traps rainfall, making it an attractive habitat for birds. Solar panels are strategically placed, generating a significant amount of energy, and this supplemented by thermal storage.

Here is a civic building that is monumental and useful, to people of every age and origin; an embodiment of Dutch ideals. It also offers an exciting architectural promenade. The inner street widens and narrows as it ascends, and vitrines displaying books and art function like shop windows on a commercial street. Patrons may carry a book from the stacks and browse on a ledge beside the staircase. For young people who are more at home with texting and tweeting, and may feel intimidated by a hushed reading room, Rozet demystifies the printed word.

■ Study models of the internal routes distribution

1-2 Internal view

3. External view in its urban context

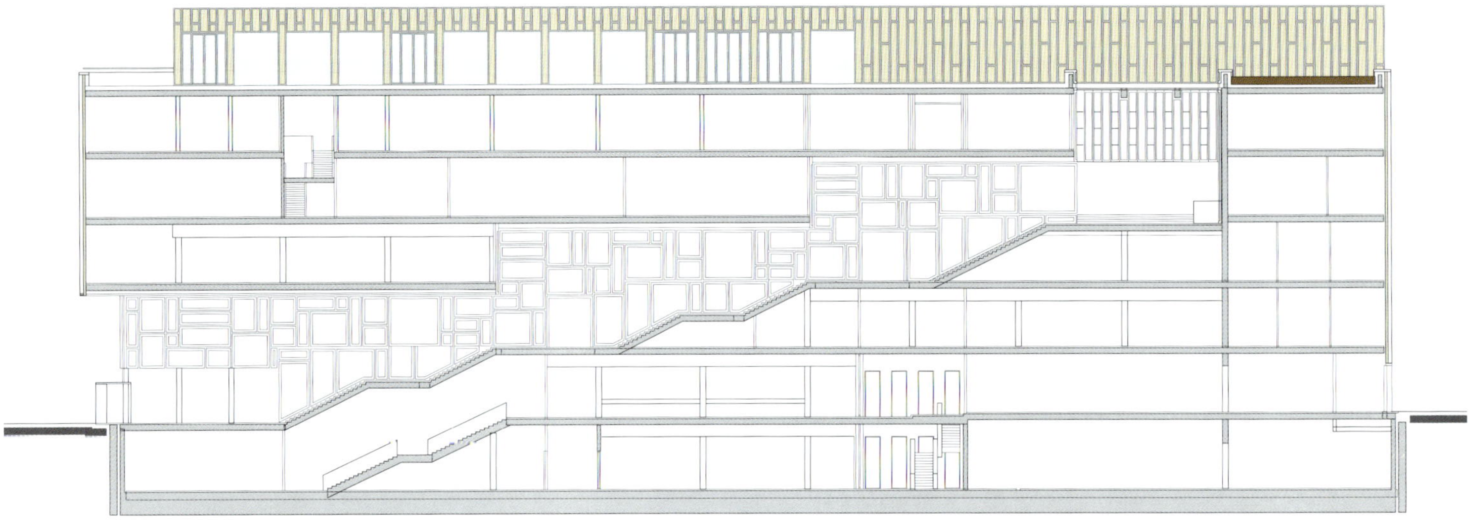

■ YY Section - Scale 1:500

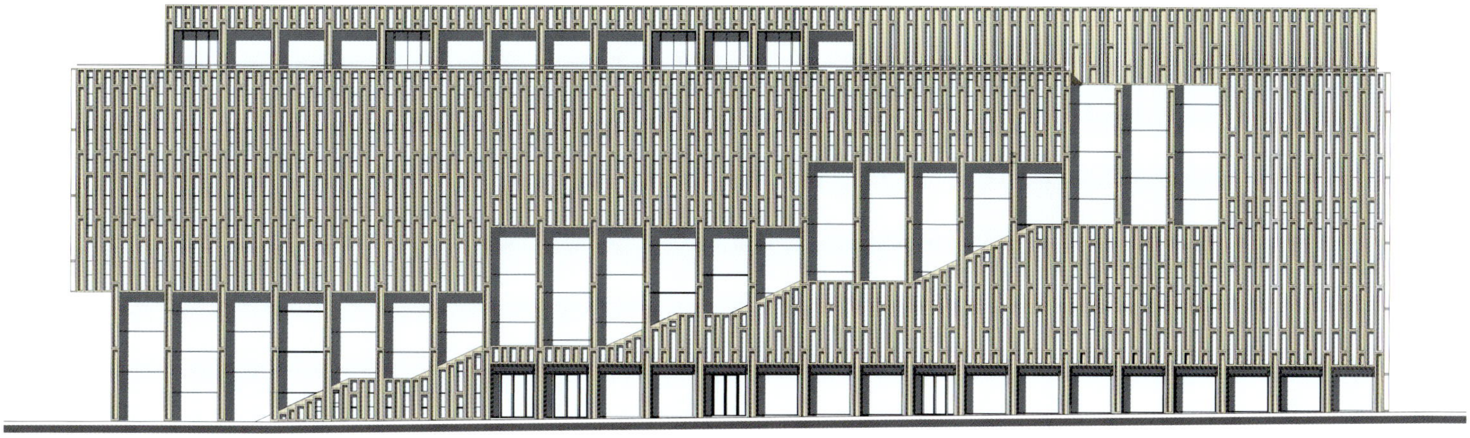

■ North elevation - Scale 1:500

8-14 jaar

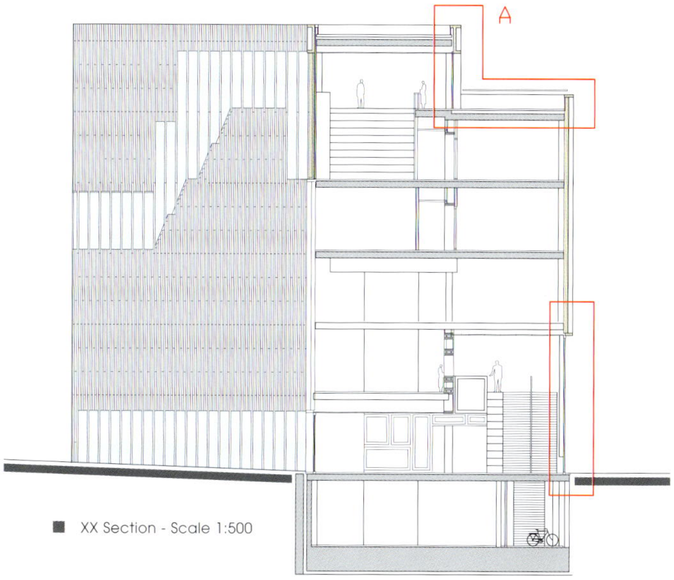

■ XX Section - Scale 1:500

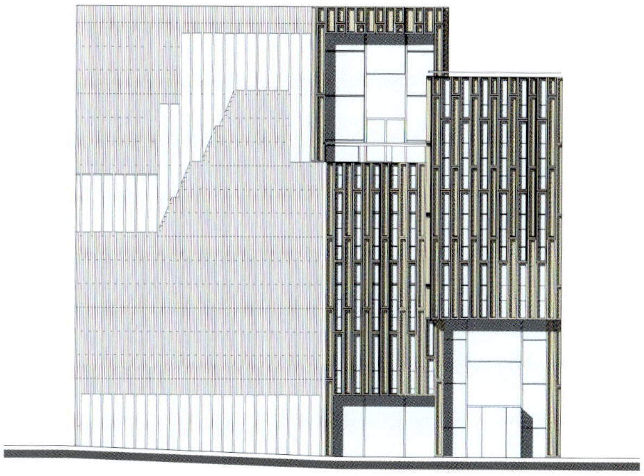

■ East elevation - Scale 1:500

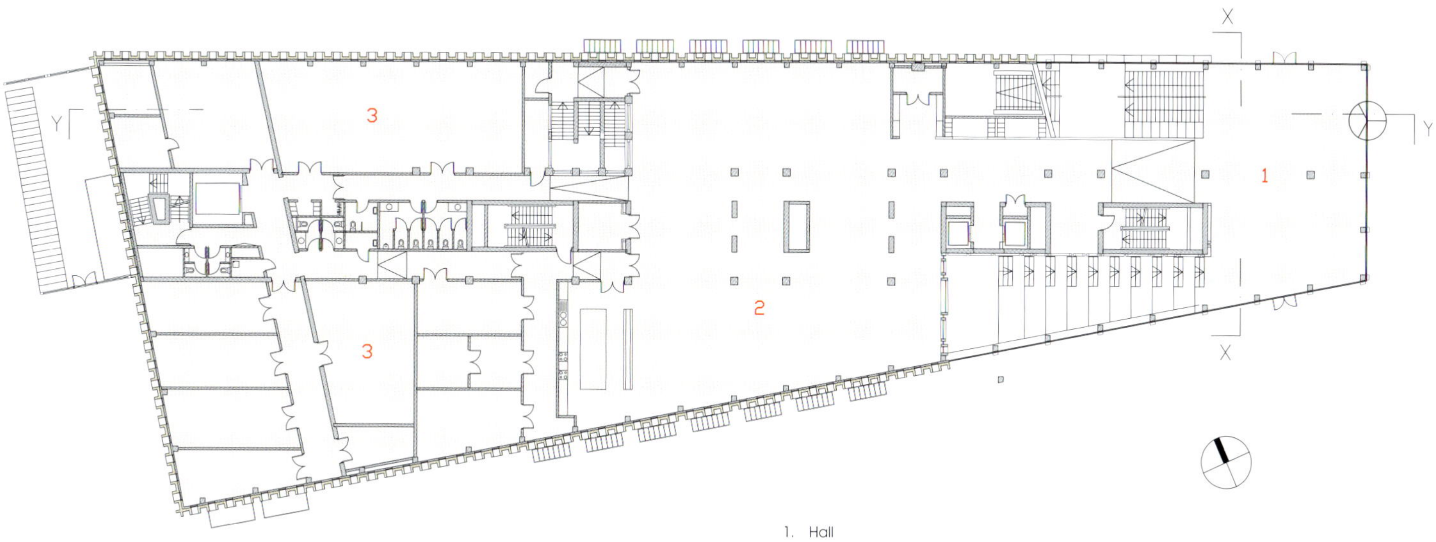

1. Hall
2- Café / restaurant
3- Ancillary facilities
4- Arts school
5- Auditorium

■ Ground floor plan - Scale 1:500

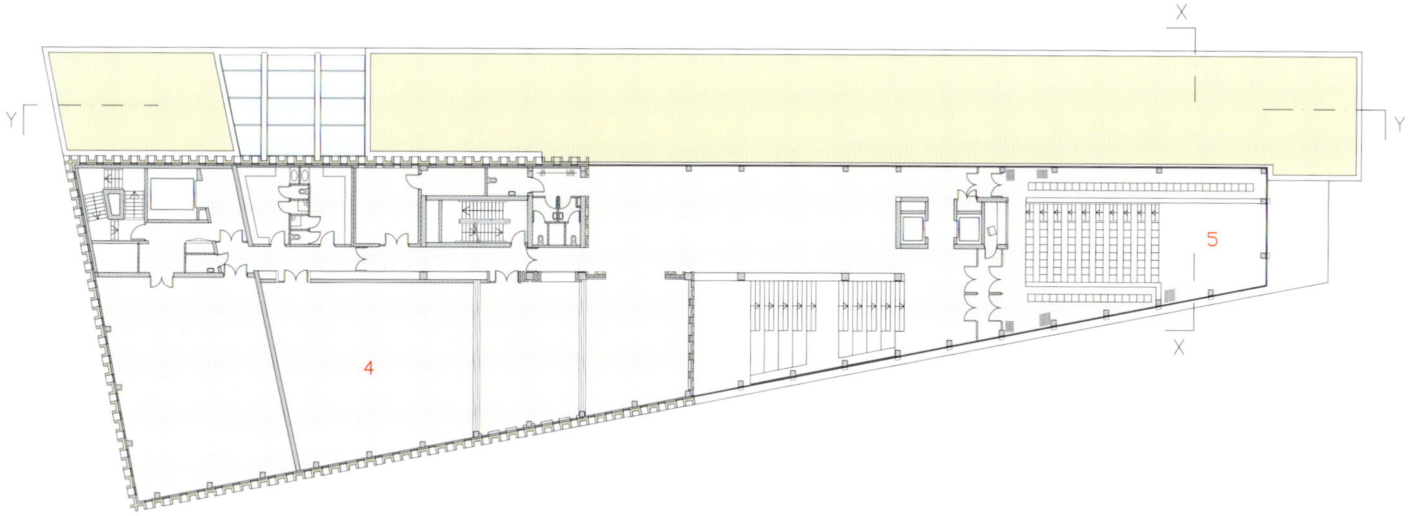

■ 5th floor plan - Scale 1:500

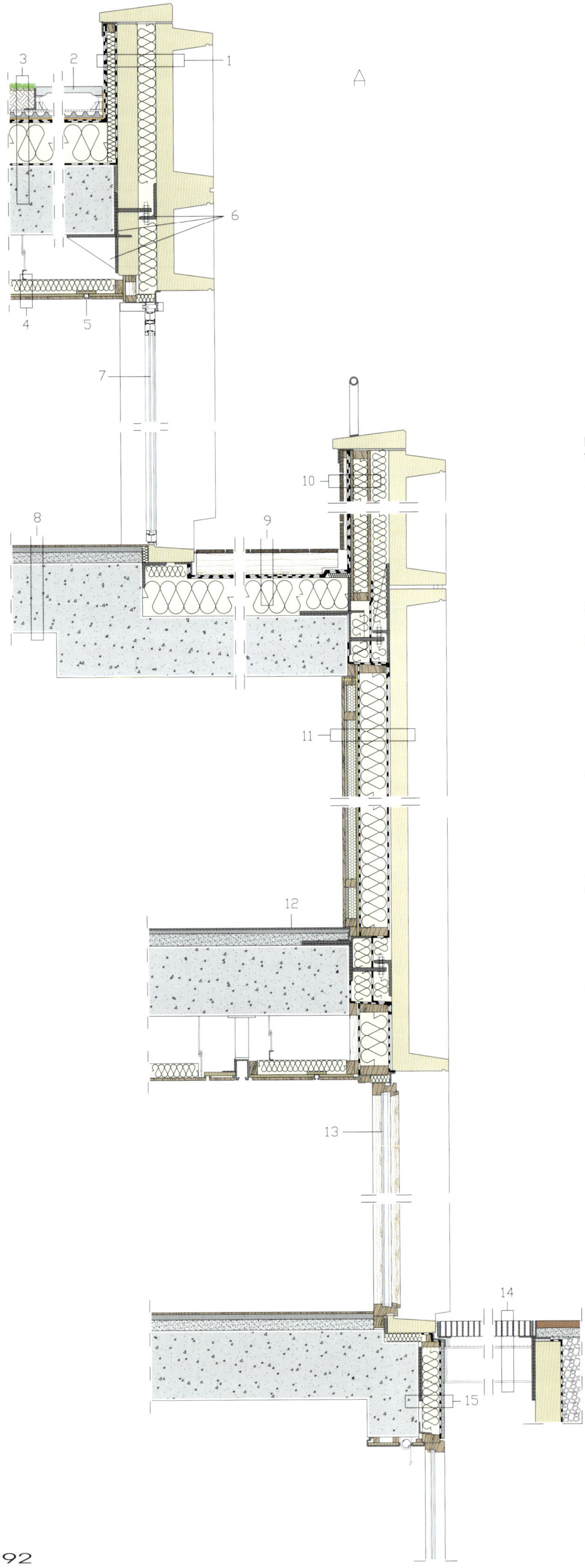

DETAIL A: CONSTRUCTION SYSTEM VERTICAL SECTION - SCALE 1:30

1. Façade comprising prefabricated 4" (100 mm) decorative concrete blocks, 4 1/8" (105 mm) rigid insulation, 4 3/4" (120 mm) concrete block, waterproofing membrane, 2" (50 mm) rigid insulation, double waterproofing membrane
2. Perimeter walkway in concrete blocks on adjustable pedestals
3. Green roof with lawn, 4" (100 mm) soil, non-woven membrane, drainage blanket, protective membrane, double waterproofing membrane, 9 1/8" (230 mm) insulation layer, waterproofing membrane, 15 3/8" (390 mm) reinforced concrete slab
4. False ceiling comprising 5/8" (15 mm) oak panel, 5/8" (15 mm) plywood panel, 3 1/8" (80 mm) insulation layer, steel C-profile support suspended by tie rods from slab
5. Curtain track
6. Structure of steel plates and L-profiles securing façade to supporting structure
7. Full height glazed façade with 5/16 - 5/8 - 5/16" (8/15/8 mm) steel double-glazing units in steel frame
8. Floor comprising 3/8" (10 mm) oak floorboards, 1 1/4" (30 mm) levelling screed, 2 3/8" (60 mm) screed, 15" (380 mm) reinforced concrete slab
9. Terrace deck comprising 3/4" (20 mm) bamboo decking, 4 3/4" (120 mm) timber beams (parallel to plane of section), double waterproofing membrane, 8 1/4" (210 mm) rigid insulation
10. 3/4" (20 mm) bamboo cladding, supporting frame of 7/8" (22 mm) timber (parallel to plane of section), double waterproofing membrane, 3/4" (18 mm) wood fiber panel, frame of 3 3/8 x 1 3/4" (85x45 mm) timber sandwiching insulation, 4 1/8" (105 mm) rigid insulation
11. Interior wall covering in 5/8" (15 mm) timber panels, fire-retardant treatment, 2" (50 mm) acoustic insulation, 5/8" (15 mm) plywood panel, vapour barrier, frames of 6 1/8 x 2" (155x50 mm) timber sandwiching insulation, waterproofing membrane, air space, concrete block
12. 3/8" (10 mm) linoleum flooring
13. Full height glazed façade with 1/4 + 1/4 - 1 - 5/8" (7+6/24/15 mm) timber double glazing units
14. Walk-on steel grille, 4 x 2 3/8" (100x60 mm) steel box beam (parallel to plane of section), 7 7/8" (200 mm) steel I-beam (parallel to plane of section)
15. 3/4" (20 mm) fiber cement cladding, waterproofing membrane, 4" (100 mm) rigid insulation, steel plate anchor, reinforced concrete beam

Bar

PARQUE BIBLIOTECA ESPAÑA

MEDELLÍN, COLOMBIA

GIANCARLO MAZZANTI ARQUITECTOS

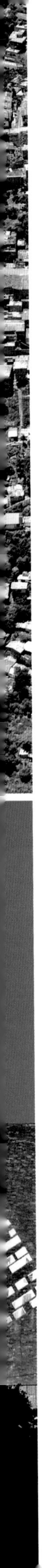

Inaugurated in 2007, the public library "Parque Biblioteca España" in the Columbian city of Medellín combines symbol and function: it bears witness to a community's desire for social renewal, and indicates how inequalities can be lessened by spreading knowledge in contemporary society. Giancarlo Mazzanti's winning project in the 2005 competition held by the Medellín city council reveals a deeply pondered view of architecture's role in society.

His architecture resonates with both the immediate urban fabric and the vast plain stretching out below. Its materials and form have an osmotic relationship with their context. The three huge blocks making up the library complex stand out against the skyline of a city sprawling over undulating slopes enclosed by the craggy summits of an Andes mountain chain. Rising amidst a jumble of makeshift houses, mainly in brick, their arrangement resembles the distant mountain range.

The three buildings house different functions: a library, auditorium, and training centre, respectively. Set on an artificial platform, they stand as one compact system offering a public service. A pinewood platform creates passageways between and access routes to the buildings. On the side facing the mountains, the walkway opens out into a sort of collective plaza for community socialising.

The buildings rise like closed jagged volumes, their sharp angles emphasising their solid mass. Geometry and outer cladding turn the complex into a single unit. The oblique planes of the multi-faceted façades create unexpected spaces between one building and another, giving rise to an ingenious play of light and shadow, views and architectural relations. Protected by the overhang of the building, deeply recessed entrances take on symbolic importance. The translucent glazed doorways are differently coloured (yellow, green and red) to denote each building's function.

The dark hues of the closely set opaque stone cladding lend the elevations an austere quality. A limited number of apparently randomly arranged, different-sized windows accentuate the buildings' imposing mass. On some façades, the number of apertures increases progressively while on others, the windows are not aligned horizontally. They seem designed to exclude any lateral source of natural light.

The library and training centre do, however, receive light from the side and the top of the building: the inner concrete structure leaves a wide gap between floors and outer envelope, allowing natural light to penetrate the whole building, so leaving intact the monolithic aspect of the outer envelope.

For everything is designed to turn attention inwards. While the views over the valley can be admired from the outside terraces and platform, the interiors are wholly concerned with the persons within, the events, activities, colours and intriguing floor plan, where corridors or balconies give onto the interior air space. Inside, the focus is entirely on the interior and what goes on in it.

■ 2nd level plan - Scale 1:400

1. Entrance
2. Reception
3. Hall
4. Workshop
5. Library
6. Auditorium
7. Plaza
8. Control room

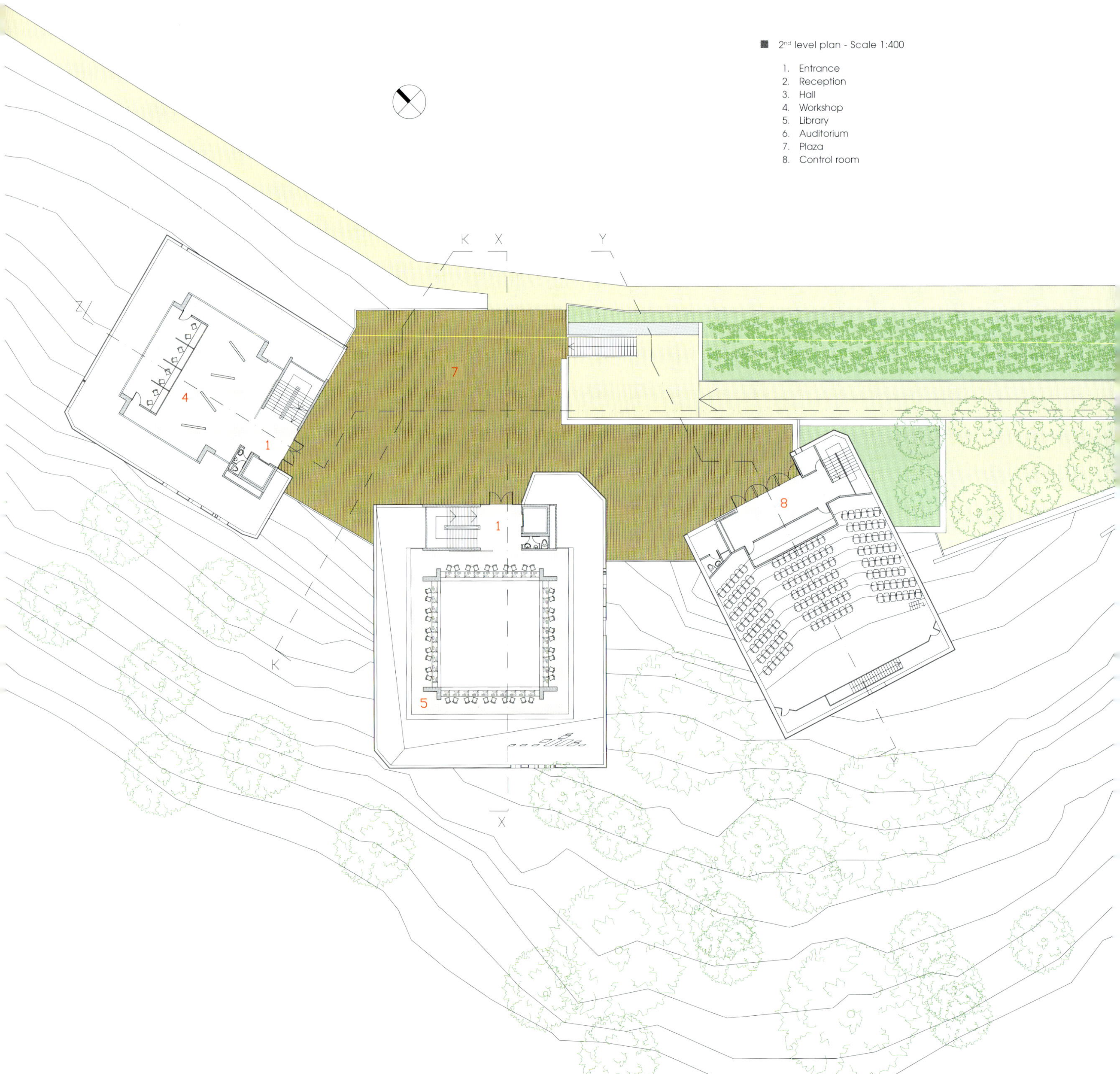

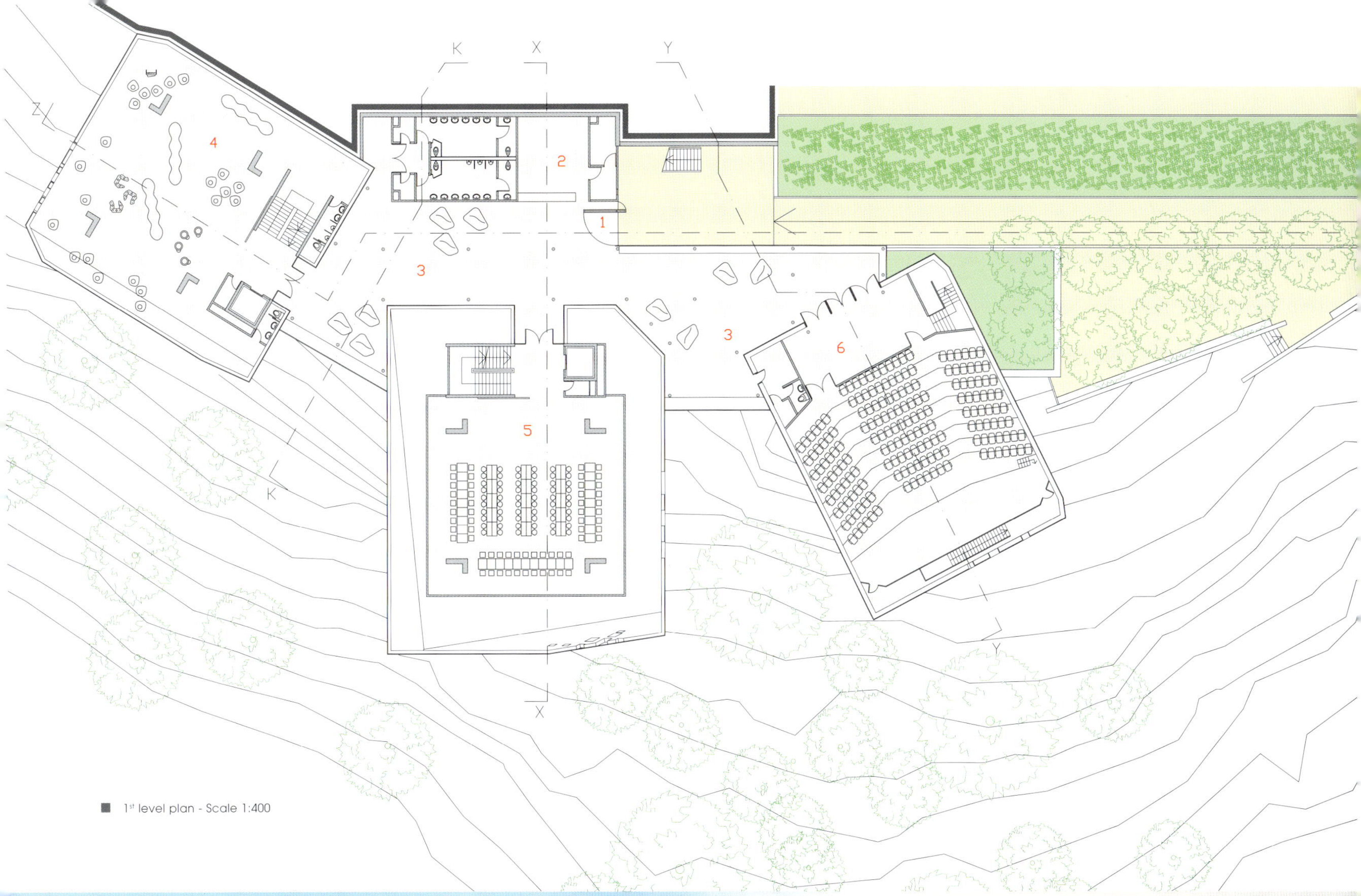

■ 1st level plan - Scale 1:400

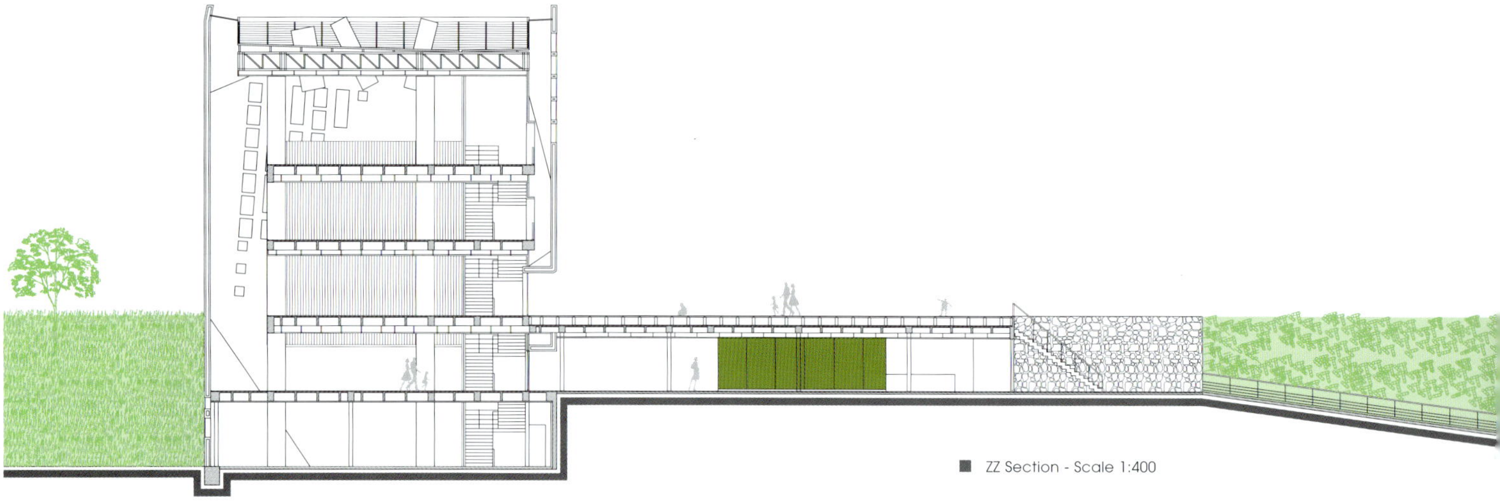

■ ZZ Section - Scale 1:400

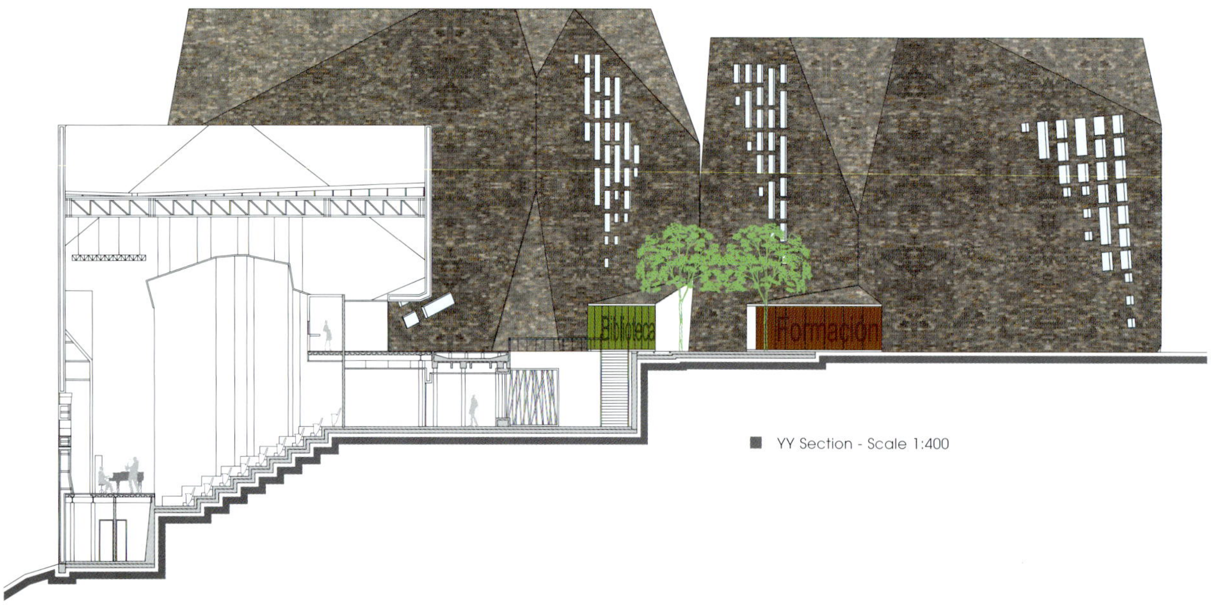

■ YY Section - Scale 1:400

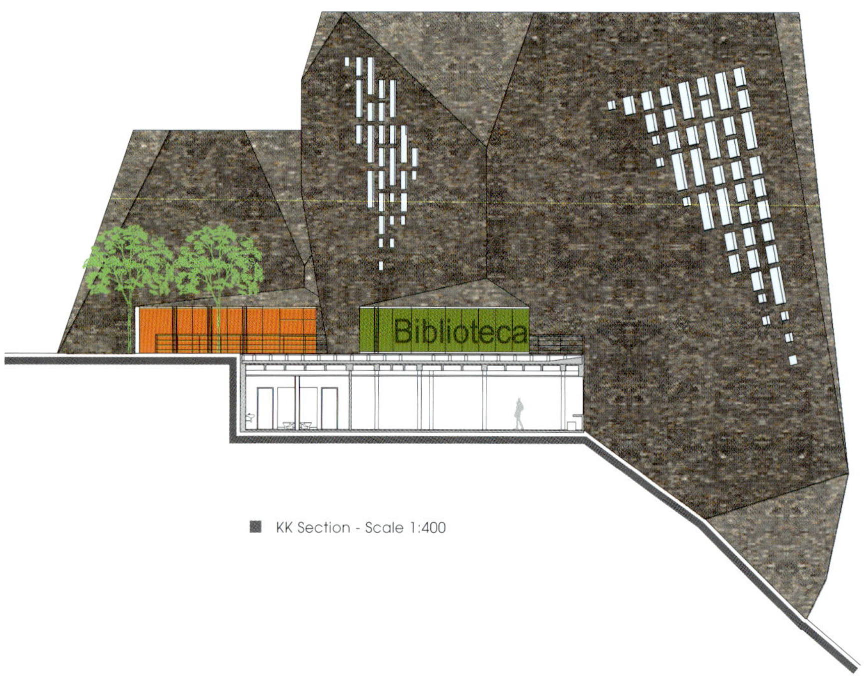

■ KK Section - Scale 1:400

■ XX Section - Scale 1:400

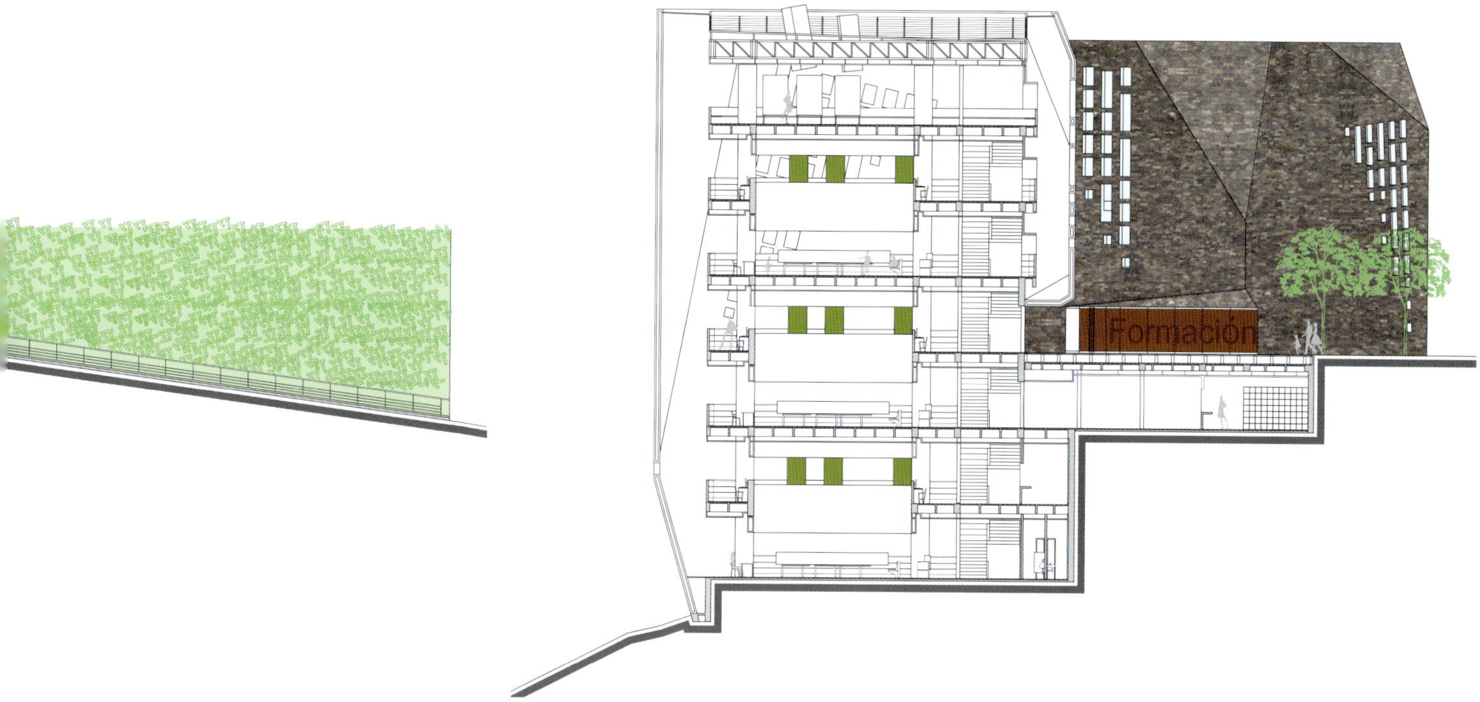

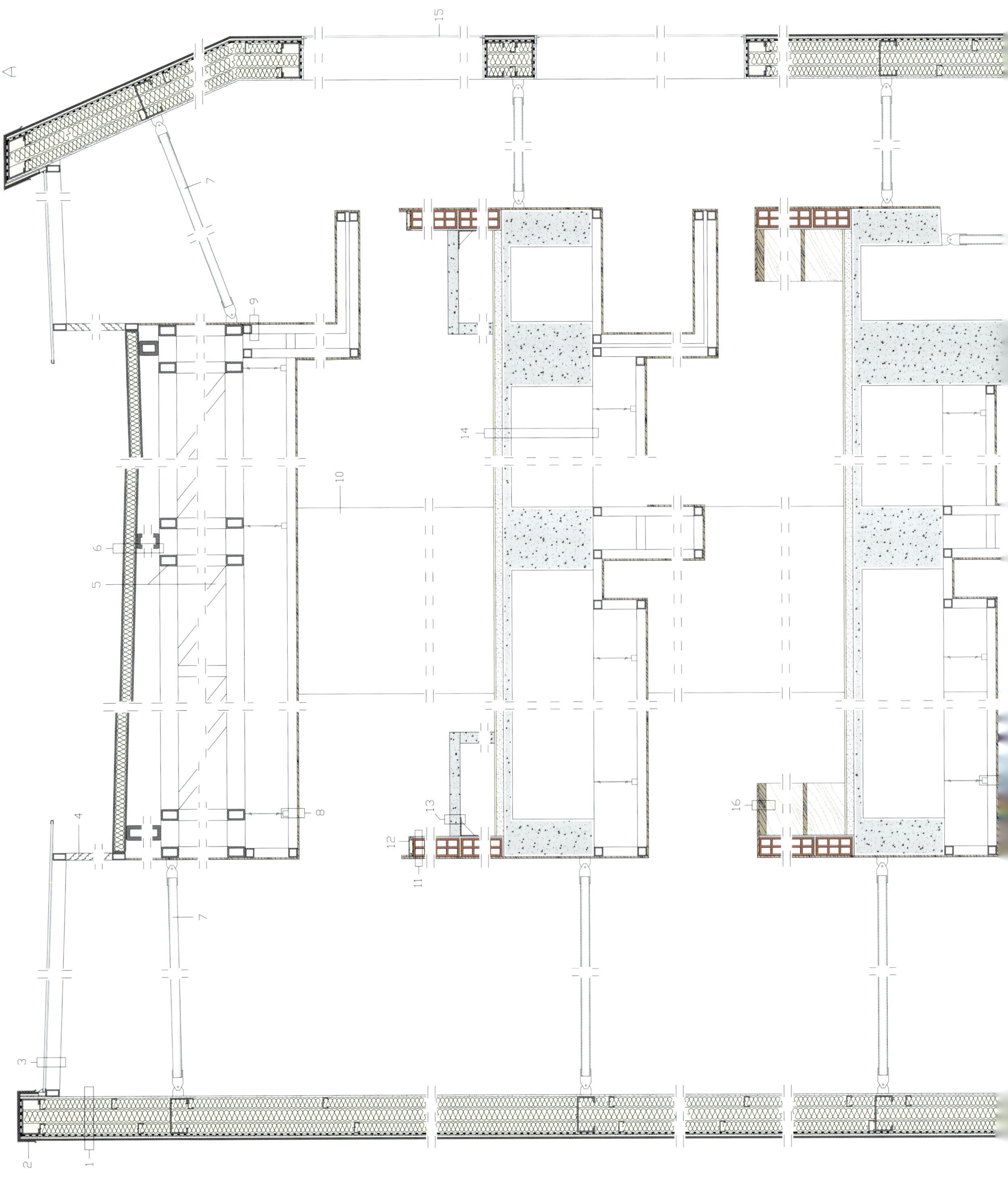
A
1
2
3
4
5
6
7
8
9
10
11
12
13
14
15
16

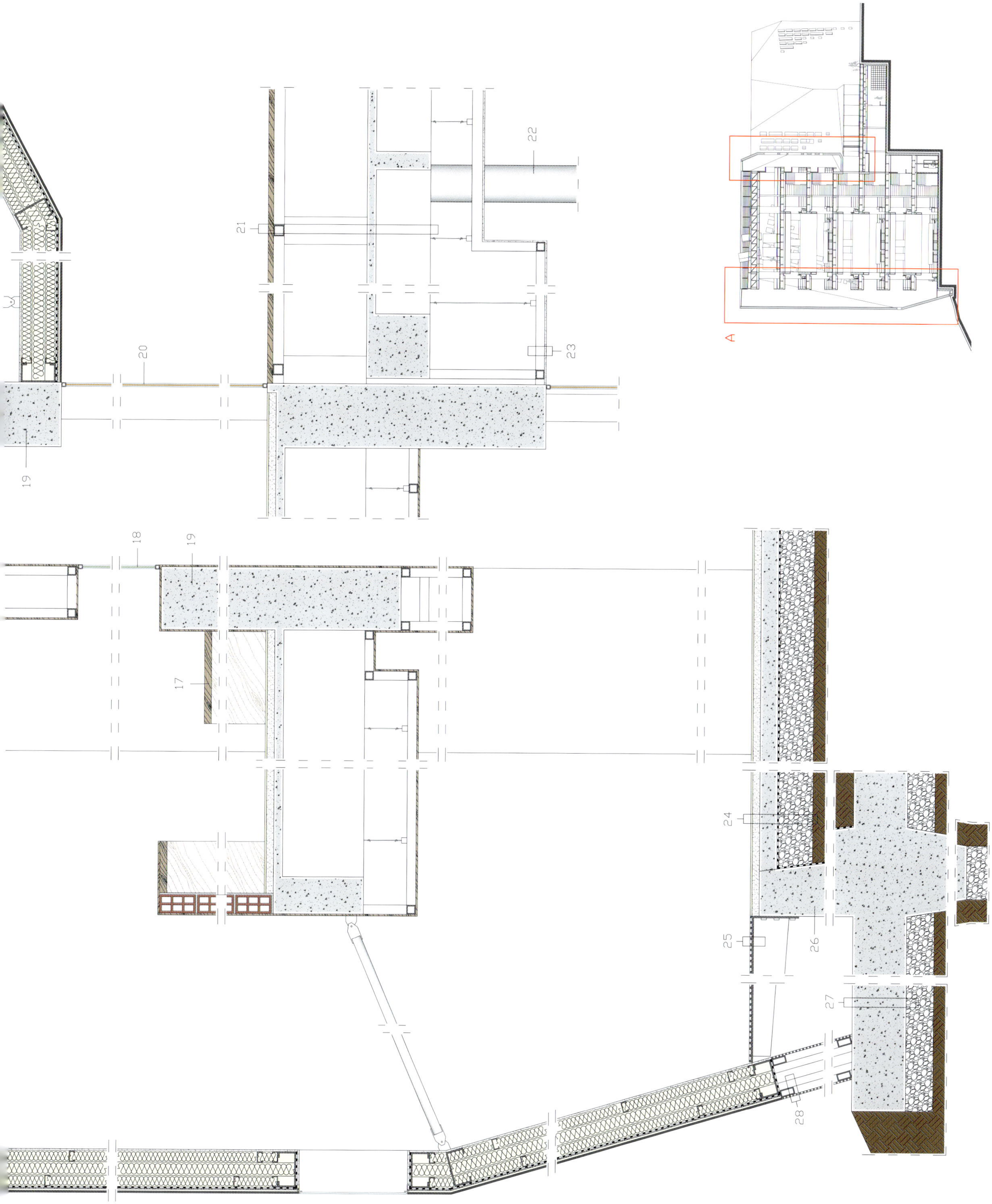
A
17
18
19
20
21
22
23
24
25
26
27
28

DETAIL A: LIBRARY, CONSTRUCTION SYSTEM VERTICAL SECTION SCALE 1:25

1. Façade formed by 3/8" (10 mm) acid-treated black stone cladding, 3/8" (10 mm) layer of latex-based glue, 1/4" (6 mm) fiber cement panel, waterproofing membrane, structural frame in 7 7/8 x 4" (200x100 mm) steel C-profiles and double infill frame in steel C-profiles and 7 7/8" (200 mm) thermo-acoustic insulation, 3/8" (10 mm) gypsum board
2. Aluminum flashing
3. Skylight formed by 3/8" (10 mm) laminated glass, supporting frame of 3 x 1 5/8" (75x40 mm) box-shaped steel profiles
4. Adjustable aluminum ventilation louvers
5. Roof formed by trussed structure of 4 x 2 3/8" (100x60 mm) steel box profiles
6. Roof formed by 3" (75 mm) sheet aluminum sandwich panels with foamed polyurethane insulation, steel box profiles in various sizes forming 2% slope
7. Steel tie rod bracing
8. False ceiling formed by 3/8" (10 mm) oak panels, supporting frame of 2 x 2" (50x50 mm) steel box profiles on tie rods suspended from load-bearing structure
9. 3/8" (10 mm) oak panelling, supporting frame of 2 x 2" (50x50 mm) steel box profiles
10. Reinforced concrete column
11. Parapet formed by 3/8" (10 mm) oak panels, 4" (100 mm) masonry blocks, render
12. 1/16" (5 mm) oak panel finish
13. 2 3/8" (60 mm) reinforced concrete seating, 4 x 4" (100x100 mm) steel L-profile support with reinforcing triangular plate
14. 3/8" (10 mm) stone flooring, 1 5/8" (40 mm) screed, 19 3/4" (500 mm) pre-cast reinforced concrete floor with steel beams and embedded slab
15. 1/4" (6 mm) fixed laminated glass window with steel frame
16. Bookcase formed by 3/8" (10 mm) oak panels, 1 5/8" (40 mm) wood beam, wood upright (parallel to plane of section)
17. Table formed by 1 5/8" (40 mm) wood panel
18. Closure formed by double 1/4 + 1/4" (6+6 mm) pane of glass separated by green film with aluminum frame
19. 13 3/8" (340 mm) thick reinforced concrete structure
20. Door formed by double 1/4 + 1/4" (6+6 mm) pane of glass separated by coloured film with aluminum frame
21. 1 1/8" (30 mm) pine decking, supporting frame of 2 3/8 x 2 3/8" (60x60 mm) steel box profiles, circular concrete spacer column, 13 3/4" (350 mm) pre-cast reinforced concrete slab
22. Ø 7 7/8" (200 mm) steel column
23. False ceiling formed by 3/8" (10 mm) gypsum board, supporting frame of 2 x 2" (50x50 mm) steel box profiles on tie rods suspended from slab
24. 3/8" (10 mm) stone flooring, 1 5/8" (40 mm) screed, 4" (100 mm) reinforced concrete slab, waterproofing membrane, 7 7/8" (200 mm) layer of compacted ballast, earth
25. Steel grille, steel L-profile support with reinforcing plate
26. Reinforced concrete foundation
27. 11 7/8" (300 mm) reinforced concrete slab, layer of compacted ballast
28. Steel ventilation grille, double supporting frame of 3 1/8 x 1 5/8" (80x40 mm) steel box profiles

33 VESTRY STREET
NEW YORK, USA

ARCHI-TECTONICS

The sober alignment of compact building fronts on the streets of TriBeCa speaks clearly of this New York neighborhood's not-so-distant past. The ubiquitous worksites speak of its far-reaching transformation. Until the 1970s, TriBeCa - an acronym for Triangle Below Canal Street - was the hub of the cotton and textile trade, as testified by the buildings on Hudson Street, West and Harrison Street. As the industry declined and disappeared from TriBeCa in the Sixties and Seventies, the plentiful, now empty, commercial spaces began to attract several artists eager to leave the pricey Soho neighborhood nearby. The influx of the art world gave a whole new lease of life to the TriBeCa, which also received a commercial and residential boost, making it now one of the most attractive, sought-after areas of New York.

Architecture firm Archi-Tectonics has added another residential piece to the mosaic on Vestry Street where several former warehouses have already been converted to housing. The 33 Vestry Street project resonates with its context but at the same time marks a departure from traditional TriBeCa features. Flanked by two converted industrial buildings, number 33 aligns with the street wall and cornice heights but stands apart for the design and materials of its façade.

One of the stated aims of the project was to be a new TriBeCa landmark while at the same time respecting the essential features of its surrounds. The building conforms in its proportional systems, extreme ceiling heights, tripartite stone façade subdivisions, and street façade alignments. At the same time, however, the street-side façade reflects a distinctive typology and distribution system. No longer a traditional residential condominium, it is rather a set of stacked custom-designed townhouses - each with its own identity, occupying a whole floor or distributed over two or three levels. Their extremely generous size (between 300 and 450 sq m) includes large outdoor spaces in the form of terraces and gardens.

The building's dual character creates an inherent tension. On the one hand, the introverted urban nature of the residence as expressed

■ Schematic study diagrams of the south facing façade

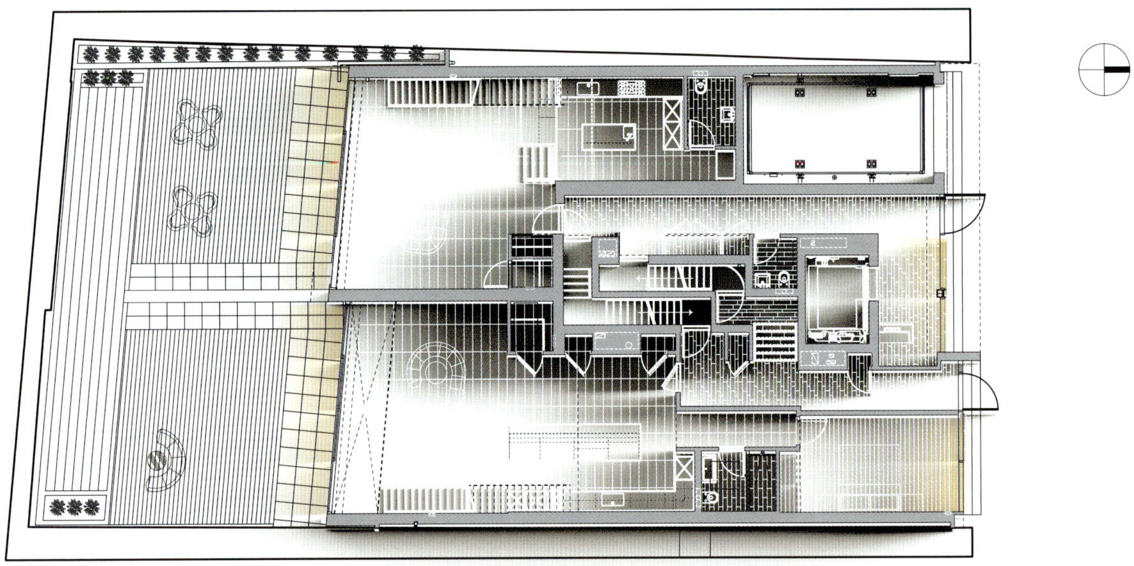

■ 1st floor plan
Scale 1:250

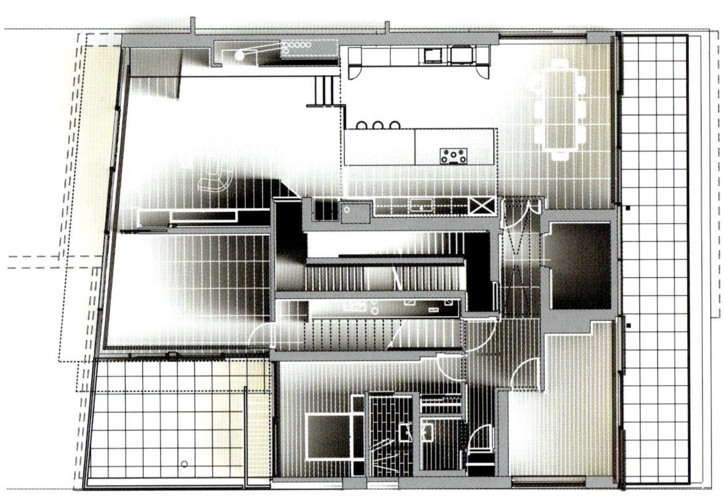

■ 8th floor plan
Scale 1:250

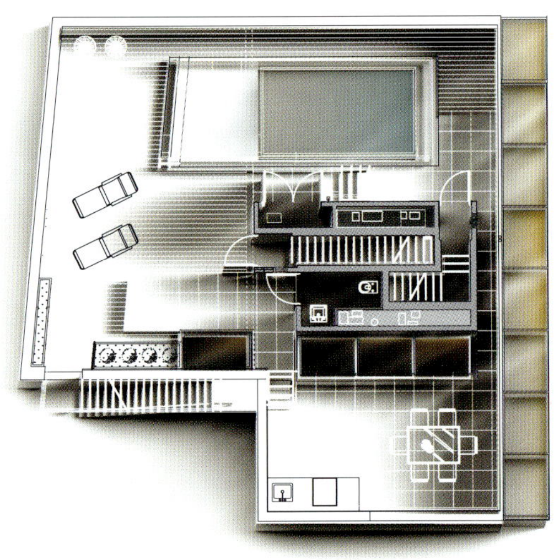

■ Roof floor plan
Scale 1:250

by the hermetic street façade; on the other, the variegated bucolic court-facing façade with large cantilevering volumes and loggias mark out the different identity of each townhouse and its occupant. The north-facing street front is a stone-glass panel curtain wall arranged in a tripartite design. In stark contrast, the south façade overlooking the garden is a three-dimensional frontage whose terraces and cantilevers provide shaded interiors.

The two systems meet in the center of the building. Here, floors and ceilings are made to slope and fold. Lower ceiling heights compress street-side spaces only to widen out to double-height volumes on the inner garden side.

The building's eight stories are stacked in staggered fashion, the many different size and design of dwelling units slotted into one another to allow for different layouts and exposure. Every floor is divided so as to ensure that where there are two apartments, each enjoys north-south orientation over both street and garden. Bedrooms and services are placed street side, illuminated during the day by natural sunlight filtering through the irregular patterns on the thin stone facing slabs. Day zones are placed courtside, their double-height volumes opening onto terraces. The composition, placement of the apertures, and large cantilevers on this inner façade give a clear indication from the outside of how the different dwelling units have been divided up. The exterior features - long narrow terraces with ample gardens - also provide clues as to the custom-designed interiors. The top floor villa, designed as a suspended volume, has an exclusive rooftop terrace with swimming pool.

Located in a booming real estate neighborhood that can easily absorb ambitious projects like this, the 33 Vestry Street program by Archi-Tectonics reflects urban living priorities but at the same time allows for custom-designed living. Here, compact sobriety signals discrete conformity to urban tenets, while open spaces and terraces answer our ancestral need for a natural environment.

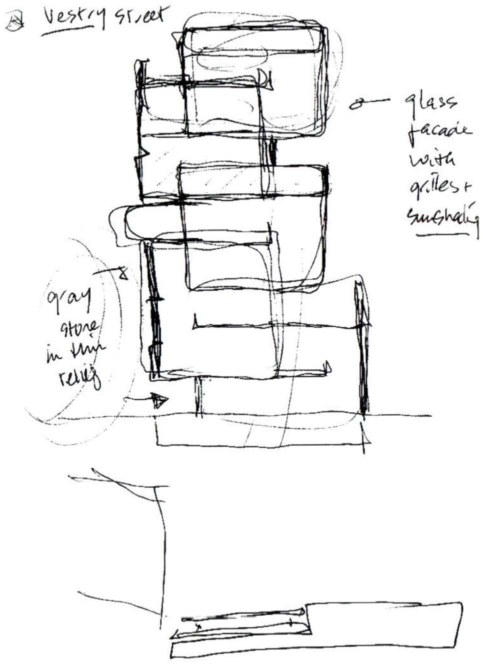

■ Perspective cross-sectional view

■ South façade - Perspective view

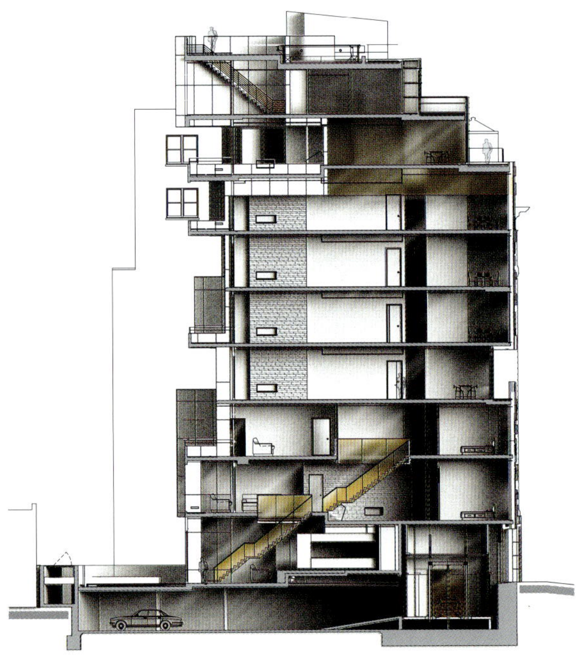

■ Cross section - Scale 1:400

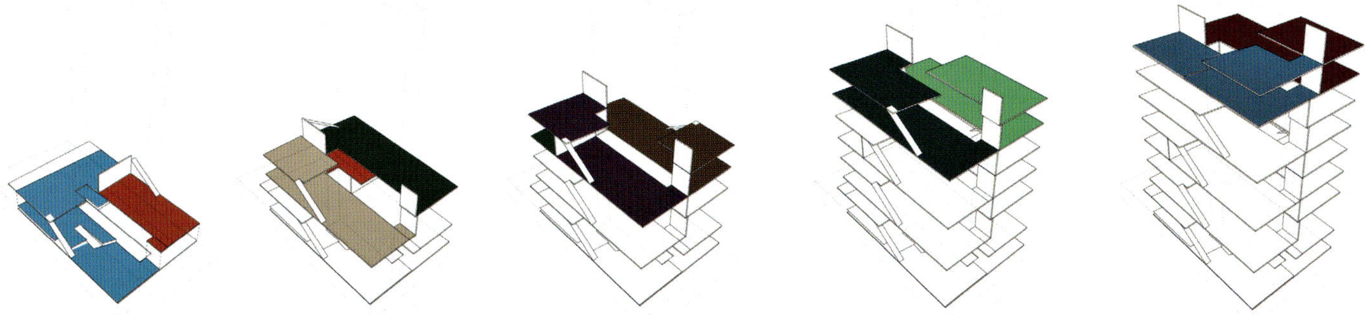

Schematic diagram of duplex apartment distribution on the various levels

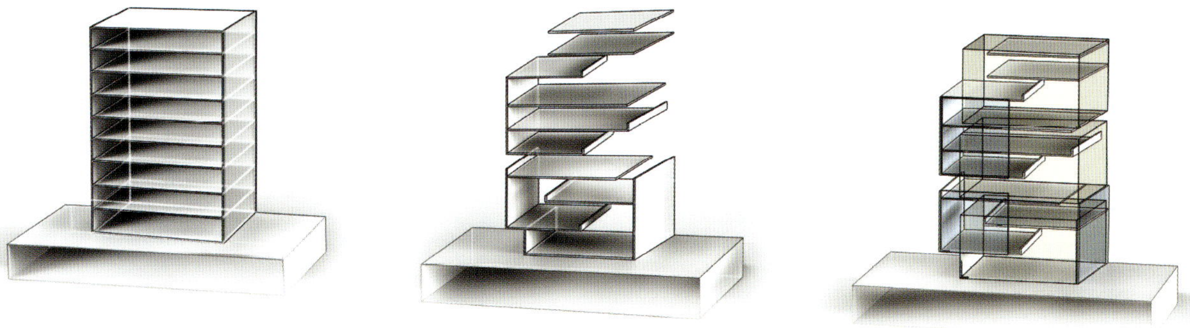

Conceptual diagrams and study sketches of how the volumes break down and recompose. The compact street frontage contrasts with the disjointed inward facing façade

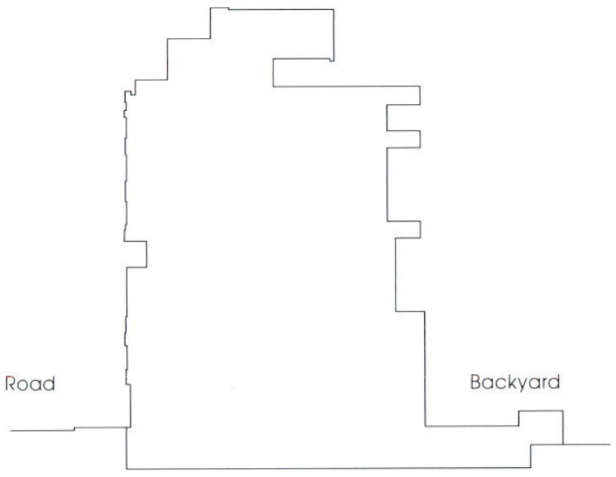

■ Wire-frame cross-sectional detail of street and court-facing elevations

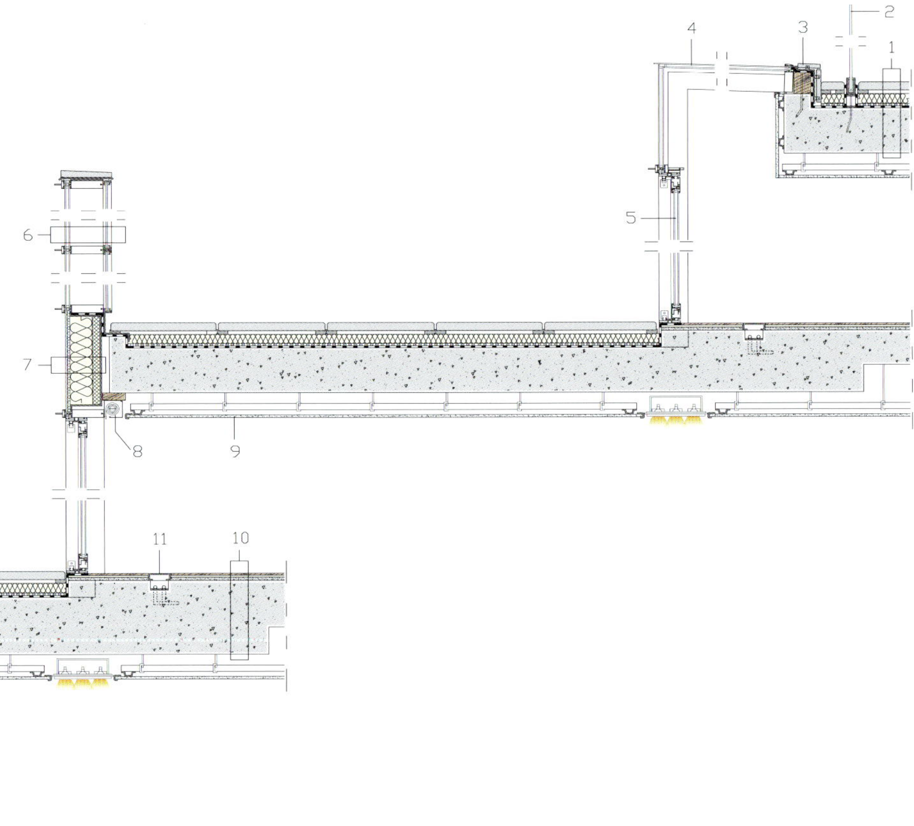

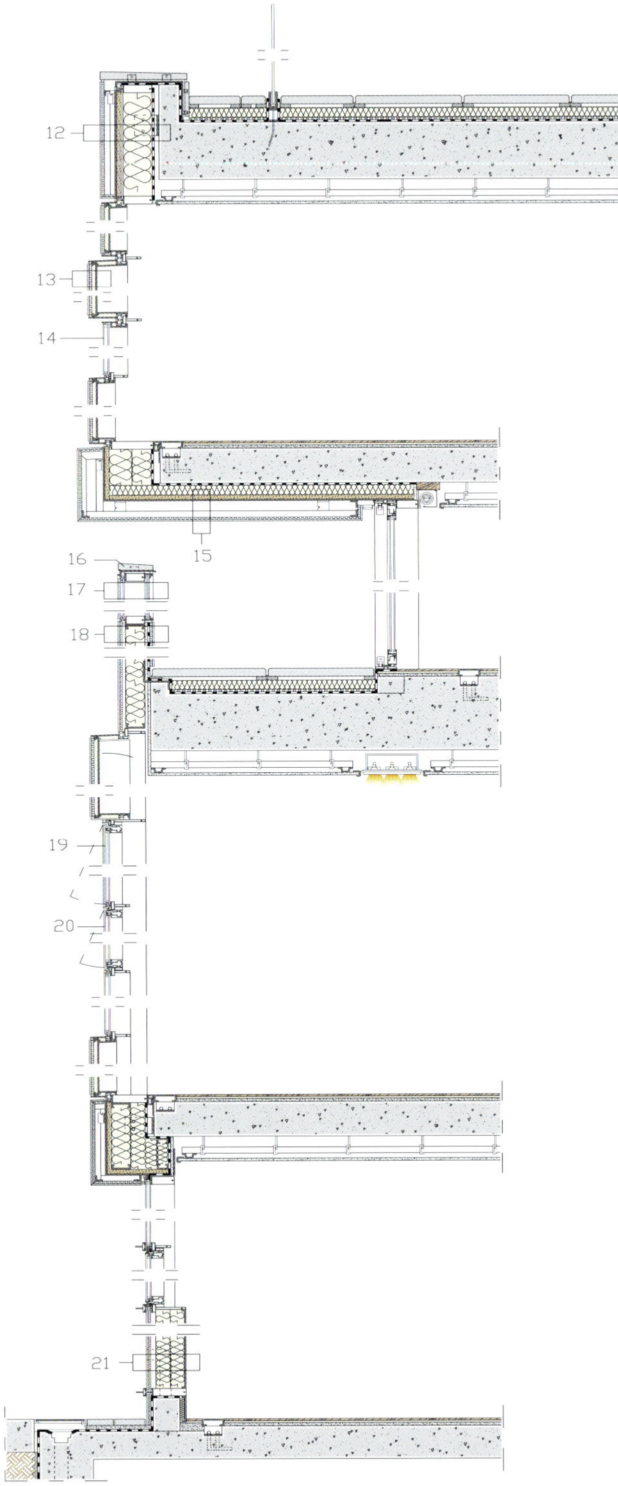

DETAIL A
CONSTRUCTION SYSTEM
VERTICAL SECTION - SCALE 1:40

1. Walk-on roof comprising 2″ (50 mm) concrete blocks on pedestals, 2 3/8″ (60 mm) rigid insulation, drainage panel, waterproofing membrane, 11″ (280 mm) reinforced concrete slab
2. Railing comprising laminated glass in steel U-profiles and steel plates anchored to slab
3. 1″ (25 mm) stone slab on steel L-profiles
4. Skylight with 1/4 - 1/2 - 5/16″ (6/14/8 mm) aluminum glazing unit in aluminum frame
5. Sliding aluminum door with 1/4 - 5/8 - 1/4″ (6/16/6 mm) glazing unit
6. Railing comprising aluminum frame and 1/4 - 5/8 - 1/4″ (6/16/6 mm) glazing unit, frame of 7 1/2″ (190 mm) aluminum, double 1/4″ (6 mm) laminated glass on aluminum profile supports
7. Floor course fascia comprising 1″ (25 mm) aluminum honeycomb stone panels, 4 7/8″ (125 mm) rigid insulation, 1 5/8″ (40 mm) flame-retardant layer, aluminum sheeting
8. Roller blind
9. False ceiling comprising 5/8″ (16 mm) gypsum board on aluminum omega profiles and frame of C-profiles suspended by tie rods from slab
10. Oak floorboards, sound-absorbing matting, leveling layer, 18 1/8″ (460 mm) reinforced concrete slab
11. Air conditioning grate
12. Façade comprising 1″ (25 mm) aluminum honeycomb stone cladding, steel upright support, 1″ (25 mm) aluminum-reinforced plywood panel, 6 1/2″ (165 mm) frame of aluminum profiles sandwiching insulation, vapor barrier, 5 1/2 x 5 1/8″ (140x130 mm) steel L-profile
13. Façade comprising 1″ (25 mm) aluminum honeycomb stone cladding, 3/4″ (20 mm) insulation layer, aluminum sheeting trim
14. Façade comprising 1/4 - 3/4 - 3/8″ (6/20/8 mm) glazing units on aluminum profiles
15. False ceiling comprising 1″ (25 mm) aluminum honeycomb stone panels on aluminum L-profiles and profile anchors, 1″ (25 mm) aluminum-reinforced plywood panel, insulation layer
16. Stone handrail on steel flashing
17. Railing comprising 1/4 + 1/4 - 1/2 - 5/16″ (6+6/14/8 mm) glazing unit with 4 3/4″ (120 mm) stone finish in aluminum frame, 3/8 + 1/8″ (9+3 mm) glass and stone panel
18. Railing comprising 1″ (25 mm) aluminum honeycomb stone panels on aluminum frame, frame of 4 3/8 x 1 1/8″ (110x30 mm) steel C-profiles sandwiching insulation, 5/8″ (16 mm) protective panel, 1″ (25 mm) aluminum honeycomb stone panel
19. Window with Schüco aluminum frame and 1/4 + 5/16 - 1/2 - 5/16″ (6+8/14/8 mm) glazing unit lined by stone panels
20. Window with Schüco aluminum frame and 5/16 - 1/2 - 5/16″ (8/14/8 mm) glazing unit
21. Façade comprising 1″ (25 mm) aluminum honeycomb stone cladding on aluminum frame, 1 1/4″ (30 mm) air space, double 3 1/8″ (80 mm) rigid insulation, aluminum sheeting finish
22. 5 7/8″ (150 mm) reinforced concrete railing, waterproofing membrane, steel flashing
23. Glazed façade with Schüco aluminum frame and 1/4 - 5/8 - 1/4″ (6/16/6 mm) glazing units
24. False ceiling comprising 1″ (25 mm) ipe boards, frame of aluminum C-profiles suspended by tie rods from slab, 2 3/4″ (70 mm) rigid insulation, vapor barrier
25. Railing comprising shaped steel plates and Ø 1/2″ (12 mm) steel tie rods and aluminum handrail
26. Aluminum casing, insulation fill
27. 9 7/8 x 9 7/8″ (250x250 mm) steel box girder

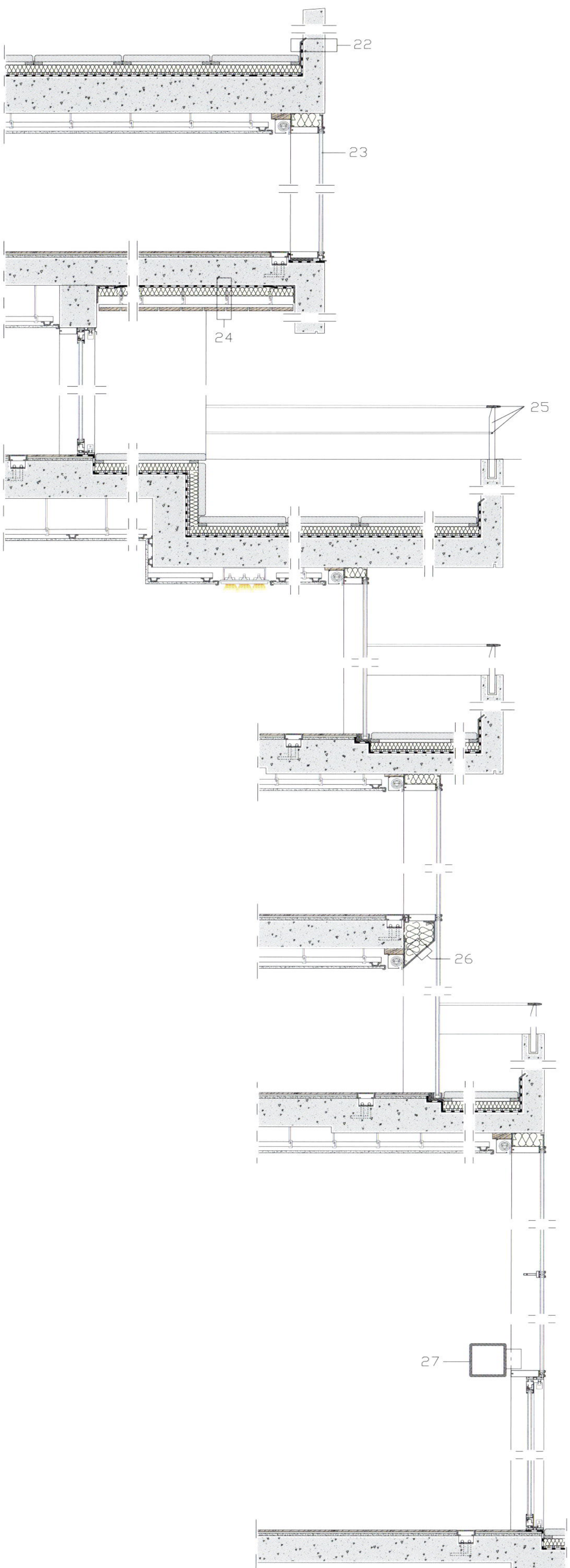

22
23
24
25
26
27

ELQUI DOMOS
ASTRONOMICAL HOTEL

PISCO ELQUI, PAIHUANO, CHILE

RODRIGO DUQUE MOTTA

Chile's narrow Elqui Valley is a thin stretch of land between the Andes and a coastal mountain chain. The landscape, its natural colours, unpolluted skies and mild climate make it an ideal place for winegrowing, astronomy and peaceful contemplation.

In operation for ten years, the Elqui Domos hotel recently decided to make over and enlarge its premises. Designed by Rodrigo Duque Motta, the new programme not only melts seamlessly into its context, it also offers guests intimate settings from which to observe the natural scenery all around.

The original hotel comprised a restaurant and seven translucent fabric domes. To these have been added four detached wooden cabins. The new project is wholly at one with its natural setting. Like the older, tent-like fabric domes, the cabins simply rest on the ground, fitting into the landscape without disruption, respectfully slipping in between vegetation and natural outcrops.

Located a short distance from the pre-existing structures, each cabin is surrounded by a small garden with native trees and bushes. The maisonettes resemble a little village nestled at the foot of a mountain.

Not one single element - from the volume itself to the materials used and the internal layout - that does not speak of intimate, total and exclusive communion with nature.

Each unit is entirely clad in dark timber slats. When doors and shutters are closed to shield occupants from the light, the dark wood cabins can hardly be distinguished from the surrounding vegetation. A short flight of steps leads to the living area. Inside, light-coloured timber-clad walls and floors frame views onto the trees in the foreground and valley beyond through a large picture window shielded by sliding shutters. Each room relates intimately yet differently with the outside. A few broad steps lead from the living area to a raised night zone. Here, inclined glazed walls and ceilings give extensive views of the heavens from the bed, creating exclusive, intimate stargazing vantage points for its occupants.

An outside staircase leads from the night zone up to a third room: a semi-outdoor space delimited only by timber slat partitions, the ultimate place in which to feel completely at one with the extensive Chilean landscape.

■ East elevation - Scale 1:100

■ Siteplan - Scale 1:400

1. Entrance
2. Lounge
3. Lobby
4. Domes
5. Observatories

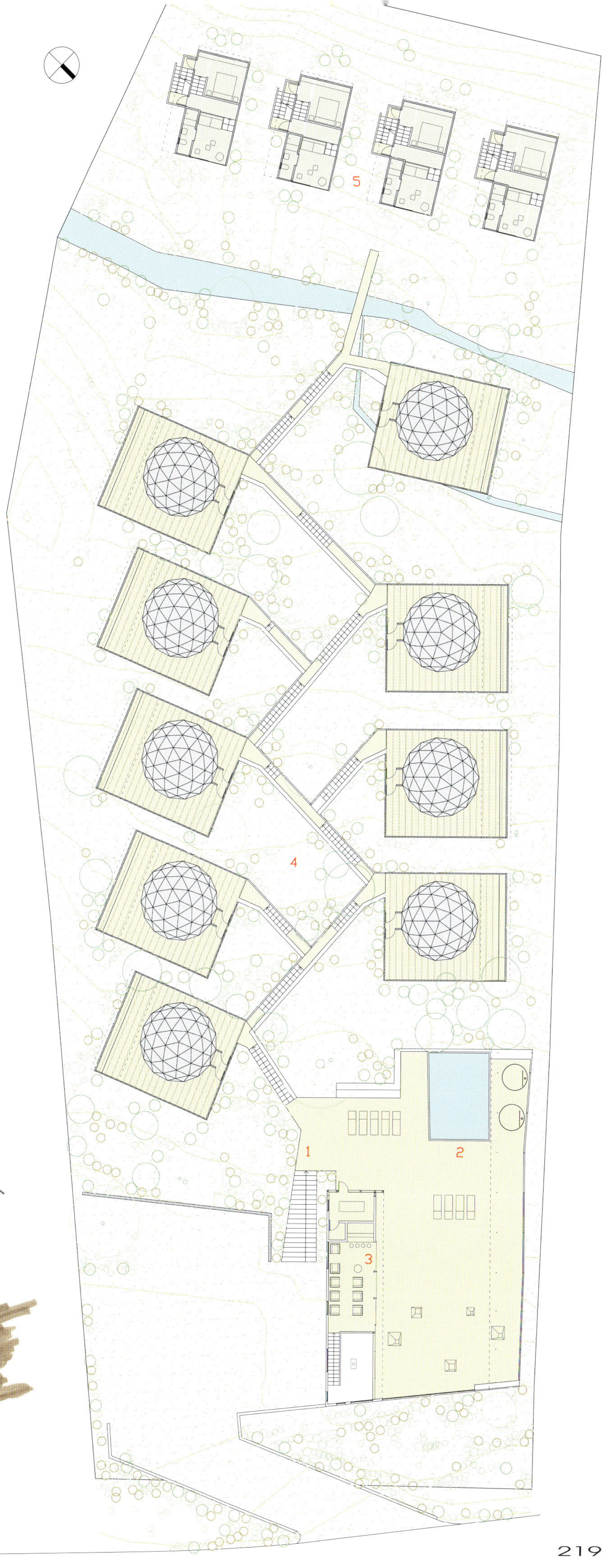

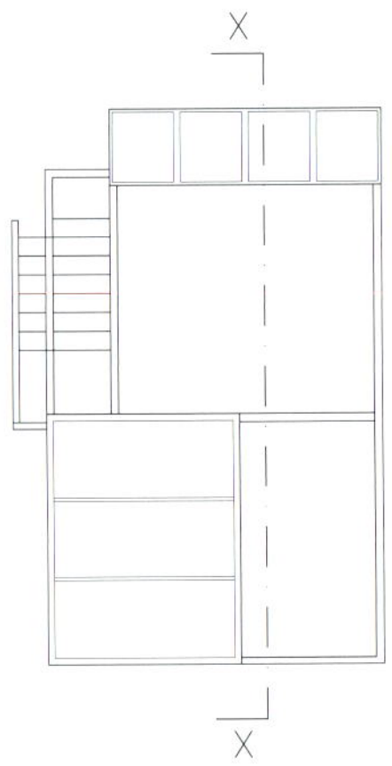

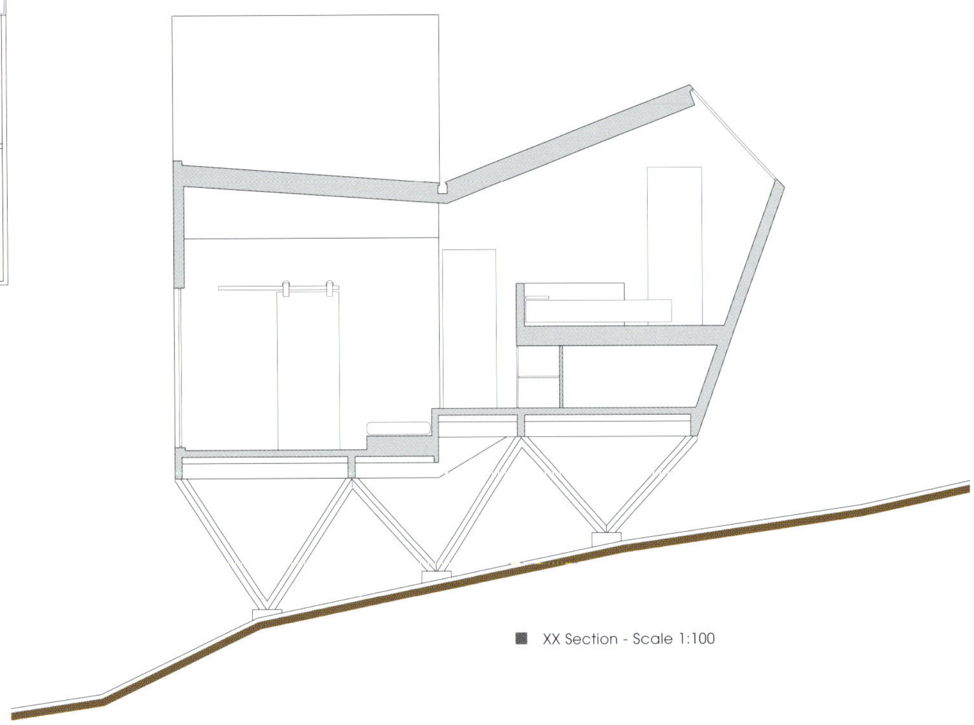

■ XX Section - Scale 1:100

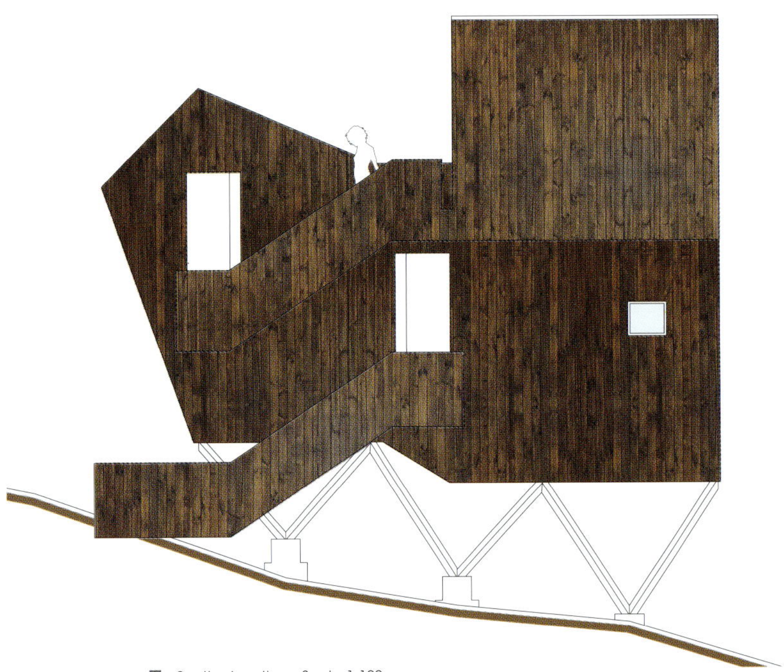

■ South elevation - Scale 1:100

DETAIL A: CONSTRUCTION SYSTEM
VERTICAL SECTION - SCALE 1:30

1. 3/4″ (20 mm) pine board cladding with feathered joints, waterproofing membrane, 3/8″ (10 mm) OSB panel, frame of 2 x 2 7/8″ (50x75 mm) timber sandwiching insulation, 3/8″ (10 mm) OSB panel, 3/4″ (20 mm) timber boarding
2. Skylight for star gazing with aluminum frame, 1 1/4 x 2″ (30x50 mm) aluminum box-profiles and 3/16″ (5 mm) glass
3. Aluminum profile supporting blackout blind
4. Roof comprising 2x4″ (50x100 mm) pine shingles on timber beams (parallel to plane of section), zinc aluminum sheeting, acoustic membrane, 5/8″ (15 mm) multilayer wood panel, 2 x 7 7/8″ (50x200 mm) timber rafters sandwiching 4″ (100 mm) thick insulation, 3/4″ (20 mm) timber boarding
5. Zinc aluminum guttering
6. 3/4″ (20 mm) feathered pine floorboards, 3/4″ (20 mm) multilayer wood panel, 2 x 7 7/8″ (50x200 mm) joists sandwiching 2″ (50 mm) insulation
7. Parapet consisting of 2 x 2″ (50x50 mm) timber finished with 3/4″ (20 mm) timber with timber handrail
8. 2 x 2 7/8″ (50x75 mm) timber cabinet frame
9. Timber beam structure on concrete plinths supporting the house

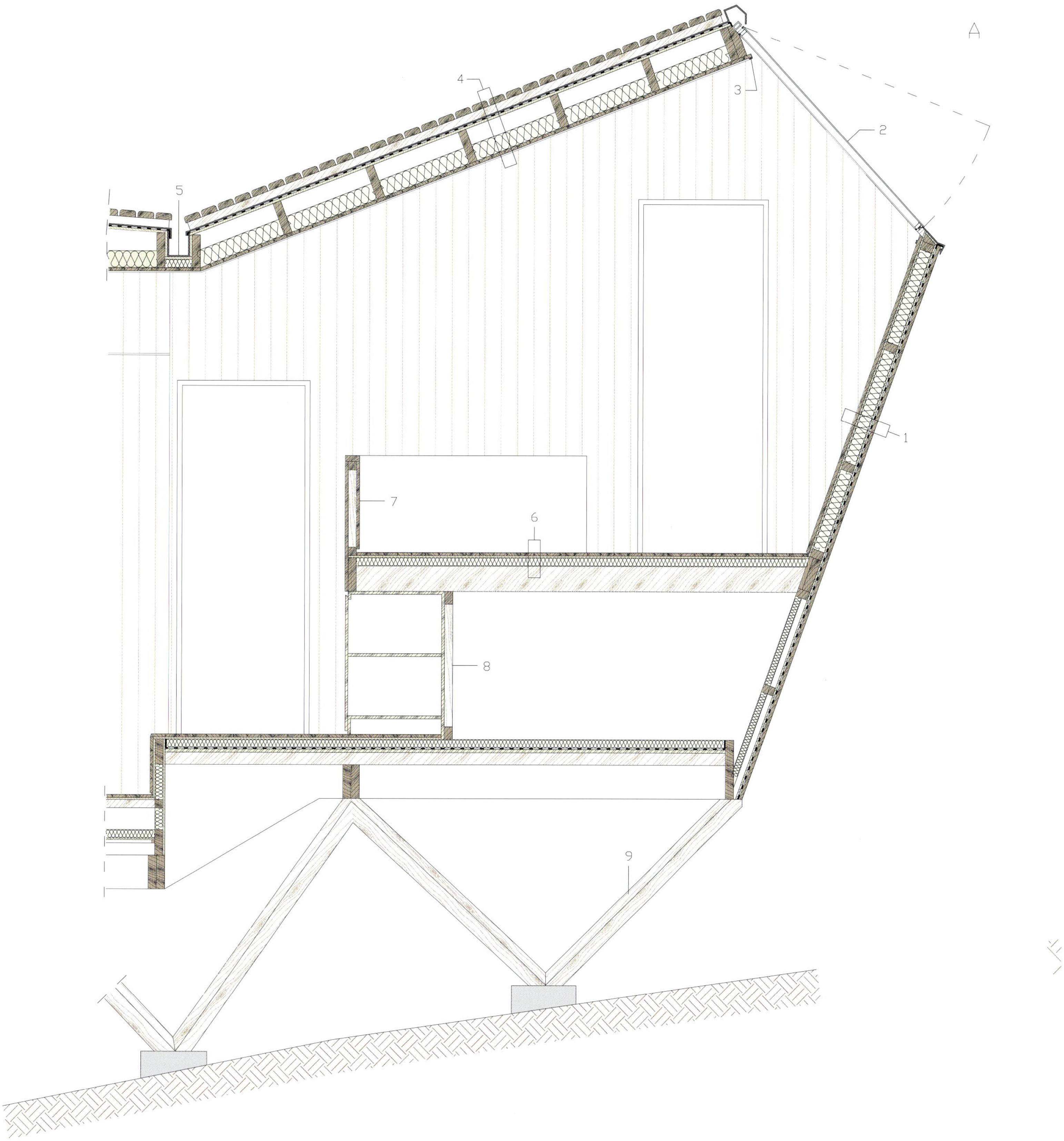
A
1
2
3
4
5
6
7
8
9

OBERHOLZ OBEREGGEN

OBEREGGEN, ITALY

PETER PICHLER ARCHITECTURE
WITH PAVOL MIKOLAJCAK

The Alps seem to have become the training ground for good architecture. It may be on account of the breathtaking landscape, or the inescapable requirement to guarantee unfailing quality of structure and finish, or the increasing environmental awareness of tourists. Whatever the reason, Alpine architecture is at the forefront of contemporary architecture.

Not that it was not before. This has always been the case practically since the Alps were discovered by the Grand Tour and its vernacular architecture became the subject of study, admired and tapped for the perfect technological solutions born of empirical know-how under inhospitable high-altitude mountain conditions. When, however, after two centuries, élite tourism gave way to mass tourism, mountain landscapes also were subjected to assault. Concrete eyesores rose up in complete disregard for the volumes and stratified materials developed down the years in keeping with their natural surroundings and age-old building traditions. A swathe of sterile, shortsighted archetypes spread across the Alps, from the Maritime Alps in the west to the eastern Giulie region, exclusively in the name of business and building.

Recently - perhaps because the low lands have been exploited to breaking point - there has been renewed interest in the mountains and what they can teach us. The focus is once again on what the albeit few, but outstanding architects, like Carlo Mollino and Edoardo Gellner, have handed down to us. We are rediscovering an environment, which however familiar - all northern Italians are very much aware they are surrounded by a semicircle of mountains - remains what it has always been: a challenge. For mountains are difficult places, requiring courage, inventiveness and real know-how as to the assembly of materials and the optimization of form.

The Milan firm Peter Pichler Architecture, in partnership with architect Pavol Mikolajcak, provides a fine example of how contemporary architecture can fit into a mountain environment intelligently and sensitively but without forgoing the ambition to build something arresting and compelling. Standing at an altitude of 2,096 m, the recently completed Oberholz Mountain Hut at Obereggen in Italy's South Tyrolean (Alto Adige) Dolomites - a Unesco World Heritage landscape - was built from sustainable materials. Started with a competition in 2015

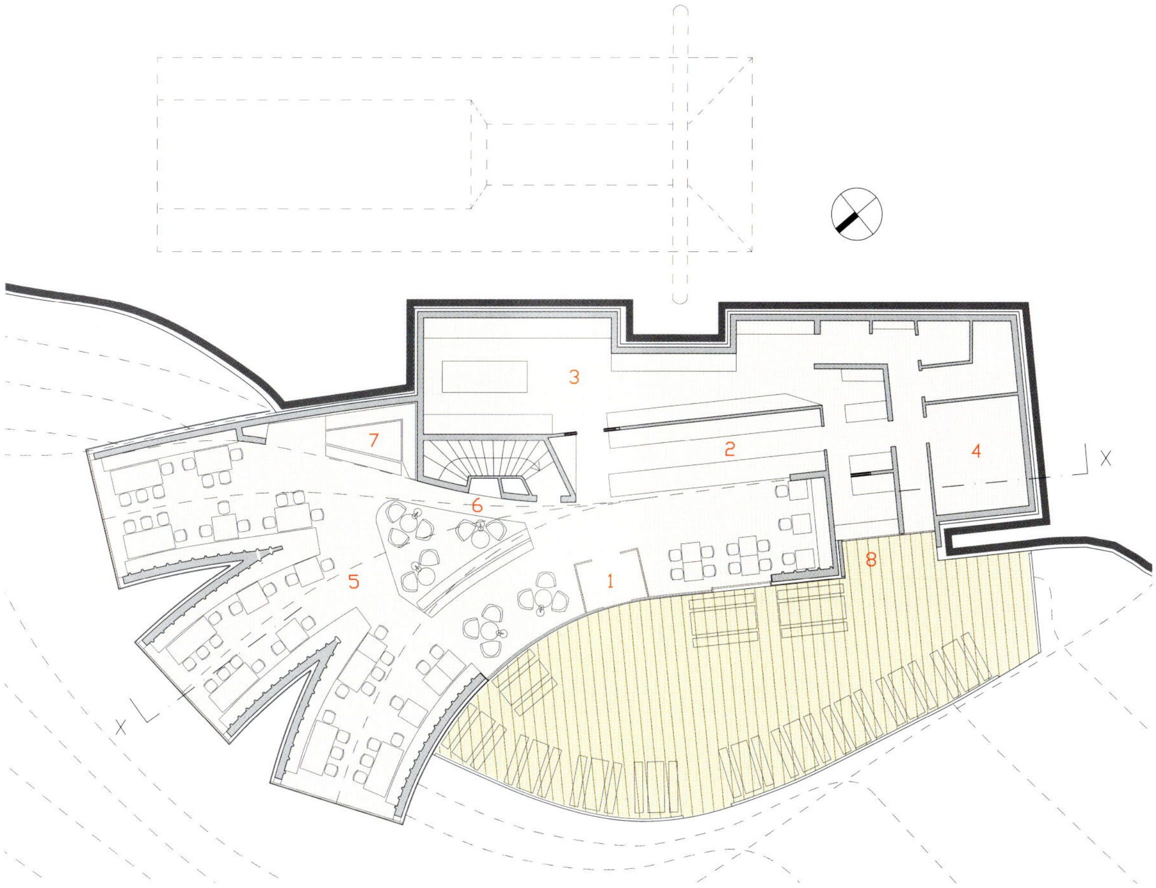

■ Ground floor plan - Scale 1:300

1. Entrance
2. Café
3. Kitchen
4. Storage
5. Restaurant
6. Fireplace / Lounge area
7. Stube
8. Panoramic café
9. Staff rooms
10. Technical room

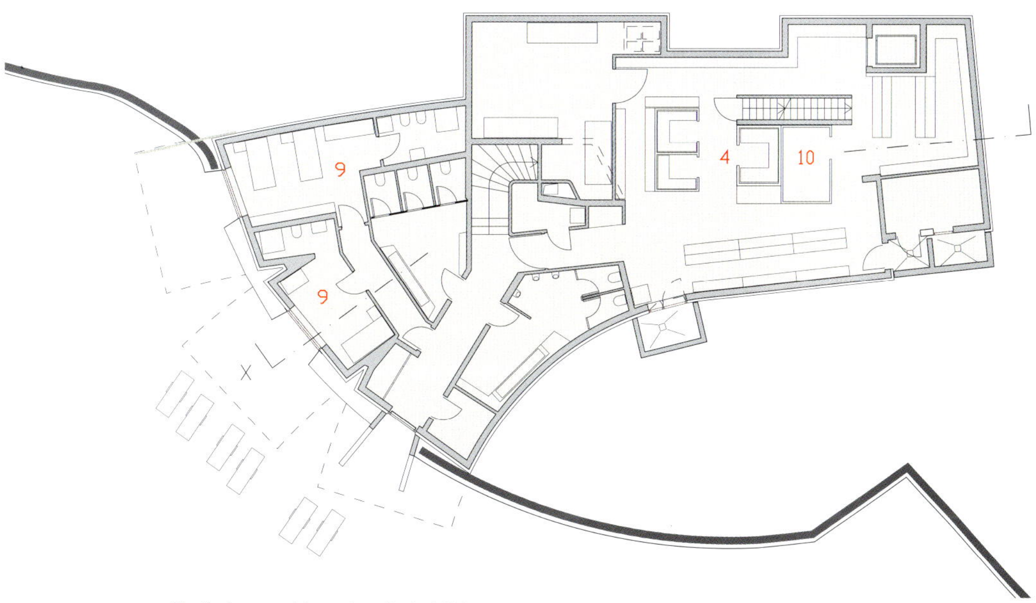

■ Underground floor plan - Scale 1:300

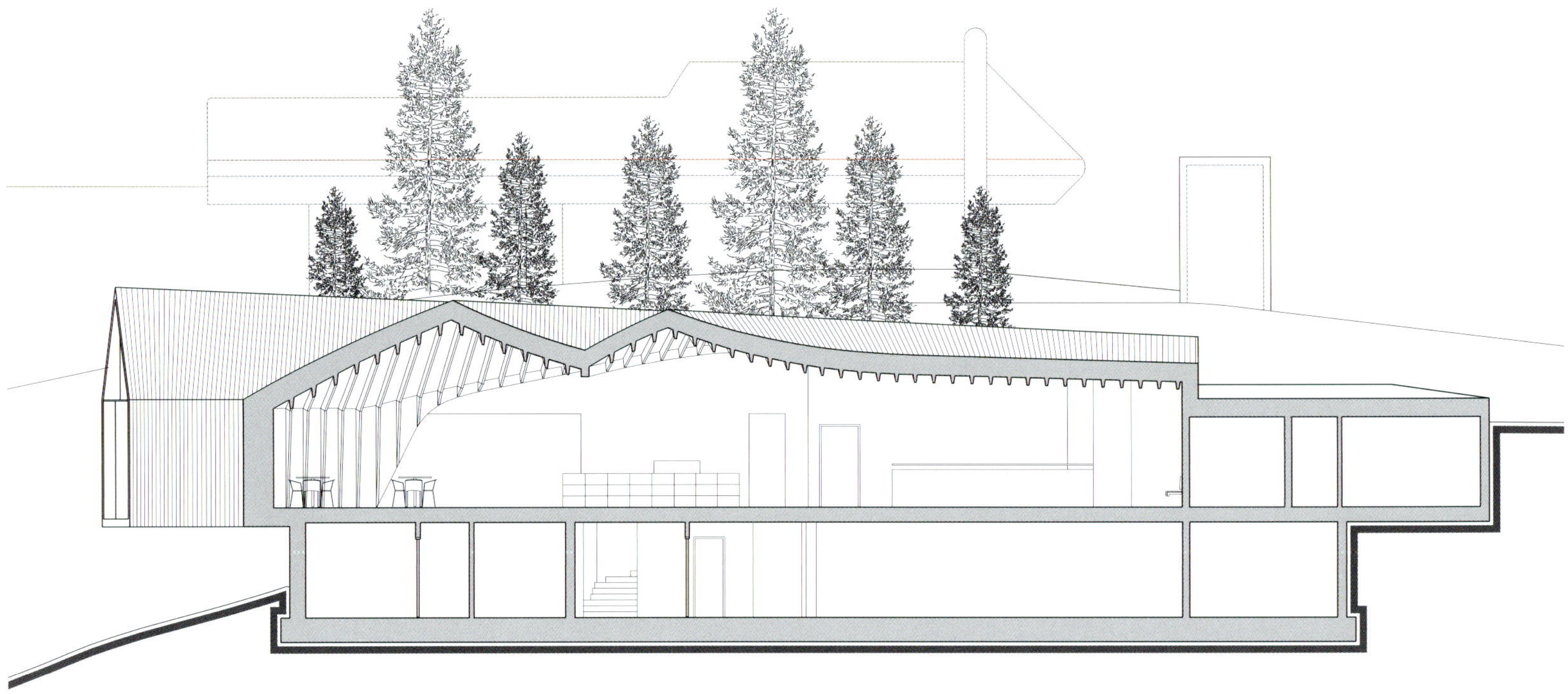

■ XX Section - Scale 1:200

and opened for the 2016/17 skiing season, it combines a new take on a hospitality facility with contemporary tourist requirements.

The hut has a dual personality: a concrete volume set partly underground in the dolomite rock and housing various service functions; and a wooden construction anchored to the concrete structure below. It is here that the architects show their prowess with archetypes, designing a unique, arresting piece of architecture.

The plan of the above-grade timber volume spreads out like a three-fingered hand, the tip of each finger projecting towards one of the major summits in the region: the Mendel, the Black Horn and the White Horn. Each fingertip has a transparent crystal glass front, its shape an almost playful reference to the *naïf* pitched roof and gable archetype. The impression from the outside is of a simple hut structure clad in juxtaposed larch slats splaying out towards the mountains like three closely set telescopes - three unobtrusive little constructions with sweeping views over the Latemar mountain chain. It is inside that the miracle becomes apparent. You find yourself standing in a magnificent Gothic cathedral, the long line of imposing red spruce trusses emphasizing the building's sinuous geometry. Three curving naves are generated by the conventional pitched roof shapes. The tapering structural ribs dissolve into the walls, giving the impression of a single volume, an impression reinforced by the varying fir-paneled widths separating the truss elements.

Functionally, the main environments - restaurant, small lounge, bar and kitchens - are on the ground level. A second small bar to the side facing the valley connects to a large open-air panoramic terrace, used both summer and winter. As mentioned, the semi-basement area is occupied by restrooms, storage and staff quarters, the unconcealed reinforced concrete frame dialoguing to great effect with the warm wood enveloping the hut interiors.

The facility can be directly reached from the chair lift a few meters away, either by means of a lift that takes visitors directly into the building, or on foot along the road leading to the *piste* running past the hut and right up to the terrace that also serves as the main entrance.

DETAIL A: NORTHERN FAÇADE
VERTICAL SECTION - SCALE 1:20

1. Glazed curtain wall comprising 3/8 - 5/8 - 5/16 - 5/8 - 3/16 + 3/16″ (10/16/8/16/5+5 mm) glazing units with exterior pane with 3/4 - 1″ (20–25 cm) fritted edging, structural frame of steel C-profiles and 3 x 6 1/4″ (75x160 mm) steel plates
2. 1 5/8 x 1 5/8″ (40x40 mm) steel L-profile edging
3. Roof constructed using LignoAlp prefabricated roofing comprising 1 1/4″ (30 mm) larch decking, 1″ (25 mm) timber (parallel to plane of section), 1 1/4 x 2″ (30x50 mm) timber beams, waterproofing membrane, 4 7/8″ (125 mm) rigid insulation, vapor barrier, 3/4″ (20 mm) larch boards
4. 3/4″ (20 mm) larch panels, structural frame of 9 1/2″ (240 mm) h steel I-beams
5. Prefabricated LignoAlp structural entrance with red fir glulam beams
6. 3/4″ (20 mm) larch panel infill, steel Z-profile anchor sandwiching 1 5/8″ (40 mm) rigid insulation, 1 1/8 x 2 3/8″ (30x60 mm) timber supports
7. Ventilation system comprising 5/8″ (16 mm) steel grille on supporting steel C- and L-profiles and composite steel plates
8. 1″ (25 mm) oak floorboards, glue, screed with embedded floor heating, 3/4″ (20 mm) rigid insulation, vapor barrier, 2″ (50 mm) foamed concrete, cantilevered 7 7/8″ (200 mm) reinforced concrete slab, 3 1/8″ (80 mm) rigid insulation, waterproofing membrane, 1″ (25 mm) timber beam (parallel to plane of section), 1 1/4″ (30 mm) larch finish

CREDITS

EXPANSION OF PORTLAND
JAPANESE GARDEN
PORTLAND, USA
KENGO KUMA AND ASSOCIATES

Location / Luogo: Portland, Oregon, USA - **Client / Committente:** Portland Japanese Garden - **Completion Date:** 2017 - **Total Construction Cost:** 29,240,000 Euros - **Gross Floor Area:** 1,432 m² - **Architect:** Kengo Kuma and Associates - **Project Architects:** Kengo Kuma, Balazs Bognar - **Architect of Record:** Hacker Architects - **Interior Design:** Kengo Kuma and Associates - **Structural and Civil:** KPFF Consulting Engineers - **Geotechnical:** GRI - **MEP:** PAE Engineers - **Landscape:** Sadafumi Uchiyama, Walker Macy - **Sustainability:** Green Building Services - **Lighting:** Luma Lighting Design - **Acoustics:** Listen Acoustics - **General Contractor:** Hoffman Construction Company - **Roofing:** Bassett Construction, Pure+Freeform, DNP - **Interior Furnishings:** Hacker Architects - **Japanese Castle Walls:** Suminori Awata, O'Driscoll Stone, Green Man Builders, Stone Sculptures, Alpine Boulder Company - **Metal-glass Curtain Wall:** Arcadia - **Ceramic Roof Panels:** Komatsu Seiren - **Main Entry Doors:** Nakamura Komuten **Main Interior Wood Screens and Ceiling:** Takumi Company - **Carpentry:** Straight Up Carpentry - **Sliding Doors:** Vitrocsa - **Tiles and Wall Fabric:** Lixil, Kawashima Selkon - **Custom Furniture:** Time & Style, George Nakashima Woodworker - **Bathroom and Kitchen Fixtures:** DXV, American Standard, INAX/LIXIL

ELBPHILHARMONIE
HAMBURG, GERMANY
HERZOG & DE MEURON

Location: Hamburg, Germany - **Client:** Free and Hanseatic City of Hamburg - **Completion Date:** 2016 - **Site Area:** 10,540 m² - **Gross Floor Area:** 125,512 m² - **Architect:** Herzog & de Meuron - **Partners:** Jacques Herzog, Pierre de Meuron, Ascan Mergenthaler, David Koch - **Project Director:** Jan Christoph Lindert - **Project Architects:** Nicholas Lyons, Stefan Goeddertz - **Project Management:** Christian Riemenschneider, Henning Severmann, Stephan Wedrich, Carsten Happel, Birgit Föllmer, Kai Zang, Peter Scherz, Jan Per Grosch - **Main Contractor:** Adamanta Grundstücks-Vermietungsgesellschaft - **Structural:** Hochtief Solutions, WGG Schnetzer Puskas Ingenieure, Rohwer Ingenieure - **Brick Façade:** Jäger Ingenieure - **Façade Maintenance:** Manfred Helmus Ingenieurpartnerschaft - **Fire Protection:** Hahn Consult Ingenieurgesellschaft **Wind Engineering:** Wacker Ingenieure - **HVAC, Mechanical, Plumbing:** Hochtief Solutions, Knott & Partner Ingenieure, Müller + Partner, CATS Computer and Technology Service, ARGE Generalplaner Elbphilharmonie, Winter Ingenieure - **Climate:** Transsolar - **Noise Control:** Taubert und Ruhe - **Acoustics:** Nagata Acoustics - **Audio-visual:** Peutz Consult, Ahnert Design Acoustic - **Scenography:** ARGE Planung Elbphilharmonie, BAA Projektmanagement, Generalplaner Elbphilharmonie, Ducks Sceno, GCA Ingenieure - **Planning:** Joint Venture Arbeitsgemeinschaft Planung Elbphilharmonie (Herzog & de Meuron, H+P Planungsgesellschaft, Hochtief Solutions) **3D Modelling:** Hochtief ViCon - **Steel Construction:** Spannverbund Gesellschaft für Verbundträger, Haslinger Stahlbau - **Stage System and Equipment:** Waagner-Biro - **Wooden Panelling:** Eichhorn **Organ:** Klais Orgelbau - **Seatings:** Poltrona Frau - **Façade Consultant and Manufacturer:** Josef Gartner (Permasteelisa Group) - **Glass for Façades:** AGC Interpane, Guardian Glass - **Lighting:** Zumtobel Group **Sanitary Equipment:** Duravit

AUDITORIUM AND CULTURAL CENTER
CUERNAVACA AND TEOTITLÁN
DEL VALLE, MEXICO
PRODUCTORA

TEOPANZOLCO AUDITORIUM

Location: Cuernavaca, Morelos, Mexico - **Client:** Cultural Secretary of the State of Morelos - **Architects:** Isaac Broid + Productora (Carlos Bedoya, Víctor Jaime, Wonne Ickx, Abel Perles) - **Gross Floor Area:** 7,000 m² - **Completion Date:** 2017 - **Structural Frame:** Colinas del Buen - **Technical Engineering:** M2 - **Theater:** Alejandro Luna and Itzel Alba - **Acoustics:** Cristian Ezcurdia, Arup - **Lighting:** Luz y Forma - **Bioclimatic System:** Bioarquitectura - **Bathroom Fittings:** Helvex, Bobrick - **Lighthing:** Brillant, Prommsa, Illux, Philips, Leviton

COMMUNITY CULTURAL CENTER

Location: Teotitlán del Valle, Oaxaca, Mexico - **Client:** Municipality of Teotitlán del Valle - **Architect:** Productora (Carlos Bedoya, Víctor Jaime, Wonne Ickx, Abel Perles) - **Gross Floor Area:** 1,700 m² - **Main Contractor:** Bonarq Diseño (Ismael Rojas) - **Structural:** Kaltia Consultores, DAE **Technical Engineering:** BioE - **Landscape:** Taller de Paisaje

REID BUILDING, GLASGOW SCHOOL OF ART
GLASGOW, UK
STEVEN HOLL ARCHITECTS

Location: Glasgow, Scotland, UK - **Client:** The Glasgow School of Art - **Architect:** Steven Holl Architects - **Design Architects:** Steven Holl, Chris McVoy - **Partners-in-Charge:** Chris McVoy, Noah Yaffe - **Project Architect:** Dominik Sigg - **Assistant Project Architect:** Dimitra Tsachrelia **Associate Architects:** JM Architects - **Project Manager:** Turner & Townsend - **Gross Floor Area:** 11,646 m² - **General Contractor:** Sir Robert McAlpine **Engineering:** Ove Arup & Partners - **Quantity Surveyor:** Turner & Townsend - **Landscape Architect:** Michael Van Valkenburgh and Associates **Planning:** Turley Associates - **Metal Panels for Exterior Cladding:** Stainless Sections - **Curtain Wall System:** Jansen Viss - **Roofing:** Bauder Total Roofing System - **Glazing:** Saint Gobain - **Wood Doors:** European Doorsets - **Acoustical Ceilings:** 2T Joiners - **Carpet:** Tretford - **Furnishings:** Azzurro, Vitra, Hal, Schmidinger - **Upholstery:** Cappellini, Gambetta, Vitra, Park - **Interior Lighting:** Skinflint Design, iGuzzini, Delta Light, Elektroled, Encapsulite, Aether, Acdc - **Downlights:** Wila, Whitecroft, Cooper, Regent, Versa Engineering, GE Lighting, Lighting Science Group, Selux, Thorn, Erco - **Windows and Façade Aluminum Systems:** Schüco - **Fixed Seatings:** Poltrona Frau

MAPUNGUBWE INTERPRETATION CENTRE
LIMPOPO, SOUTH AFRICA
PETER RICH ARCHITECTS

Location: Mapungubwe, South Africa - **Completion:** 2009 - **Gross Floor Area:** 984 m² - **Construction Costs:** 1,050,000 Euros - **Client:** SANParks (South African National Parks) - **Architect:** Peter Rich - **Design Team:** Lineo Leratholi, Desrae Dunn, Abdullah Abass, Anne Fitchett, Heinrich Kammeyer, Franz Prinsloo - **Structural:** John Ochsendorf (Massachusetts Institute of Technology), Michael Ramage (Cambridge University), James Bellamy, Henry Fagan and Mark Mallin (Henry Fagan & Partners) - **Technical:** James Bellamy

CREDITS

GRACE FARMS
NEW CANAAN, USA
SANAA KAZUYO SEJIMA + RYUE NISHIZAWA

Location: New Canaan, Connecticut, USA - **Completion Date:** 2015 - **Architect:** SANAA, Kazuyo Sejima + Ryue Nishizawa **Design Team:** Shohei Yoshida, Takayuki Hasegawa, Tommy Haddock - **Executive Architect:** Handel Architects **Project Manager:** Paratus Group - **Construction Manager:** Sciame - **Structural:** Robert Silman Associates - **Landscape:** Olin, Larry Weaner Landscape - **MEP and Lighting:** Buro Happold - **Civil:** McChord Engineering - **Sustainability:** Transsolar - **Acoustics:** Harvey Marshall Berling Associates, Nagata Acoustics - **Geotechnical:** Langan Engineering - **Geothermal:** Alderson Engineering **Soils and Wetlands:** Environmental Planning Services - **Conservation Planning and Herpetologist:** Michael W. Klemens - **Graphics:** Pentagram **Building Envelope:** Front - **Glazing:** Roschmann Steel & Glass - **Roofing:** Zahner

KIBERA HAMLETS SCHOOL
NAIROBI, KENYA
SELGASCANO & HELLOEVERYTHING

Location: Nairobi, Kenya - **Client:** Kibera Hamlets - **Site Area:** 150.36 m² - **Built area:** 136 m² - **Architects:** SelgasCano, helloeverything - **Local Architect:** Abdul Fatah Adam (Studio.14) - **Financed** by Second Home London, Louisiana Museum and Kibera Hamlets School, with the contribution of the sale of crafts made by local women - **Built and Run** by members of Kibera Hamlets

FREDERIKSBERG COURTHOUSE
COPENHAGEN, DENMARK
3XN

Location: Frederiksberg, Denmark - **Client:** Bygningsstyrelsen - **Completion Date:** 2012 - **Gross Floor Area:** 8.200 m² - **Architect:** 3XN **Project Team:** Kim Herforth Nielsen, Jan Ammundsen, Bo Boje Larsen, Dorthe Toft Boesen, Marie Hesseldahl Larsen, Eva Hviid-Nielsen, Audun Opdal, Bodil Nordstrøm, Laila Fyhn Feldthaus, Olaf Kunert, Noel Wibrand, Stine de Bang, Tine Skov, Andreas Herborg Nielsen, Robin Vind Christiansen, Rune Bech, Umut Üsüdür, Berglind Halla Elfudottir - **Engineer:** Lemming & Eriksson - **Landscape Architect:** Schønherr Landskab **Light Artist:** Steven Scott - **Solar Shading:** Viking Markiser, Photosolar - **Solar Cells:** Direct Energy - **Internal Windows Foil:** Modulex - **Window Frames:** Hueck - **Signs:** DanSign - **Green Roof:** Vegtech - **Doors:** Jeldween - **Façade Cladding:** Strøjer Tegl - **Wallpanels in Courtrooms:** Moelven

COPENHAGEN INTERNATIONAL
SCHOOL NORDHAVN
COPENHAGEN, DENMARK
C. F. MØLLER

Location: Copenhagen, Denmark - **Client:** Copenhagen International School - **Completion Date:** 2017 - **Gross Floor Area:** 26,000 m² - **Architect:** C.F. Møller Architects - **Landscape Architect:** C.F. Møller Landscape - **Main Contractor:** Per Aarsleff - **Structural:** Niras - **Information and Communications Technologies:** CN3 - **Energy Management:** KT Elektric Aalborg, DTEK - **Partitions:** Troels Hansen - **Railings:** LS-Trapper og Stål - **Floors:** Miko Gulve, Pihl Coating - **Paints:** Malerfirma Peter Munck & Søn - **Carpentry:** Tømrer MGB Entreprise - **Ceilings:** JS Ventilation - **Interior Glass Partitions:** Alutec Glas Aluminium - **Doors:** Jeld-Wen - **Fire Insulation:** City Lak - **Sunshades and Curtains:** Blendex - **Sports and Theater Equipment:** Virklund Sport - **Technical Equipment:** SSI-Skandinavisk Skoleinventar - **Playground Equipment:** Kompan - **Solar Panels:** SolarLab - **Greenhouses:** Drivhuse-Drivadan - **Wood Fins, Glass Panels and Sandwich Elements:** Eiler Thomsen Alufacader

RENOVATION OF LES DOCKS
MARSEILLE, FRANCE
ALFONSO FEMIA WITH 5+1AA

Location: Marseille, France - **Client:** JPMorgan, Constructa Urban Systems - **Gross Floor Area:** 21,000 m^2 - **Cost:** 21,000,000 Euros - **Completion Date:** 2015 - **Architectural and Landscape Design:** 5+1AA Alfonso Femia Gianluca Peluffo - **Architects:** Alfonso Femia, Gianluca Peluffo, Simonetta Cenci, Nicola Spinetto - **Project Director:** Nicola Spinetto - **Project Leader:** Sara Traverso - **Design Team:** Alfonso Femia, Gianluca Peluffo, Simonetta Cenci, Sara Gottardo, Nicola Spinetto, Sara Traverso, Fanélie Pardon, Valeria Parodi, Sara Massa, Luca Bonsignorio, Carola Picasso, Lorenza Barabino - **Collaborators:** Alessandro Bellus, Francesco Busto, Suzanne Jubert, Etienne Bourdais, Gabriele Filippi, M. Cristina Giordani, Valentina Grimaldi, Roberto Mancini, Aude Rasson, Giulia Tubelli - **Developer:** Constructa Urban Systems **Main Contractor:** Dumez Méditerranée (société de VINCI Construction France) - **Structural:** Secmo - **Services Engineering:** Garcia Ingénierie **Quality and Safety:** Bureau Veritas - **Economy Control:** R2M - **North Façade:** Tapiro design - **Artist:** Danilo Trogu - **Wood Flooring:** Xilo1934 **Metal Frames, Rings and Ceramic Structure:** Bodino Engineering Metal Sheet - **Working and Lettering Panels:** Brovetto A. e Figlio **Window Frames:** Effegieffe, Chiri, Secco Sistemi - **Lighting:** Castaldi Lighting - **Frames:** FerroMurano - **Gardening:** Gruppo Giardini, Vannucci Piante **Elevators:** Kone France - **Sheet Steel Structure:** Landragin - **Ceramics:** Casalgrande Padana

PARISH COMPLEX
IN THE DIOCESE OF LODI
LODI, ITALY
CORVINO+MULTARI

Location: Dresano, Milan, Italy - **Clients:** Conferenza Episcopale Italiana, Diocese of Lodi - **Completion Date:** 2017 **Architect:** Corvino+Multari (Vincenzo Corvino, Giovanni Multari) - **Design Team:** Michele Natale, Giovanni Podestà, Marco Poerio, Giovanna Castaldo, Salvatore Carleo **Construction Management:** Ivan Chiesa, Mino Carella, Claudio Rotta - **Main Contractor:** Eco Costruzioni - **Structure:** Studio Salvatoni - **Plant and Equipment:** Luigi Sgobaro - **Acoustics:** Gianpiero Majandi - **Process Director:** Roberto Spagliardi - **Works of Art:** Nino Longobardi - **Lighting:** iGuzzini **Flooring:** Favaro1, Casalgrande Padana - **Concrete:** Colabeton - **Insulation and False Ceilings:** Saint-Gobain - **Roof Systems:** Riverclack **Windows and Door Frames:** Serramenti Del Chiese, Domal - **Curtain Wall:** Wicona - **Sun-shading:** Sunbell - **Skylights:** Velux - **Sound Systems:** RCF **Taps and Fittings:** Grohe - **Acoustic Insulation:** Top Noise Acoustic - **Marble:** Marmo Elite - **Cast Bronze and Aluminum:** Fonderia Nolana Del Giudice **Wood Furniture:** F.lli Schiavone - **Glass:** AGC - **Doors:** Secco Sistemi - **Electrical Equipment:** Vimar

LA SEINE MUSICALE
PARIS, FRANCE
SHIGERU BAN ARCHITECTS EUROPE
WITH JEAN DE GASTINES ARCHITECTES

Location: Paris, France - **Client and Main Contractor:** Bouygues Construction - **Completion Date:** 2017 - **Site Area:** 23,000 m^2 - **Gross Floor Area:** 36,500 m^2 - **Building Area:** 16,000 m^2 - **Architects:** Shigeru Ban Architects Europe with Jean de Gastines Architectes - **Project Managers (Shigeru Ban Architects Europe):** Philippe Monteil, Nicolas Grosmond, Geoffroy Boucher - **Project Team (Shigeru Ban Architects Europe):** Alessandro Boldrini, Masashi Maruyama, Sara Lazzarin, Amélie Fritzlar, Alexis de Dumast, Veronica Arianna, Mathieu Chapus, Patrick Allan **Client Project Manager:** Jean-François Laurent - **General Consultant:** Setec - **Timber:** Blumer-Lehmann - **MEP:** Artelia - **Stage and Hall Equipment Design:** dUCKS scéno - **Acoustics:** Lamoureux Acoustics - **Concert Hall Acoustics:** Nagata Acoustics - **Façade:** RFR, T/E/S/S atelier d'ingénierie - **Landscape:** Bassinet Turquin Paysage - **Movable Partition Walls:** Algaflex - **Aluminum Composite Panels:** Alucobond - **Scenographic Machinery:** Amg-Fechoz - **Furniture:** Artek, Vitra - **Scenic Curtains and Fabrics:** Azur Scenic **Sail Structure:** Baudin Chateauneuf - **Mosaic Tiles:** Bisazza - **Signage:** Boscher - **Auditorium Seats:** Concept D - **Door Frames and Fixtures:** Dorma, Malerba - **Elevators:** Fain, Kone - **False Ceilings and Plaster Boards:** Fermacell, Knauf, Placoplatre, SINIAT - **Acoustical Fabrics:** Fidivi, Texaa - **Auditorium Wood Finishing:** Frapont - **Auditorium Façade Wood Structure:** Hess - **Photovoltaic Panels:** Issol - **Metalic Meshes:** Jakob - **Wood and Resin Flooring:** Lopez Pigueras, Prima Pavimenti - **Glass Façades:** Tvitec, Saint-Gobain - **Fire Safety Glass:** Pilkington - **Acoustical Plaster Ceiling:** Werey Stenger - **Glass Façades:** Guardian Glass

LIYUAN LIBRARY
JIAOJIEHE, BEIJING, CHINA
LI XIAODONG ATELIER

Location: Jiaojiehe, Beijing, China - **Client:** Luke Him Sau Charitable Trust, Pan Xi - **Completion Date:** 2011 - **Architect:** Li Xiaodong Atelier **Design Team:** Li Xiaodong, Liu Yayun, Huang Chenwen, Panxi - **Gross Floor Area:** 175 m^2 - **Construction Cost:** 125,000 Euros

THE ROY AND DIANA VAGELOS EDUCATION CENTER
NEW YORK, USA
DILLER SCOFIDIO + RENFRO

Location: New York, USA - **Gross Floor Area:** 10,220 m^2 - **Completion Date:** 2016 - **Contractor:** FJ Sciame Construction - **Owner's Representative:** Group PMX - **Architect:** Diller Scofidio + Renfro - **Partner in Charge:** Elizabeth Diller - **Principal Designers:** Ricardo Scofidio, Charles Renfro, Benjamin Gilmartin - **Project Director:** Anthony Saby - **Project Architect:** Chris Hillyard - **Executive Architect:** Gensler - **Principal in Charge:** Madeline Burke-Vigeland **Project Architect:** Kristian Gregerson - **Technical Direction:** Ambrose Aliaga-Kelly - **Structure:** Leslie E. Robertson Associates **MEP, Security, Business and Technology:** Jaros Baum & Bolles (JB&B) - **Landscape:** SCAPE/Landscape Architecture - **Curtain Wall:** Buro Happold Consulting Engineers - **Lighting:** Tillotson Design Associates - **Acoustics:** Cerami & Associates - **Elevators:** Jenkins & Huntington - **Building Permits and Authorizations:** Milrose Consultants - **Graphic Designers:** 2x4, Gensler - **Civil and Geotechnical:** Thornton Tomasetti - **Sustainability:** Vidaris **Curtain Wall:** Josef Gartner / Permasteelisa Group - **Glass:** BGT Bischoff Glastechnik - **Metal Panels:** Imetco - **Precast Cladding:** David Kucera Incorporated - **Doors:** Blumcraft - **Interior Finishes:** Clipper Wall, Legere Group, Twenty2 - **Flooring:** Daltile, Johnsonite, Wausautile - **Wood:** Tru Grain, M. Bohlke Veneer Corporation - **Lighting:** Prescolite, Gammalux, 1212 Studio, Lutron - **Elevators:** TEI Group

ROZET CULTURAL CENTER
ARNHEM, THE NETHERLANDS
NEUTELINGS RIEDIJK ARCHITECTS

Location: Arnhem, The Netherlands - **Client:** City of Arnhem - **Completion Date:** 2013 - **Construction Cost:** 31,000,000 Euros - **Gross Floor Area:** 12,000 m^2 - **Architect:** Neutelings Riedijk Architects - **Interior Architect:** deMunnik-deJong-Steinhauser architecten - **Models:** Neutelings Riedijk Architects **General Contractor:** Wessels Rijssen - **Structural:** ABT, van de Laar - **Building Physics:** DGMR - **Building Services:** Ingenieursburo Linssen **Costs:** Bremen Bouwadviseurs - **Construction Management:** ABT - **Design Rosette:** Catalogtree - **Renders:** A2 Studio - **Precast Concrete:** Westo **Outer Frames:** Rollecate - **Wooden Flooring:** Finesse - **Interior:** Gielissen Interiors & Exhibitions - **Heating:** Van Losser Installaties - **Electrical Installation:** Leerkes - **Escalator:** Mitsubishi Elevator Europe

PARQUE BIBLIOTECA ESPAÑA
MEDELLÍN, COLOMBIA
GIANCARLO MAZZANTI ARQUITECTOS

Location: Santo Domingo Savio, Medellín, Colombia - **Client:** Alcaldía de Medellín - **Completion:** 2007 - **Gross Floor Area:** 2,960 m² **Construction Costs:** 1,027 $/m² - **Architect:** Giancarlo Mazzanti Arquitectos - **Design Team:** Andrés Sarmiento, Juan Manuel Gil, Fredy Pantoja, Pedro Saa, Gustavo Vásquez, Iván Ucros, Camilo Mora, Alejandro Piña - **Structural:** Sergio Tobón, Alberto Ashner - **Acoustical:** Raul Dario Franco **Mechanical:** Jorge Ramirez - **Main Contractor:** Arquitectura & Concreto - **Concrete:** Argos - **Metalwork:** Acesco, Socoda - **Stone:** Stone Slate from Bogota - **Glass:** Golden Glass - **Elevators:** Andino - **Fiber Cement Cladding:** Colombit - **Woodwork:** Refocosta - **Wood Furniture:** Pizano **Fiberglass Furniture:** Fibrit - **Ligthing:** High Lights

VESTRY 33 RESIDENTIAL BUILDING
NEW YORK, USA
ARCHI-TECTONICS

Location: New York, USA - **Client:** Vestry Acquisitions - **Completion Date:** 2014 - **Architect:** Archi-Tectonics - **Principal in Charge:** Winka Dubbeldam **Design Team:** Thomas Barry, David Barr, Wouter van Daele, Jose Munoz, Monty Forman, Jordan Bartelt, Lucy Flather - **Architect of Record:** Michael Zenreich Architects - **Main Contractor:** Vanguard Construction and Development Company - **Renders:** Archi-Tectonics, Seventh Art Group - **Structural:** Cantor & Seinuk Engineers - **Mechanical:** Stanislav Slutsky Engineers - **Curtain Wall:** Israel Berger and Associates **Curtain Wall:** Archiglaze - **Glass:** Cricursa - **Roofing:** Kemper Systems - **Elevators:** Kone - **Doors:** Tre-Più - **Railings:** Atlantis Rail - **Lighting:** Reggiani **Stones:** Stone Source, Hastings Tile and Stone - **Fireplaces:** Montigo Fireplaces - **Façade Aluminum System:** Schüco - **Kitchen Cabinet:** bulthaup

ELQUI DOMOS ASTRONOMICAL HOTEL
PISCO ELQUI, PAIHUANO, CHILE
RODRIGO DUQUE MOTTA

Location: Pisco Elqui, Paihuano, Chile - **Client:** Elqui Domos - **Architect:** Rodrigo Duque Motta - **Design Team:** Martin Holmes, Catalina Ventura, Jorge Siviero - **Site Area:** 4,000 m² - **Completion Date:** 2011 - **Engineering:** Alex Popp - **External Cladding, Timber Structures:** Arauco - **Windows:** Indalum **Lighting:** Sodimac

OBERHOLZ OBEREGGEN
OBEREGGEN, ITALY
PETER PICHLER ARCHITECTURE

Location: Obereggen, Bozen, Italy - **Client:** Obereggen AG - **Completion Date:** 2016 - **Site Area:** 1,432 m² - **Built Area:** 634 m² - **Architects:** Peter Pichler Architecture with Pavol Mikolajcak - **Interior Design:** Peter Pichler Architecture - **General Contractor:** Pfeifer Bau - **Structural:** Andreas Erlacher - **Electrical:** Elektro Gibitz - **HVAC:** Wiedenhofer, Heizstudio - **Lighting:** Von Lutz - **Lighting:** Artemide - **Lounge Chairs:** HAY **Woodwork Contractor:** LignoAlp

Architecture in Context
Contemporary Design Solutions based on
Environmental, Social and Cultural Identities
Contemporary Architecture in Detail

ISBN: 978-84-16851-72-0

All the original drawings in this volume have been elaborated by The Plan Editions

Promopress is a brand of:
Promotora de prensa internacional S.A. C/ Ausiàs March 124. 08013
Barcelona, Spain
Tel.: 0034 932451464. Fax: 0034 932654883. Email: info@promopress.es
www.promopresseditions.com
Facebook: Promopress Editions
Twitter: Promopress Editions @PromopressEd

First published in English: 2018

Translators: Kieren Edward Bailey, Stephanie Johnson, Chris Turner

Front cover: Reid Building, Glasgow School of Art © Iwan Baan
Back cover (L-R clockwise): Grace Farms © Iwan Baan - Renovation of Les Docks
© Luc Boegly, courtesy of Alfonso Femia with 5+1AA

D.L.: B 9484-2018

Printed in China

Image Credits

Expansion of Portland Japanese Garden © Jeremy Bittermann, courtesy the author
Elbphilharmonie p. 25 © Jorg Modrow, p. 29 © Maxim Schulz, pp. 33, 34-35, 37, 38, 39 © Iwan Baan
Auditorium and Community Center © Luis Gallardo, courtesy PRODUCTORA
Reid Building, Glasgow School of Art © Iwan Baan
Mapungubwe Interpretation Centre © Robert Rich, courtesy Peter Rich Architects
Grace Farms pp.81, 83, 85 © Iwan Baan, p.82 © Dean Kaufman
All images courtesy Sanaa
Kibera Hamlets School pp.86-87, 89, 93 left top and bottom, 94, 95 © Iwan Baan, pp. 91, 93 right © helloeverything, courtesy the author
Frederiksberg Courthouse © Adam Mørk, Courtesy 3XN
Copenhagen International School Nordhavn © Adam Mørk, courtesy C.F. Møller
Renovation of Les Docks © Luc Boegly, courtesy of Alfonso Femia with 5+1AA
Parish complex in the diocese of Lodi pp.134-135, 137 right top and bottom, 140-141, 142 top and middle © Studio F64 - Paolo Cappelli & Maurizio Criscuolo Fotografi Associati, pp. 137 left top and bottom, 142 bottom, 145 © Corvino+Multari
All images courtesy Corvino+Multari
La Seine Musicale © Didier Boy de la Tour, courtesy Shigeru Ban Architects Europe
Liyuan Library © Li Xiaodong, courtesy the author
The Roy and Diana Vagelos Education Center © Nic Lehoux, courtesy the author
Rozet Cultural Center © scagliolabrakkee, courtesy Neutelings Riedijk Architects
Parque Biblioteca España pp.194-195, 197 bottom, 199, 201 © Sergio Gomez, p. 197 top © Carlos Tobon, p. 205 © Lorenzo Castro
All images courtesy El Equipo Mazzanti
Vestry 33 Residential Building © Floto & Warner Photography, courtesy Archi-Tectonics
Elqui Domos Astronomical Hotel © Cristóbal Palma
Oberholz Obereggen pp. 226-227, 232 © Oskar Dariz, p. 230 © Jens Rüßmann
All images courtesy Peter Pichler Architecture

Text Credits

Expansion of Portland Japanese Garden by Raymund Ryan
Elbphilharmonie by Michael Webb
Auditorium and Community Center by Raymund Ryan
Reid Building, Glasgow School of Art by Yehuda Emmanuel Safran
Mapungubwe Interpretation Centre by Francesco Pagliari
Grace Farms by Yehuda Emmanuel Safran
Kibera Hamlets School by Caterina Testa
Frederiksberg Courthouse by Caterina Testa
Copenhagen International School Nordhavn by Luca Maria Francesco Fabris
Renovation of Les Docks by Giorgio Tartaro
Parish complex in the diocese of Lodi by Giovanni Menna
La Seine Musicale by Michael Webb
Liyuan Library by Caterina Testa
The Roy and Diana Vagelos Education Center by Michael Webb
Rozet Cultural Center by Michael Webb
Parque Biblioteca España by Francesco Pagliari
Vestry 33 Residential Building by Caterina Testa
Elqui Domos Astronomical Hotel by Caterina Testa
Oberholz Obereggen by Luca Maria Francesco Fabris

Cover Credits

Front cover: Reid Building, Glasgow School of Art © Iwan Baan
Back cover (L-R clockwise): Grace Farms © Iwan Baan - Renovation of Les Docks
© Luc Boegly, courtesy of Alfonso Femia with 5+1AA